Marylanders
to
Kentucky

Henry C. Peden, Jr.

Published by

FAMILY LINE PUBLICATIONS
Rear 63 East Main Street
Westminster, Maryland 21157

GENEALOGY * LOCAL HISTORY * EARLY MAPS

MARYLAND * PENNSYLVANIA * DELAWARE * WASHINGTON, D.C.

Send for Free Catalogue.

International Standard Book Number: 0-940907-18-6

Published by
Family Line Publications
1991

Printed in the United States of America

The exploration of Kentucky by Dr. Thomas Walker in 1750 and Daniel Boone in 1773, plus the creation of the Transylvania Land Company by Col. Richard Henderson in 1775, led to the eventual settlement of Kentucky primarily by people from Virginia, Maryland, North Carolina, Tennessee and Pennsylvania. In 1776 Kentucky was designated as Kentucky County, Virginia, and in 1780 it was divided into the counties of Fayette, Jefferson and Lincoln. By 1790 these three counties had been subdivided into the counties of Mason, Bourbon, Woodford, Fayette, Madison, Jefferson, Mercer, Nelson and Lincoln. In 1792 Kentucky became the 15th state.

Significant numbers of Marylanders began to migrate to Kentucky after 1775, lured by its rich and plentiful land, but the greatest migration occurred after the Revolutionary War. Reasons for the movement west were as diverse as the people themselves. The causes were mainly social, economic, political and religious. In 1785 a group of Catholic settlers, mostly from St. Mary's County, migrated to Nelson County, Kentucky. This "Maryland League," and others that followed, went overland to Pittsburgh, then down the Ohio River in flatboats to Maysville, and through the wilderness to Nelson County. A detailed accounting of these early pioneers can be found in Benjamin J. Webb's, *The Centenary of Catholicity in Kentucky* (1884), and Bayley Ellen Mark's, *Economics and Society in a Staple Plantation System: St. Mary's County, Maryland, 1790-1840* (Ph.D. Dissertation, University of Maryland, 1979). Settlers were also lured to Kentucky from Maryland by the Land Lottery of 1789. It offered 40,000 acres divided into lots of not less than 150 acres, at $15 per ticket, with first prize being 800 acres. This lottery was advertised in the *Maryland Journal and Baltimore Advertiser* on February 17, 1789, and similar lotteries were advertised over the next ten years.

Although migrations westward were still impaired by hostile Indian uprisings, which did not end until General Wayne's victory at Fallen Timbers in Ohio in 1794, settlers still moved west, and their numbers increased, especially with the completion of the Wilderness Road from the Cumberland Gap into southeastern Kentucky. On December 1, 1796, the *Fredericktown Weekly Advertiser* noted that travellers would find no difficulty in procuring the necessities they needed on the Wilderness Road and the abundant crops in Kentucky would afford the emigrants a certainty of being supplied with every necessity of life.

Significant migrations to Kentucky from Maryland and other states also occurred after 1805 - primarily because the American Revolution, then an event of the past, had given birth to the new Federal Government which was lending its might to the protection and fostering of new homes in the west. The area had already become more or less "settled and safe" as Indian troubles were also a thing of the past. The end of the War of 1812 brought further movement westward as the need for "elbow room" pushed these adventuresome people to and through Kentucky, just as the bounty lands granted to soldiers of the Revolutionary War had done.

iii

Marylanders played an important role in the settlement of Kentucky during its first 50 years from 1775 to 1825. No historical compilation can be expected to locate and list every one of the thousands of these early settlers who moved west to Kentucky from Maryland, but this book has been compiled with the purpose in mind of aiding those genealogists who are searching for Kentuckians of Maryland descent. In addition persons with the same surname have been grouped together, as a indication of possible relationship. The reader is cautioned that this is not meant to imply that they were all necessarily related to one another.

In this compendium of Kentuckians with Maryland roots, a variety of primary and secondary sources has been used. Revolutionary War pension abstracts, land records, marriage records, cemetery records, newspaper advertisements, queries from descendants, and genealogical journals were the major sources of information. Other sources are cited within the text, with occasional references to additional material available on specific families. Appreciation is also expressed for contributions by Robert W. Barnes and F. Edward Wright.

The following keys to the most frequently used source materials are used in this book in order to conserve time and space. Each of these keys (reference codes) is followed by one or more numbers which, in most instances, refer to the page or the volume and page. For example, Ref: KA 6:2, p. 16 refers to Kentucky Ancestor, Vol. 6, No. 2, page 16. A list of the coded references follows:

AAG.....Newman, Harry Wright. Anne Arundel Gentry, Vol. I and II. (Westminster, MD: Family Line Publications, 1990. Originally published in 1970 and 1971).

BCF.....Barnes, Robert W. Baltimore County Families, 1659-1759 (Baltimore: Genealogical Publishing Co., 1989).

BCK.....Biographical Cyclopedia of the Commonwealth of Kentucky (Chicago-Philadelphia: John M. Gresham Co., 1896).

BCLR....Baltimore County Land Records abstracted by Robert W. Barnes, of Perry Hall, Maryland (1989).

DAR.....DAR Patriot Index, Volume I (Washington, D.C.: National Society, Daughters of American Revolution, 1966).

HCLR....Harford County Land Records abstracted by Henry C. Peden, Jr., of Bel Air, Maryland (1990).

HCP.....Peden, Henry C. Jr. Revolutionary Patriots of Harford County, Maryland, 1775-1783. (Bel Air, MD: Published by Author, 1985).

KA......Kentucky Ancestor. (Frankfort, Kentucky: Kentucky Historical Society Quarterly, 1965-1981).

KB......Westerfield, Thomas W. and McDowell, Sam. Kentucky Biography and Genealogy. (Owensboro, Kentucky: Genealogical Reference Company, 9 vols., 1969-1982. Originally published as Kentucky: A History of the State, by W. H. Perrin, J. H. Battle, and G. C. Kniffin in the 1880's).

KBG.....Kentucky Blue Grass Roots. (Frankfort, Kentucky: The Kentucky Genealogical Society Quarterly, 1979-1980).

KC......Webb, Benjamin J. The Centenary of Catholicity in Kentucky. (Louisville: Charles A. Rogers Co., 1884).

KCR.....Kentucky Cemetery Records, Vol. I, by the Kentucky Society, Daughters of the American Revolution. (Lexington, Kentucky: The Keystone Printery, Inc., 1960).

KM......Sprague, Stuart Seely. Kentuckians in Missouri. (Baltimore: Genealogical Publishing Co., 1984).

KP......Fowler, Ila E. Kentucky Pioneers and Their Descendants. (Baltimore: Genealogical Publishing Co., 1967).

KPG.....Kentucky Pioneer Genealogy and Records: Genealogical Journal Devoted to Kentucky. (Hartford, Kentucky: Cook and McDowell Publications, 1979-1980).

KPR.....Kentucky Pension Roll of 1835: Report from the Secretary of War in Relation to the Pension Establishment of the United States. (Baltimore: Genealogical Publishing Co., 1968).

KR......Ardery, Mrs. William B. Kentucky Records: Early Wills and Marriages. (Baltimore: Genealogical Publishing Co., 1965. Originally published in 1926).

KYM.....Clift, G. Glenn. Kentucky Marriages, 1797-1865. (Baltimore: Genealogical Publishing Co., 1974. Originally published in 1938).

LU......Lu, Helen M. and Neumann, Gwen B. Revolutionary War Period Bible, Family and Marriage Records Gleaned from Pension Applications. (Dallas: Published by Authors, 1980).

MGS.....Maryland Genealogical Society Bulletin. (Baltimore: Maryland Genealogical Society Quarterly, 1984-1990).

MM-1....Barnes, Robert W. Maryland Marriages, 1634-1777. (Baltimore: Genealogical Publishing Co., 1976).

MM-2....Barnes, Robert W. Maryland Marriages, 1778-1800. (Baltimore: Genealogical Publishing Co., 1979).

MMG.....Maryland Magazine of Genealogy. (Baltimore: Maryland Historical Society, 1979-1982).

MPA.....McGhee, Lucy Kate. Maryland Pension Abstracts of Revolution, War of 1812, and Indian Wars. (Washington, DC: Published by Author, 1966).

MRP.....Clark, Raymond B. Jr. Maryland Revolutionary Pensioners (St. Michaels, MD: Published by Author, 1982).

MRR.....Newman, Harry Wright. Maryland Revolutionary Records (Baltimore: Genealogical Publishing Co., 1980. Originally published in Washington, D.C. in 1938).

MS......Burns, Annie Walker. Maryland Soldiers of the Revolutionary, 1812, and Indian Wars Who Drew Pensions While Residing in Kentucky. (Washington, DC: Published by Author, 1939).

MW......Wright, F. Edward. Maryland Militia, War of 1812. (Silver Spring, MD: Family Line Publications, 1979).

NAW.....Wright, F. Edward. Marriages and Deaths from Newspapers of Allegany and Washington Counties, Maryland, 1820-1830 (Westminster, MD: Family Line Publications, 1988).

NGS.....National Genealogical Society Quarterly. (Arlington, Virginia: The National Genealogical Society, 1932-1963).

RSK.....Quisenberry, Anderson C. Revolutionary Soldiers in Kentucky. (Baltimore: Genealogical Publishing Co., 1982. Originally published in the Year Book of the Kentucky Society of the Sons of the American Revolution, 1896).

SRM.....Passano, Eleanor Phillips. An Index to the Source Records of Maryland: Genealogical, Biographical, Historical. (Baltimore: Genealogical Publishing Co., 1984. Originally published in 1940).

WMNA....Wright, F. Edward. Western Maryland Newspaper Abstracts, 1786-1800. (Silver Spring, MD: Family Line Publications, 3 vols., 1985-1987).

Henry C. Peden, Jr.
Bel Air, Maryland

MARYLANDERS TO KENTUCKY, 1775-1825

ABELL. In 1788, Robert ABELL migrated with his family to Kentucky and settled in the Catholic settlement of Rolling Fork in Nelson County. His father, Samuel ABELL, was a Protestant and had been High Sheriff of St. Mary's County, Maryland. His mother, Ellen O'BRIEN, was a Catholic. Robert ABELL was elected a representative from Washington County, Kentucky to the constitutional convention in 1799. He had also represented Nelson County in the State Legislature of 1792. His wife, whom he married in St. Mary's County, Maryland on November 3, 1777, was Margaret MILLS, or MILES. Their ten children were Samuel, Jesse, James, Robert A., Ignatius, Benjamin, John, Mary, Ellen, and Janet. Robert ABELL returned to Maryland in 1802 for a visit, was taken ill and died. (Ref: MM-1:1; KC:102)

Barton ABELL, Abner ABELL, and Absalom ABELL were also in Kentucky prior to 1800 (Ref: KC:110).

ACTON. Smallwood ACTON was born in Prince George's County, Maryland in 1758 and served in the Revolutionary War under Capt. John LOWE. He served for six months in 1776 and marched under Gen. William SMALLWOOD from Piscataway to Baltimore, then to Philadelphia and New York and back. He stated in his pension application that he saw Gen. George WASHINGTON many times. In 1777 he was drafted in the militia and again marched north and was in the Battle of Germantown where he was wounded in the leg. He moved to Clark County, Kentucky circa 1800, having received bounty land warrant 34590-160-55. He married Nancy KANE (CANE) in Clark County on December 16, 1823, and was a pensioner as of June 7, 1832. He died September 28, 1844. His widow applied and received pension W26658 in 1855, at age 81 (Ref: MS:26; LU 1:8; MRR:7, 109).

ADAMS. Sallie ADAMS of Maryland married John C. MICKLE of Virginia, and their son, Dr. J. G. MICKLE was born June 4, 1835 in Christian County, Kentucky. (Ref: KB 6:92)

Nancy ADAMS (1800-1872) of Maryland married William DITTO of Tennessee, and their son, W. N. DITTO, was born March 2, 1835 in Tipton County, Tennessee and subsequently moved to Hickman County, Kentucky. (Ref: KB 6:143)

Alexius ADAMS of Maryland was a Catholic elder in Bardstown, Kentucky in 1820. (Ref: KC:63)

Eli ADAMS and James ADAMS were in the Catholic settlement of Cartwright's Creek in (now) Washington County, Kentucky in 1788. (Ref: KC:80)

Richard ADAMS was in the Cox's Creek settlement of Kentucky by 1795. His son, Rev. Joseph ADAMS, was ordained a priest in the cathedral of St. Joseph in 1840. (Ref: KC:114, 131)

James Bowles ADAMS was born June 5, 1812 in Hagerstown, Maryland, son of Eli ADAMS and Amelia BERRY, who moved to Washington County,

2

Kentucky in 1816. (Ref: KA 13:4, p. 211) They were possibly related to Revolutionary War soldiers John ADAMS and Peter ADAMS (brothers) who migrated from Hagerstown, Maryland to Washington County, Kentucky around 1816. Peter never married but left a will (probated December 15, 1856) which mentioned the children of his brother James, namely Martha, Malinda, James, Martin and Heland. (Ref: KPG 2:2, p. 110)

John ADAMS was born December 8, 1760 in York County, Pennsylvania and served in the Revolutionary War in 1777 in Frederick County, Maryland under Capt. Samuel HUGHES. He married ELINOR WORLUND in Hagerstown, Maryland and moved to Washington County, Kentucky around 1816. Their children were John, Bill, Ann, Eli (whose children were James B., Susan, Josephus and Elinor), Otho, and James. John ADAMS received pension S30816 in 1831 in Washington County, Kentucky (Ref: MS:56; KA 10:1, p. 53; KPR:1835; MRR:7).

AKER. Elizabeth AKER married John NEIKIRK, who was born in Hagerstown, Maryland and migrated to Kentucky with the Aker family prior to 1815. Their son, William NEIKIRK, was born in Pulaski County, Kentucky in 1819 (Ref: KB 5:220).

ALDRIDGE. Elizabeth ALDRIDGE, a daughter of William and Elizabeth ALDRIDGE of Maryland, married George J. HUME of Kentucky. William ALDRIDGE was a Revolutionary pensioner in 1831, age 77, in Boone County, Kentucky. (Ref: RSK:39; MRR:7; KPR:1835) He migrated to Jefferson County, Kentucky when it was only a fort, but left there because of Indians and moved to Millersburg, Kentucky. He moved soon after to Verona in Boone County, Kentucky. He was a farmer and raised eight children, including Elizabeth. He also served in the War of 1812 and fought in the Battle of Blue Licks (Ref: KB 8:89).

ALEXANDER. James R. ALEXANDER filed his claim for a pension based upon his Revolutionary War service on May 14, 1833 in Allen County, Kentucky. He said he was age 76 and was born November 23, 1756 in a house which stood on the dividing line of Maryland and Pennsylvania. He was living in Cecil County, Maryland when called into service in 1776 and served in Capt. Walter ALEXANDER's Company, became a Sergeant, and was discharged December 1, 1776. He studied medicine in New Jersey and returned home to his father in North Carolina. In 1780 he was a Surgeon in Mecklenburg County, North Carolina under Col. William DAVIDSON. He married Dorcas GARRISON on November 26, 1789 in York District, South Carolina. He died in Allen County, Kentucky on March 11, 1836. (Ref: Pension File W2901; MRR:7, 109) His Bible was inscribed: "James R. Alexander, Allen County, Kentucky, Private and Surgeon in Company of Capt. Alexander in Maryland Line." It included these records: Silas, born May 10, 1791; Amanda, born February 6, 1793; Charles Grandison, born August 27, 1794; Mary Sample, born April 10, 1796; Mark Alexander, born December 29, 1797; Abigail B., born November 8, 1799; Hannah, born August 19, 1801; James Rankin, born July 5, 1803; John G., born March 4, 1806; and, Dorcas Reese, born December 28, 1807 (Ref: MS:4; KPR:1835).

ALLEN. William Porter ALLEN was born October 18, 1829 in Ohio

3

County, Kentucky, son of Capt. Levi ALLEN, a native of Sumner County, Tennessee. Capt. Allen (1794-1861) was in the War of 1812. His father, Theophilus ALLEN (1770-1835) and his grandfather, Rhodom ALLEN, were natives of Maryland. (Ref: KB 3:115)

Another William ALLEN was a Private in the Maryland Militia and applied for a pension in 1831 in Mason County, Kentucky, at age 77 (Ref: KPR:1835. Source RSK:119 erroneously states he was in the Virginia line).

ALLOWAY. William ALLOWAY, of Maryland, migrated to Kentucky when Louisville was a small town, and was one of the first mechanics in the State. His son, Joel ALLOWAY, was born in Shelby County, Kentucky and was a carpenter and farmer, and married Elizabeth GRIGSBY of Nelson County, Kentucky (Ref: KB 7:144).

ALVEY. John ALVEY and Thomas S. ALVEY migrated from St. Mary's County, Maryland and settled in the Catholic settlement on Hardin's Creek, Kentucky circa 1786. (Ref: KC:56)

Josias ALVEY (born 1757) and Thomas Green ALVEY (born 1750) both served in the Maryland Line during the Revolutionary War. Clement ALVEY married Mary Ann MUDD circa 1810 in Kentucky (Ref: MRR:7, 109).

AMBROSE. William AMBROSE and wife Ann were early settlers of Maryland and Kentucky. Their children were: James AMBROSE married Charlotte -----, and had a son William who married Isabel HARRISON; Ann AMBROSE married Isaac DAY; and Rachel AMBROSE married George NEWLAND (Ref: MGS 15:1, p. 16).

AMOS, AMOSS. Nicholas Day AMOS, only son of Thomas AMOS and Elizabeth DAY, was born in Baltimore County, Maryland on September 19, 1742. He took the Oath of Allegiance to the State of Maryland during the Revolutionary War in 1778 and was an Ensign in the 8th Battalion of Harford County. (Ref: HCP:5) Nicholas married in Baltimore County on October 28, 1761 to Christiana DITTO, daughter of Abraham DITTO and Nancy BOWLES. Their children were: Elizabeth AMOS (1762-1812) married Aquila PARKER (1755-1834) in Maryland and died in Bourbon County, Kentucky; Mary AMOS married Joshua BARTON in Maryland in 1783; Mordecai AMOS, born in Maryland, was in Jessamine County, Kentucky in 1800, and in Barren County, Kentucky circa 1808; Thomas AMOS married Catherine DEVORE in 1788 in Jefferson County, Kentucky, and died in Bourbon County, Kentucky in 1830 (she died in 1853 in Howard County, Indiana); Nancy AMOS married John CONWAY; Nicholas Day AMOS, Jr., born in 1771, married Ann JONES, and died in 1847 in Bourbon County, Kentucky; Christiana AMOS married M. MALOTT and died prior to 1819; Benjamin AMOS married Elizabeth GRIFFIN in 1797 in Bourbon County, Kentucky; Abraham AMOS left Kentucky early and was a preacher in 1804 in Clermont County, Ohio; Elijah AMOS was born in 1782 in Harford County, Maryland, married Rebecca NEALE in 1800 in Bourbon County, Kentucky, and their children were Thomas, Ditto, Martha, Cassana, Harrison, William and Elizabeth (When his wife died in 1840, Elijah married Cassander CULLISON and their children: Caroline A., Hester J., and

Mary A.; Sarah AMOS was born in 1776, married Daniel THOMAS in 1801 in Bourbon County, Kentucky, and died in 1844 in Rush County, Indiana; Ditto AMOS married Martha NEALE, moved to Rush County, Indiana and died in Clinton County, Indiana; and, William AMOS married Margaret BARNETT in 1802 in Bourbon County, Kentucky. The family of Nicholas Day AMOS, Sr. moved from Harford County, Maryland to Washington County, Maryland prior to 1792 and they migrated to Hinkston Creek near Ruddle's Mill in Bourbon County, Kentucky circa 1795. (Ref: KA 3:2, p. 89; KA 3:4, p. 186; Additional family history is contained in Maurine Schmitz and Glendola Peck's The Amos Family (compiled in 1964 and available at the Maryland Historical Society Library in Baltimore).

ARTHUR. William ARTHUR was born in 1798 in Lancaster, Pennsylvania and died in Covington, Kentucky in 1834. His wife, Eliza PARSONS, was the second daughter of William and Sarah PARSONS of Harford County, Maryland. A son, Judge William E. ARTHUR, was born March 3, 1825 and subsequently moved to Cincinnati, Ohio. He married (1) Addie SOUTHGATE in 1855, and (2) Etha SOUTHGATE, sister of Addie, in 1860 (Ref: BCK:23-25).

ASBURY. Hannah ASBURY (1759-1832), of Maryland, married George DAWSON (1754-1799) and migrated to Adair County, Kentucky around 1790. Their son, Anak DAWSON, of Maryland, married Nancy CHAPMAN, of Virginia, in Allen County, Kentucky or Simpson County, Kentucky and had twelve children. One son, James M. DAWSON, was born 1823 in Scottsville, Kentucky (Ref: KB 4:188).

AUD. The Aud family migrated from St. Mary's County, Maryland to the Catholic settlement on Pottinger's Creek in Nelson County, Kentucky in 1785. Zachariah AUD married Margaret WATHEN, a widowed daughter of Francis COOMES, in 1799. A son, Athanasius A. AUD was born near Fairfield, Kentucky, on February 21, 1803. A daughter, Clotilda AUD, married Thomas MONTGOMERY, an orphaned nephew of Austin MONTGOMERY, who lived in Washington County, Kentucky. Zachariah AUD died on April 3, 1822. In 1820 Ambrose AUD and Thomas AUD were elders in Bardstown, Kentucky. (Ref: KC:38, 39, 63, 114, 130)

Also, James AUD (born July 20, 1780) married Nancy MOORE (born January 17, 1785) and they were in Breckinridge County, Kentucky by 1818, and moved to White County, Illinois in 1822 (Ref: KA 2:1, p. 351).

AUSTIN. Samuel AUSTIN (1801-1884) migrated to Kentucky from Maryland with his parents in 1815, settling in Ohio County. He moved to Butler County where he married and subsequently became the first County Judge (Ref: KB 3:2).

AYDELOTT. George Howard AYDELOTT married Christiana B. Hill (1752-1818) on January 8, 1770 and died in Kentucky in 1803. After George's death, she married Joshua HOBBS. George was probably a son of John AYDELOTT (1715-1791) and Sarah HOWARD (daughter of George HOWARD) of Somerset County, Maryland. (Ref: MGS 16:4, p. 225).

AYRES. Daniel AYRES of Fauquier County, Virginia, married Rebecca Dorcas (Howard) MORRISON on February 17, 1806. She was born in Frederick County, Maryland on December 30, 1785 and died in Bourbon County, Kentucky on March 28, 1807. The second wife of Daniel AYRES was Matilda JACOBS (of Harper's Ferry, West Virginia) whom he married in 1808 in Kentucky. Daniel AYRES died in 1813 (Ref: KA 5:4, p. 214).

BAILEY. Major Robert BAILEY, of Bucksville, Kentucky, and formerly a resident of Hagerstown, Maryland, died at Hurt's Tavern, 8 miles north of Nashville, Tennessee, on July 12, 1827 after a short illness. (Ref: NAW:92-93)

Stephen BAILEY was born on the bank of the Potomac River in Maryland and settled on the Ohio River, three miles east of Carrollton, Kentucky, in 1780. He married a Miss ADAMS of Massachusetts, who was a relative of President John Quincy ADAMS. Stephen's son, Thomas BAILEY, married Mary A. DEAN in Carroll County, Kentucky (Ref: KB 8:6).

BAIRD. Miles BAIRD was born in Maryland in 1774, migrated to North Carolina when a young man, and married in 1800 to Mary (or Margaret) RUSH. A son, Terrell BAIRD, was born July 13, 1804 and died September 8, 1826. In 1813 they moved to (now) Simpson County, Kentucky. A son, Benjamin BAIRD, was born there on November 29, 1814, married Eliza A. WILSON (June 14, 1822 - 1861) of Boyle County, Kentucky, and died on May 3, 1878. The Baird family is buried on the Alice Adams HALCOMB farm on the Russellville Road in Simpson County, Kentucky (Ref: KB 4:173; Simpson County, Kentucky Records by the Simpson County Historical Society, 1975, p. 257).

BALD. William BALD was among the early Catholic settlers who migrated from St. Mary's County, Maryland to Nelson County, Kentucky in 1785 (Ref: KC:28).

BARCLAY. Joshua G. BARCLAY and wife Sarah WHEELER, both of Maryland, migrated to Kentucky at an early date and settled in Bardstown. They later moved to Louisville and in 1832 to Milton in Trigg County. Joshua died in 1851 and Sarah died in 1862. They had ten children, including John R. BARCLAY who was born 1822 in Louisville, Kentucky (Ref: KB 7:148).

BARKER. William BARKER was a Private in the 3rd Maryland Line during the Revolutionary War. He applied for and received pension S35775 in 1818 (age 61) in Fayette County, Kentucky (Ref: MRP:2; RSK:65; KPR:1835; MRR:9; Archives of Maryland, Vol. 18, p. 85).

BARKLOW. Leroy BARKLOW (whose father was in the War of 1812 and was wounded at the Battle of New Orleans) married Harriet BELMIRE. Both were natives of Union County, Kentucky. The Barklows originated in Maryland (Ref: KB 4:30).

BARNARD. William L. BARNARD was a Private in the Maryland Militia during the Revolutionary War. He applied for and received pension S16315 in 1831 (age 75) in Ohio County, Kentucky. (Ref: MS:61;

6

RSK:136; KPR:1835)

Ignatius P. BARNARD was the son of Joshua BARNARD and the grandson of Ignatius P. BARNARD who settled in Ohio County, Kentucky around 1820, having migrated there from Maryland. His great grandfather was a soldier of the Revolution (Ref: KB 3:119).

BARNES. Nicodemus BARNES first made application for pension for Revolutionary War services while residing in Christian County, Kentucky on November 14, 1843, age 83. He was born about 20 miles from Baltimore, Maryland in October, 1760 and enlisted for 6 months under Colonel LACY. He afterwards went to North Carolina, and then Chester, South Carolina, where he married, wife's name not given. After 10 years he moved to Rowan County, Tennessee, and 6 years later moved to Wayne County, Kentucky and then to Clinton County, Kentucky. (Ref: MS:31; MRP:3; MRR:9)

Robert BARNES, of Maryland, migrated to Clark County, Kentucky around 1806. His wife was Jane PEDDICORD. She died in 1825 and Robert died circa 1830. Their son, Alfred BARNES, was born in Maryland on June 1, 1790. He married Helen LACKLAND, daughter of Aaron, in 1816. Helen BARNES died in 1849 and Alfred BARNES migrated to Callaway County, Missouri in 1853 (Ref: KA 12:4, p. 213; MGS 27:3, p. 382).

BARNETT. Daniel BARNETT was born in 1748 and was a Private in the 7th Maryland Line during the Revolutionary War in Frederick County, Maryland. He applied for and received pension S35777 on June 11, 1818. He died in Woodford County, Kentucky on January 23, 1823 (Ref: MS:54; RSK:169; MRR:9; KPR:1835; Archives of Maryland, Vol. 18, p. 190).

BARNEY. Joshua BARNEY (July 6, 1759 - December 1, 1818) was a son of William BARNEY and Frances HOLLAND of Baltimore. He had a very distinguished career in the American Navy during the Revolutionary War. A full description of his career is given in the "Pittsburgh Statesman" newspaper following his death on December 1, 1818, while on his way to Kentucky. His widow (and second wife), Harriet COLE, received pension W79. (Ref: LU 2:78; Henry C. Peden's Revolutionary Patriots of Baltimore Town and Baltimore County, Maryland, 1775 - 1783, p. 14 (Westminster, MD: Family Line Publications, 1988).

BARR. The Barr family originated in Maryland and migrated to Kentucky in 1787, settling in Fayette County. William BARR married Ann WATSON and their son, John Watson BARR, was born in Versailles, Kentucky, December 17, 1826, and subsequently became a Judge of the U. S. District Court (Ref: KB 9:5).

BARRETT. Susan M. BARRETT married A. R. HOCKER in Ohio County, Kentucky, both natives of that county. Their parents moved to Kentucky from eastern Maryland in 1792 (Ref: KB 3:149).

BARRICKMAN. Jacob BARRICKMAN, son of Peter BARRICKMAN (name may have been BERGMANN originally) and Ann URSELLA, was born February 17, 1763 in Frederick County, Maryland. He married Jane SWAN (born

March 1, 1769 in Pennsylvania) on March 24, 1784 and had the following children, all born in Campbell County, Kentucky except the last child who was born in Franklin County, Indiana: Martha BARRICKMAN, born March 24, 1785, married Joseph STILWELL in 1811; Mary BARRICKMAN, born September 18, 1786, married James CRAIG in 1804; Sarah BARRICKMAN, born December 25, 1791, died August 6, 1821; Jane BARRICKMAN, born October 8, 1794, married David TEMPLETON; John BARRICKMAN, born February 15, 1796, married Sarah SHEPARD in 1827; Jacob BARRICKMAN, Jr., born February 17, 1799, married Jennett Hannah TEMPLETON in 1820; Keturah BARRICKMAN, born January 15, 1803, died 1901, married James TEMPLETON in 1832; Nancy BARRICKMAN, born April 14, 1805, married Thomas WILSON in 1837; James Taylor BARRICKMAN, born February 17, 1808, died 1863, married Louisa NEAL in 1837; William BARRICKMAN, born September 12, 1810, died September 8, 1838; and, Eliza May BARRICKMAN, born May 16, 1813, married Joseph MILES in 1837, and died in 1893 (Ref: KA 11:1, p. 29).

BARTLEY. Thomas BARTLEY applied for a Revolutionary pension in 1832 (age 78) in Monroe County, Kentucky. He stated he was a butcher's apprentice in Philadelphia, Pennsylvania for John HOUSEMAN at the time he enlisted in the Army. He lost his discharge in Hagerstown, Maryland, where he lived three years after the war. He subsequently moved to Virginia for four years and in 1783 joined Gen. ST. CLAIR for six months (and he was wounded.) He was brought to Georgetown, Kentucky by Major BODDINGER. He returned to Virginia, enlisted for three years and then returned to Kentucky. He married and never returned to Maryland. In 1855 his widow Margaret made an application for his pension in Monroe County, Kentucky (Ref: MS:62) However, Source MRP:3 states Thomas did receive pension S18707, although Source MS:62 states his pension application (R591?) was rejected. An article by Saundra L. Bennett of Boise, Idaho appeared in the South Central Kentucky Genealogical and Historical Society Quarterly "Traces," 18:4, Winter, 1990, pp. 126-127, and it stated that Thomas BARTLEY was married to Margaret "Peggy" BURCHUM on January 1, 1801 in Barren County, by Rev. John MULKEY. Source LU 2:96 states her name was BURNHAM and they married in 1799. Thomas was born in April, 1759, in London, Charing Cross, England. He came to America at age 13, landing in Baltimore and enlisted in the Revolutionary War in Maryland on July 28, 1776, and enlisted again later in Philadelphia. A prisoner of war in May, 1779, he was exchanged at Charles Town in November, 1781. He also fought in the Indians Wars and served under General WAYNE until 1788, when he was discharged. His wife Peggy was a daughter of Bennaize and Elizabeth BURCHUM. Thomas BARTLEY died on August 10, 1849 and Peggy BARTLEY died in August, 1869, in Monroe County, Kentucky. Their children were William, George, Isaiah, Thomas, Sally, Martha, Elizabeth, Abijah, and Benjamin (Ref: MS:62; LU:96; MRP:3).

BATEMAN. Thomas BATEMAN applied for a Revolutionary War pension on November 9, 1825 (age 78) while residing in Jefferson County, Kentucky. He stated he enlisted for three years in 1776 and served under Capt. TANNEHILL in the 6th Maryland Line, and was discharged in 1779. He stated his wife was age 67 in 1825 and they had the following children: Polly JETER, age 43; Sally SHAW, age 39; Hannah

GIBBINS, age 37; John BATEMAN, age 35; Rachel DUNAGIN, age 33, and
Thomas BATEMAN, age 26. Thomas received pension S35182 (Ref: MS:51,
MRP:3, KPR:1835)

Also, a Nancy BATEMAN married Joseph HARRISON in Fleming County,
Kentucky on June 7, 1814. Both families were from southern Maryland
(Ref: MGS 27:4, p. 498).

BATESEL. The Batesel family was in Maryland by 1745, and some migrated to Virginia and Nelson County, Kentucky. One Joseph BATESEL
was born in 1807 in Kentucky and migrated to Lawrence County, Missouri around 1840, where he married (1) Mary ROGERS in 1841, and
(2) Malinda BROWNING in 1847 (Ref: KA 13:1, p. 44).

BEALL. The Beall family was prominent in southern Maryland. Nathan
BEALL and wife Sarah BEALL migrated with their eleven children in
1798 and settled in Jefferson County, Kentucky. Washington BEALL,
son of Nathan, was born February 9, 1790 in Maryland and died in
1866 in Kentucky. He married Mary CARTER and had seven children,
one of whom, George W. BEALL, was born December 17, 1825. (Ref: KB
5:47)

Another Beall family to settle in Kentucky was that of James M.
BEALL who was born in Montgomery County, Maryland on May 11, 1795
and died in Logan County, Kentucky on December 4, 1880. He was
married four times: (1) Sarah A. ALLEN, 1796-1824, daughter of Dr.
B. A. ALLEN, in 1822; (2) Sarah N.-----, 1800-1828, in 1827; (3)
Sarah Ann McCUDDY, 1809-1851, daughter of I. B. McCUDDY, in 1830;
(4) Lucy MONDAY, 1807-1890, in 1856. All are buried in Maple Grove
Cemetery in Russellville, Logan County, Kentucky. (Ref: KCR:287)

Also, Walter BEALL and family moved from Maryland to Nelson County,
Kentucky during the 1780's and possibly were related to the James
BEALL born circa 1816 (Ref: MGS 25:4, p. 420; MGS 27:3, p. 384).

BEAN. Leonard BEAN was a Revolutionary soldier who was born in 1758
and enlisted in Maryland in 1777/1778 in the 3rd Maryland Regiment.
His wife, Eda KILGOUR, widow of William KILGOUR, was born in 1760.
Leonard applied for and received pension S35189 in 1818 (age 76)
in Mason County, Kentucky. (Ref: MS:63; RSK:118; KPR:1835. Source
MRR:110 states her name was Eda KELLOW) Their children were: John
Albert BEAN; Harrison BEAN; William Gallenous BEAN; Letitia BEAN,
married John CRUTCHER; Charlotte BEAN, married Joseph TOLLE;
Matilda BEAN, married Frank McCLURE; and, Fanny BEAN. (Ref: KP:184;
Mason County, Kentucky Court Order Book N, p. 53, April, 1833;
Mason County, Kentucky Court Order Book P, p. 8, June, 1851)

Conrad BEAN applied for a Revolutionary pension while living in
Washington County, Kentucky on May 27, 1833, age 81. He enlisted
July 1, 1777 in Baltimore County, Maryland, under Lt. RUTTER, about
7 miles from the City. (Ref: MS:56; RSK:164; LU 3:5; MGS 4:33;
MRR:9; KPR:1835) Conrad BEAN married Jenny (or Jane) BOSTON in
Washington County, Kentucky on December 1, 1810. Jacob BEAMS (BEAN)
was their bondsman, and John LANCASTER of Marion County, Kentucky,
said he knew them for several years. (Ref: MS:56; MRR:110)

Bennett BEAN was among the early Catholic settlers to move to Cartwright's Creek in (now) Washington County, Kentucky from St. Mary's County, Maryland circa 1785 (Ref: KC:80).

BEARD. Sarah BEARD, of Somerset County, Maryland, died in Jefferson County, Kentucky in 1802. Her will (written on October 13, 1796 and probated on October 4, 1802) named her sons John BEARD, Charles BEARD and Thomas BEARD, and her daughters Rachel MOORE and Mary BEARD, citing that Charles, Mary and Thomas were the youngest children. Charles BEARD, a son of Sarah, wrote his will on May 20, 1802 and it was also probated on October 4, 1802. It named his youngest brother Thomas BEARD, eldest brother John BEARD, and sisters Rachel MOORE and Mary BEARD, and brother-in-law John MOORE. (Ref: "Jefferson County, Kentucky Will Abstracts, 1783 to 1813" abstracted by William J. Gammon in 1917 (NGS 6:3, p. 50).

BEATTY. William BEATTY, Jr., son of William BEATTY of Frederick County, Maryland, was born January 17, 1739 and married Mary Dorothea GROSH in 1757. Both were only age 18. Their eldest son, William, died in the Revolutionary War. Their youngest son, Adam, was born May 10, 1777 and moved to Washington County, Kentucky as early as 1802, studied law and became a Judge. He married Sally GREEN, eldest daughter of Capt. John GREEN (also a Marylander who migrated to Kentucky) on July 2, 1804. (Ref: KB 5:2-5)

Family records of a James BEATTY (born 1742 in Maryland and died 1820 in Kentucky) can be found in the DAR Library in Washington, D.C., and other Beatty's in the holdings of the Maryland Historical Society Library in Baltimore (Ref: SRM:22).

BEAUCHAMP. Elizabeth BEAUCHAMP, born 1811, was a daughter of Jesse and Elizabeth BEAUCHAMP of Maryland. She married Jonathan BROWN in Fayette County, Kentucky in 1826. Their children were William R. BROWN, George W. BROWN, Benjamin F. BROWN, Catherine DUGAN, and Mary E. CRUME. (Ref: KB 5:64)

Newell BEAUCHAMP (1760-1827) was born in Delaware and served in the Revolutionary War. His father, Coston BEAUCHAMP, was born in Maryland. In 1785, Newell migrated to Nelson County, Kentucky. His wife was Annice DOWNHAM. A son, Robinson P. BEAUCHAMP, was born near Bardstown, Kentucky on April 15, 1814 and married Ellen ROGERS (daughter of Edmund ROGERS of Virginia and Barren County, Kentucky) in 1845. (Ref: KB 2:75-76. Note: Additional information on the Beauchamps in Maryland can be found in the DAR Magazine, Vol. 66, p. 234 (Ref: SRM:22) and a genealogy prepared by Stith Thompson in the Filson Club Quarterly, Vol. XXVIII (1954), pp. 142-180, and published in Genealogies of Kentucky Families, pp. 9-47 (Baltimore: Genealogical Publishing Co., 1981).

BEAVEN. Edward BEAVEN and wife Ellen GREEN, along with his brother Col. Charles BEAVEN of the Revolutionary War, were the first Catholic settlers on Hardin's Creek in Kentucky, having migrated there circa 1786. Col. Beaven returned to Maryland after a few years, probably to St. Mary's County. Richard BEAVEN was also an early

10

settler. (Ref: KB 5:50 and KC:45-46)

Thompson BEAVEN was a Bardstown elder in 1820, and Samuel BEAVEN and Benjamin BEAVEN were in Breckinridge County, Kentucky between 1810 and 1820 (Ref: KC:63, 142).

BEAVER. Charles BEAVER (or BEAVEN) was a Revolutionary War soldier from Harford County, Maryland. He applied for a pension on September 1, 1820 (age 66), stating that he had served from 1776 to 1780 in the 6th Maryland Regiment. He was granted pension S36414 and subsequently transferred to the Kentucky Agency in 1828. (Ref: MS:56; MRP:4) However, Sources RSK:163 and KPR:1835 indicate that a Charles BEVER was a Lieutenant in the Maryland Line, pensioned in 1819 (age 80) and transferred from Maryland to Washington County, Kentucky in 1823. Source HCP:16 states Charles BEAVER was a Private in Capt. WEBB's Company in Harford County in 1775, and Source MRR:9 states he was a Lieutenant (born 1755).

BECK. Thomas BECK applied for a Revolutionary War pension in 1833 (age 70) while residing in Caldwell County, Kentucky. He stated he served under Capt. Simon WEEKS in 1777 and was called out frequently over the next three years to defend the coast along the Chesapeake Bay. He had also learned to beat the drum and performed this service. Thomas was born in 1763 in Kent County, Maryland and married Nancy or Ann ----, on December 20, 1792. In 1794 they moved to Ohio County, Virginia near Wheeling and lived there for about 8 years before moving to Livingston County (now Caldwell), Kentucky. Thomas BECK died on November 10, 1840. In 1846, his widow (age 75) applied for a pension and William P. GEORGE and George G. CASH both attested to her marriage to Thomas BECK in 1792 in Maryland. She submitted the following from her family Bible: Thomas and Ann BECK married December 20, 1792; Ann BECK, born September 24, 1793; Margaret E. BECK, born October 24, 1795; Maria BECK, born June 24, 1797; James BECK, born January 18, 1799; William G. BECK, born August 1, 1801; Elenor BECK, born February 10, 1804; Lewis G. BECK, born September 8, 1805; Adam BECK, born April 4, 1807; Beulah H. BECK, born March 13, 1814; George H. BECK, born May 4, 1815; Thomas J. BECK, born November 28, 1817; Lawson CASH and Maria BECK married April 13, 1819; Burrel CASH, born January 11, 1820; Marcus L. CASH, born February 17, 1822; William G. CASH, born June 16, 1825; Nelson CASH, born December 18, 1827; Lewis G. CASH, born March 27, 1839 (sic); Lewis G. CASH, born September 13, 1832 (sic); James B. CASH, born April 26, 1835; Lawson CASH, Jr., born April 3, 1837; Thomas BECK died November 10, 1840, age 75; Lewis G. CASH died September 8, 1833; and, Lawson L. CASH died July 17, 1841. Thomas BECK was granted a pension at $36.66 per year to begin March 4, 1831 and Ann Beck was granted pension W8354 in the same amount to begin March 4, 1836. (Ref: RSK:50; MS:23; KA 10:3, p. 154; LU 3:15; MRP:3; KPR:1835; MRR:10) Since Thomas BECK mentioned that he lived in Ohio County, Virginia, he was probably related to the Lt. John BECK, a Revolutionary War soldier from Kent County, Maryland who also went to Ohio County, Virginia. He gave bounty land warrant #852 (which was partly in Ross County) to his brother Alexander BECK, who died in 1839 in Adams County, Ohio (Ref: KA 12:2, p. 100).

BECKITT. Thomas BECKITT from Maryland was an early Catholic settler circa 1786 on Hardin's Creek in (now) Washington County, Kentucky (Ref: KC:56).

BELL, BEALL. Walter BELL of Maryland was an early Catholic settler circa 1785 on Cartwright's Creek in (now) Washington County, Kentucky. (Ref: KC:80)

David BELL, at the age of 20, drove a team from Maryland to Ohio County, Kentucky in 1815. A veteran of the War of 1812, David BELL (BEALL) married Mary IGLEHEART in Kentucky, and died there in 1871. Their son, John D. BELL, was born in Ohio County, Kentucky on October 12, 1825 (Ref: KB 3:122)

David BEALL was a Private in the 34th Regiment of Prince George's County, Maryland, 1813-1814 (Ref: MW 6:15, 19, 22).

BELT. Joseph I. BELT was born in Prince George's County, Maryland on March 21, 1799, the youngest son of Joseph BELT (a Revolutionary soldier) and Rachel BRASHEAR. They migrated to Scott County, Kentucky around 1813. (Ref:7:28)

Joseph C. BELT (relationship unknown) married Mary ARMSTRONG circa 1824 in Fleming County, Kentucky. They had a son, George W. BELT (born July 23, 1825); moved to Platte County, Missouri by 1839 (Ref: KM:60)

Additional information on the Belt and Brashear families is in the Cary Genealogical Collection, Maryland Historical Society Library.

BENNETT. Joseph BENNETT of Maryland married Peggy DAVIS, daughter of Robert Tevis DAVIS, in Madison County, Kentucky in 1791. Their children were Moses, Joel, Jesse, Mary, Milton, Rebecca, Emily, Margaret, Elizabeth, Nancy, Serelda and Elijah. They migrated to Boone County, Missouri by 1821. (Ref: KA 14:1, p. 45)

Charles N. BENNETT was born in Ohio County, Kentucky on June 23, 1811, the eldest son of five children born to Samuel BENNETT and Lucretia BARNETT. Samuel BARNETT, son of John, came to Kentucky from near Baltimore, Maryland with his father's family in 1798. He died May 11, 1837 and his widow died on November 15, 1854 (Ref: KB 3:122-123).

BERRY. Edward BERRY was among the early Catholic settlers from Maryland to settle on Hardin's Creek, Kentucky circa 1786. (Ref: KC:56) Judson H. BERRY was born in Charles County, Maryland on November 25, 1786 and died in Union County, Kentucky on July 20, 1855; buried in a cemetery near Sturgis, Kentucky on U.S. Route 60. Chloe SMALLWOOD (1786-1851) is also buried there. The Smallwood family was very prominent in early Maryland (Ref: KCR:363).

BICKETT. Henry BICKETT of Maryland married Elizabeth GRAVES of Kentucky and their son Edmund G. BICKETT was born in Marion County, Kentucky on November 16, 1817. They were in Missouri by 1846 (Ref: KM:114).

BIDDLE. Richard BIDDLE and John CLARK of Bourbon County, Kentucky were bound unto William BRIERLY of Harford County, Maryland in the amount of $800 on November 6, 1811. Robert CLARK, of Harford County, deceased, left heirs, namely, Nancy BIDDLE (wife of Richard) and John CLARK (Ref: HCLR Liber HD #X, p. 228).

BISHOP. In an affidavit in 1832 in Nelson County, Kentucky, Solomon BISHOP, age 78, stated he knew and served in 1775 with Thomas JONES and Gen. Marquis CALMES in Maryland and Virginia (Ref: MS:54).

BLACK. James BLACK, born in Maryland, married Rachel RENICK of Virginia circa 1805 and lived in Barren County, Kentucky in 1810 (and other Kentucky counties later) before moving to Nashville, Tennessee in 1819. Their children, born in Kentucky, were Willis, James, Robert, William, Eliza and Emily. (Ref: KPG 1:3, p. 42)

Rudolph BLACK was living in Bracken County, Kentucky when he applied for and received pension S30774 on December 1, 1833, age 71. He stated he was born in Anne Arundel County, Maryland on March 14, 1762 and enlisted in Baltimore County, Maryland in 1778. After the Revolutionary War he moved to Frederick County, Maryland and then to Bracken County, Kentucky (Ref: MS:14. Source MRR:10 correctly states Rudolph BLACK served in Maryland. Source RSK:44 erroneously states he was in the Virginia Militia).

BLACKLOCK. Joseph BLACKLOCK, Nathaniel BLACKLOCK and William BLACKLOCK of Maryland were early Catholic settlers on Cartwright's Creek in (now) Washington County, Kentucky in 1788. Patrick BLACKLOCK was a Bardstown elder in 1820 (Ref: KC:63, 80).

BLADES. Samuel BLADES, a native of Maryland, migrated to Kentucky and settled in Jessamine County and then Bracken County where he died. His daughter, Mary BLADES, was born in Jessamine County and married John CLARKE (1804-1875) of Bracken County in 1829. Their son, John Blades CLARKE (born 1833) became a Judge (Ref: BCK:123-1-24).

BLANDFORD. Ignatius BLANDFORD and Charles T. BLANDFORD of Maryland were early Catholic settlers on Cartwright's Creek in (now) Washington County, Kentucky in 1788. Walter BLANDFORD had settled on Cox's Creek by 1800 and, being a carpenter, he had direction over the building of the old church of St. Michael. Even though his residence was in Bullitt County, he remained a member of the congregation of St. Michael until it was completed in 1812. (Ref: KC:80, 141)

Richard BLANDFORD was a Private in the Maryland Militia and applied for and received pension S10392 in 1831, age 78, in Nelson County, Kentucky (Ref: MRP:4; RSK:143; KPR:1835) He served from Charles County, Maryland (Ref: S. Eugene Clements and F. Edward Wright's Maryland Militia in the Revolutionary War, pp. 160-162. Silver Spring, Maryland: Family Line Publications, 1987).

BOARMAN. Felix BOARMAN (1805-1881), son of Roswell BOARMAN (1766-1850) and Miss McATEE, and a grandson of Capt. James BOARMAN, was born in Maryland and migrated with his parents to Lincoln and Marion Counties, Kentucky in 1812. Felix married Nancy CLEMENTS, daughter of John CLEMENTS and Polly HOCKER. (Ref: KB 5:55)

Sylvester BOARMAN was born October 5, 1801 in Charles County, Maryland and died in Hardin County, Kentucky on September 12, 1854. He is buried in Old Harcourt Cemetery between White Hill and Glendale, Kentucky (Ref: KCR:186. Additional data is in "The Descendants of William Boarman" compiled by C. F. Thomas in 1935, which is available at the Maryland Historical Society Library).

BODLEY. Thomas BODLEY, Cuthbert BANKS, William MORTON, Frederick RIDGELY, Daniel VERTNER and William POLLARD had originally purchased 31,000 acres at a Register's Sale of Non-Residents Land in Frankfort, Kentucky in 1800. They appointed James MORRISON of Lexington, Kentucky on November 18, 1805, to sell it for them (Ref: HCLR Liber DJ #S, p. 211).

BOHANNON. John BOHANNON went from Maryland to Kentucky circa 1800. His wife was Helen COOK. Their son, Henry BOHANNON, was a farmer, surveyor, justice and sheriff in Woodford County, Kentucky. He married Philadelphia GALE, daughter of Robert F. GALE and Elizabeth WOOD, and their son, Harvey BOHANNON, was born in Shelby County, Kentucky on November 3, 1829 and married Cynthia Ann SCROGGIN in 1849 (Ref: KB 3:85; KB 7:155).

BOLTON. John BOLTON of Maryland was an early Catholic settler on Hardin's Creek in (now) Washington County, Kentucky circa 1786 (Ref: KC:56).

BOONE. Charles BOONE and Susan HOWARD moved from Maryland to Nelson County, Kentucky in 1798 and subsequently moved to LaRue County, Kentucky. Their daughter, Mildred BOONE, was born in February, 1816, married Sylvester JOHNSON in 1835, and died July 29, 1875. (Ref: KB 5:26, 242)

John BOONE and Washington BOONE were among the early Catholic settlers from St. Mary's County, Maryland to migrate to Hardin's Creek, Kentucky in 1785 with the "Maryland League." (Ref: KC:28, 56).

BORING. Eli BORING (1793-1851) and Cecilia LOUDENSLAGER (1800--1878), both natives of what is now Carroll County, Maryland, migrated to Brooke County, West Virginia where their son, Prof. H. BORING, was born March 10, 1825. He later moved to Hopkins County, Kentucky (Ref: 4:62).

BOSLEY. Dr. Henry P. BOSLEY was born March 21, 1823 to Gideon BOSLEY, Jr. (July 9, 1784 - November 29, 1830) and Elizabeth FLEECE (1790-1864) of Lincoln County, Kentucky. Gideon was a soldier in the War of 1812. His father, Gideon BOSLEY, Sr., married a Miss COLE of Baltimore, Maryland and later settled in Lincoln County, Kentucky about five miles from Stanford. Another son of Gideon BOSLEY, Jr. was Charles F. BOSLEY (1814-1882) of Washington County, Kentucky. (Ref: KB 5:58) Additional data on the Bosley family can

14

be found in St. Paul's Parish Register in Baltimore (Ref: SRM:34).

BOSTICK. Hezekiah BOSTICK was born circa 1796 in Maryland and married Elizabeth FLOOD or Elizabeth TRUITT. He migrated to Kentucky where these children were born, presumably in Jefferson County: Amelia Elizabeth BOSTICK (born circa 1820) married Samuel BAILEY; William P. BOSTICK (born circa 1823) married Sarah J. YOUNG and died in Louisville, Kentucky in 1884; Ellen Amanda BOSTICK (July 25, 1827 - May 2, 1919, Houston, Texas) married (1) James R. BIRKHEAD and (2) Charles A. GRAY; and, Ellis Hezekiah BOSTICK (August 22, 1831-October 27, 1885) married Katherine B. MOORE and died in New Orleans (Ref: KA 10:1, p. 48).

BOSTON. The Boston family of Maryland descend from one Henry BOSTON who arrived in Somerset County, Maryland in 1663. Many of his descendants migrated in later years to Kentucky, as follows: Jacob BOSTON (1766-c1835) and brother Jesse BOSTON (1772-1830), sons of Jacob BOSTON (1722-1788) of Worcester County, Maryland, migrated to Spencer County, Kentucky circa 1825; Thomas Williamson BOSTON (1786-1867), son of Levin BOSTON (1747-c1820), migrated to Barren County, Kentucky circa 1817; Silas BOSTON (c1801-c1835), son of Jesse BOSTON (1745-c1815), migrated to Spencer County, Kentucky circa 1825; James BOSTON (c1778-1833), son of Esau BOSTON (1753--1795), migrated to Louisville, Kentucky in 1804 and his children settled Beech Grove, Kentucky (Ref: KB 7:213, and for considerably more genealogical information, see Matthew M. Wise's The Boston Family of Maryland, 1967, available at the Maryland Historical Society Library).

BOULDIN. Joseph ALEXANDER of Henry County, Virginia married (1) Ann C. BOULDIN in 1807, and (2) Sarah BOULDIN in 1818 in Charlotte County, Virginia, a daughter of Thomas and Lucy BOULDIN. Thomas BOULDIN emigrated from England and settled in Maryland, but afterward moved to Virginia. In 1824 Joseph ALEXANDER migrated to Cumberland County, Kentucky (Ref: KB 5:35).

BOUNDS. Thomas J. BOUNDS (born 1800 in Maryland) married Hester A. PURNELL (born 1804 in Maryland) and migrated to Woodford County, Kentucky where their son Charles L. BOUNDS was born in 1831. By 1832 they had moved to Marion County, Missouri. (Ref: KM:165) The Bounds and Purnell families were from the Eastern Shore of Maryland (Ref: SRM:35).

BOWLES. In St. Mary's County, Maryland in 1774 the children of John BOWLES were William, John Baptist, Joseph, Jane, James J., Susan, Henrietta, and Mary. They subsequently migrated to Kentucky and Missouri. Joseph BOWLES married Alice RALEY and died in Washington County, Kentucky. John Baptist BOWLES married Henrietta WHEATLEY and had these children: Walter BOWLES was born in 1788 in Maryland and married Rose McATEE in Union County, Kentucky in 1831; James W. BOWLES was born in 1795 near Bardstown, Kentucky, married Susan LUCKETT, settled in St. Charles, Missouri; Leo BOWLES married Theresa McATEE and settled in St. Charles, Missouri; Clara BOWLES was born in 1797 and married Dennis O'NAN in 1823 in Union County, Kentucky; Catherine BOWLES married Stephen T. McATEE and settled in St. Charles, Missouri; Matilda BOWLES married Walter BARRON in 1823, Union County, Kentucky; and, Cecelia BOWLES married James W. DRURY and settled in St. Charles, Missouri. (Ref: An article on the Bowles family by James F. O'Nan in KA 10:2, 1974, pp. 83-84)

The brothers Ignatius BOWLES, John BOWLES and William BOWLES migrated from St. Mary's County, Maryland in 1785 and were among the early Catholic settlers in the "Maryland League" on Pottinger's Creek in (now) Washington County, Kentucky (Ref: KC:28, 31)

Samuel BOWLES applied for a Revolutionary War pension while residing in Bourbon County, Kentucky in 1832, age 82. He stated he volunteered for one year in 1775 in Sussex County, Delaware under Capt. David HALL, and then moved to Worcester County, Maryland and entered the service in 1776 under Capt. James CORDERRY. In 1777 he served with Capt. Mathew PURNELL and in 1778 he was drafted under Capt. Solomon LONG and was attached to the 3rd Maryland Regiment. He was sick in the hospital at Germantown for about 5 months. In 1839 he transferred from Kentucky to Galloway County, Missouri to be near his children. In 1854 his widow, Nancy, stated she married Samuel on February 15, 1815 in Worcester County, Maryland and her maiden name was POWELL. Samuel BOWLES died May 16, 1841. Pension W10444 was later issued on May 22, 1855 to his widow (Ref: MS:8; MRP:5; KPR:1835. Source RSK:42 misspelled his name "Bowels").

BOWLING. Thomas BOWLING was born in Maryland in 1763 and married first in 1783 to Ann NEVITT in Prince George's County, Maryland. He migrated to Pottinger's Creek in (now) Washington County, Kentucky with the "Maryland League" in 1785. His second wife was Ellen BROWN, widow of John HUTCHINS, and they were in Nelson County, Kentucky circa 1806. By his first wife he had a son Charles D. BOWLING, and by his second wife he had William, Francis, Robert, Ann and Eleanor (Ref: KA 5:4, p. 220; KC:28-30).

BOWMAN. Leonard BOWMAN of Maryland was among the first settlers of Clark County, Indiana where he lived and died. His son, Ransom BOWMAN, was born in Indiana, married and had an only child, William M. BOWMAN, who was born February 7, 1831 and settled in Lyon County, Kentucky. (Ref: KB 4:146)

Roswell BOWMAN of Maryland was an early Catholic settler circa 1786 on Hardin's Creek in (now) Washington County, Kentucky. (Ref: KC:56)

Joseph BOWMAN was a resident of Washington County, Kentucky. The Elizabeth-Town Advertiser (Maryland) on December 3, 1801 contained this notice: "Chancery Court case, Jacob WOOLFKILL agst. Joseph BOWMAN, to convey part of tract "The Resurvey on Manheim" in Washington County, Maryland (and) the defendant resides in Kentucky." (Ref: WMNA 2:69).

BOYER. John Gottlieb BOYER was a Private in the Maryland Line during the Revolutionary War, and applied for a pension in 1831 (age 71) in Fayette County, Kentucky, subsequently receiving it, as did his widow (W8378) after his death. His Bible record contained the following information: John G. BOYER married Anna Mary ZEALER on April 10, 1786; Alfred Z. BOYER married Elizabeth Jane LOCOM on December 16, 1829; Alfred Z. BOYER married Zerelda McCOY on September 24, 1834; John Gottlieb MOYER, born August 4, 1762; Anna Mary BOYER, born February 17, 1769; Mary BOYER, born February 28, 1787; Margret BOYER, born October 12, 1788; Ezra BOYER, born April 4, 1790; Henry BOYER, born December 5, 1791; Jacob BOYER, born March 10, 1793; and, William BOYER, born December 9, 1794 (Ref: MRP:5; LU 4:58-59; KPR:183-184; MRR:111).

BOYLE. Mathew J. BOYLE was a Catholic settler from Maryland on Cartwright's Creek in (now) Washington County, Kentucky circa 1785 (Ref: KC:80).

BRADSHAW. John BRADSHAW and family of Maryland migrated to Kentucky prior to 1800 and had many conflicts with the Indians. His daughter, Agnes BRADSHAW, married Dr. Samuel ROSS, and their son, B. B. ROSS, was born in 1839 in Shelbyville in Shelby County, Kentucky (Ref: KB 7:233).

BRANDENBURG. Mathias BRANDENBURG migrated to Kentucky from Frederick County, Maryland. His brothers were William and Jacob BRANDENBURG. William BRANDENBURG was born in 1758 and was a Private in the Maryland Militia. Jacob Brandenburg married Dorcas AYRES before 1820 in Maryland (Ref: MRR:12, 111. Note: For more biographical material, see History of Frederick County, Maryland, by T. J. C. Williams and Folger McKinsey. Baltimore: Regional Publishing Co., 1979).

BRASHEAR. Judge BRASHEAR of Maryland married Elizabeth LEACH and they were in Scott County, Kentucky by 1807. Their son L. C. BRASHEAR was born there January 21, 1808 and they were in Missouri by 1816 (Ref: KM:142).

BRATTON. James BRATTON married Rachel GREATHOUSE on June 11, 1805 in Warren County, Kentucky. Their marriage was proven through a Maryland Revolutionary War pension application, probably that of William BRATTON (born 1755) who was a Seaman in the Navy (Ref: MRR:12, 111).

BREATHETT. Susan C. H. BREATHETT, daughter of William BREATHETT and Miss WHITSETT, was born near Hagerstown, Maryland. They migrated to Kentucky where Susan married William M. BLAKEY of Culpeper County, Virginia, and a son George T. BLAKEY was born February 5, 1822 in Logan County, Kentucky. William BLAKEY died in 1824 and Susan BLAKEY died in 1830. George later became Sheriff of Logan County (Ref: KB 4:136).

BREVARD. The Brevard family were Huguenots and settled in Baltimore, Maryland. John BREVARD went to North Carolina and served in the Revolutionary War. His son, Cyrus N., was born in Lincoln County, North Carolina in 1808 and died in Smith County, Tennessee in 1866. Some Brevards went to Fulton County, Kentucky. (Ref: KB 6:75. Note: Additional data on the Brevard families of Maryland and North Carolina can be found in the "Genealogy of the Mays

Family" at the Maryland Historical Society Library in Baltimore (Ref: SRM:41).

BREWER. William BREWER of southern Maryland was an early Catholic settler in Nelson County, Kentucky in 1785, and Thomas BREWER had settled on Cox's Creek, Kentucky by 1800. (Ref: KC:28, 114)

George W. BREWER of Maryland was married to Sarah FOX of Virginia and their son, Judge Milton BREWER, was born on September 27, 1820 in Spencer County, Kentucky. By 1841 they were in Missouri. (Ref: KM:152)

James BREWER was born circa 1760 in St. Mary's County, Maryland, married Mary YATES, and died after 1810 in Washington County, Kentucky (Ref: MGS 20:2, p. 171).

BRICE. The Brice family of Maryland settled in Campbell County, Kentucky. "Indenture made 30 August 1820 between William MILES and Elizabeth his wife, daughter of Henry BAKER, deceased, of the County of Campbell of the one part, and Peter MILES of the County of Baltimore in the State of Maryland of the other part. William and Elizabeth for $500 sell all the land in the State of Maryland aforesaid which the said Elizabeth MILES is entitled to as the only daughter and child of Mary BRICE, deceased, who intermarried with Henry BAKER, deceased, and which was devised to the said Mary by the name of Mary BRICE, by the last will and testament of her father Thomas BRICE, now deceased, executed on the 10 October 1775 which said last will and testament is recorded in Harford County in the State of Maryland. Sealed and delivered in presence of Richard SOUTHGATE and W. W. SOUTHGATE." (Ref: Campbell County Deed Book E, p. 377, published in KA 6:2, p. 66) The will of Thomas BRICE was written October 10, 1775 and probated April 16, 1776 in Harford County, Maryland, naming his wife ELizabeth BRICE and daughters Mary BRICE, Christian BRICE and Margaret BRICE, all under age 16. (Ref: Will Book AJ No. 2, p. 29).

BRIERLY. George BRIERLY was born in 1757 and enlisted in the Revolutionary War in Harford County, Maryland, serving under Capt. Benjamin AMOS. George married Mary GARRISON on March 27, 1793. Mary was born in 1761 and was living as late as November 22, 1856. In 1832 George BRIERLY produced the depositions of Abraham WILLIAMS, Thomas MOUNTJOY and George MEFFORD in Mason County, Kentucky to prove his military service. (Ref: Mason County, Kentucky Court Order Book M, p. 4, published in KP:181; LU 4:92; MS:63; MRR:111) George BRIERLY took the Oath of Allegiance to the State of Maryland in 1778 in Harford County (Ref: HCP:25).

BRIGHT. John Hanson BRIGHT (1789-1837) married Teresa CISSELL, daughter of Peter and Eleanor CISSELL. The Bright family was from St. Mary's County, Maryland and subsequently settled in the Kentucky counties of Union, Graves, Marion and Washington. (Ref: KA 16:2, p. 118)

Henrietta BRIGHT of Maryland married Joseph GRAY (born 1773) of New Jersey and raised a family in Bath County, Kentucky. A son,

John GRAY (born 1807) married Matilda BELLAMY (Ref: KPG 2:4, p. 231).

BRIMMAGE. John BRIMMAGE was born in Queen Anne County, Maryland on June 8, 1760 and served in the militia during the Revolutionary War. He moved to Anson County, North Carolina and enlisted there in 1781. Afterwards, he moved to Effingham County, Georgia and Pendleton County, South Carolina and Lincoln County, Tennessee. In 1795 he moved to Graves County, Kentucky. He received pension S38568 for his services (Ref: MS:40; KPR:1835).

BRISCOE. The Briscoe family of southern Maryland was very prominent in colonial Maryland. Henry BRISCOE was born in St. Mary's County on February 3, 1763 and enlisted into the military at Leonardtown in 1781 for six months. He migrated to Jefferson County, Kentucky in 1802 and in 1832 he applied for and received pension S30888. He moved to Clark County, Illinois in 1835 and was still alive in 1837 when he requested that his pension be transferred there. (Ref: MS:51; KPR:1835)

Ralph BRISCOE was born November 24, 1747, in Trinity Parish, Charles County, Maryland, a son of John BRISCOE and Ann WOOD. He married (1) Ann MACKALL, daughter of John MACKALL and MARTHA DUKE, circa 1770 and (2) Sarah T. DELASHMUTT in Frederick, Maryland in 1792. They moved to Kentucky in 1812. (Ref: MGS 25:1, p. 129)

Catherine BRISCOE (born 1802 in Maryland) married Benjamin EMISON (born 1801) of Scott County, Kentucky. Their son, James A. EMISON, was born January 15, 1824 and they were in Clay County, Missouri by 1850 (Ref: KM:143).

BROOKHART. David BROOKHART of Kentucky was married to Miss Terace FUNK of Allegany County, Maryland by Rev. KURTZ in March, 1820. (Ref: NAW:31).

BROWN. George BROWN of Maryland was an early Catholic settler on Hardin's Creek in (now) Washington County, Kentucky in 1786. (Ref: KC:56)

James BROWN was born in Maryland on October 10, 1780 and died in Jefferson County, Kentucky on April 9, 1853. His wife was Urath O. LAWRENCE, daughter of Samuel and Sarah LAWRENCE. Urath was born in Maryland on June 27, 1791 and died in Kentucky on January 3, 1854. They are buried in the Brown and Lawrence Cemetery in Jefferson County, Kentucky, as are the following: James Lawrence BROWN, March 10, 1827 - April 13, 1861; Francis C. BROWN, died July 4, 1830, age 1 year and 2 months; Elizabeth C. BROWN, died September 18, 1822, age 10 years and 6 months; Samuel L. BROWN, died September 26, 1817, age 1 year; Alfred BROWN, died March 15, 1820, age 10 years; Emeline BROWN, died January 8, 1826, age 10 months; Mary Ann BROWN, December 11, 1817 - July 20, 1850, married Thomas Seabrook FORMAN, 1808-1849; Norborne Galt BROWN, infant son of Arthur and Matilda BROWN; Theodore BROWN, April 29, 1853 - July 7, 1853, and Horace BROWN, June 6, 1856 - March 20, 1857, sons of Theodore and Sally BROWN. (Ref: KCR:228-9)

William BROWN was born February 15, 1790 in Baltimore, Maryland and died June 20, 1859 in Jefferson County, Kentucky. His wife Catherine -----, was born July 27, 1793 in Fairfield County, Virginia and died November 7, 1840 in Kentucky. They are buried in the Old Cemetery at 16th and Jefferson Streets in Louisville, Kentucky. (Ref: KCR:232)

Edward BROWN was born March 16, 1734 in Maryland, married Margaret DURBIN and moved to Madison County, Kentucky circa 1795. He died August 14, 1823. (Ref: KA 10:2, p. 99)

Richard BROWN was raised in that part of Maryland which became the District of Columbia. He moved to Virginia and married Sarah WOMACK. They lived in Adair County, Kentucky from 1805 to 1827 and moved to Montgomery County, Illinois. He died in 1843. Their children were Elisha, Elizabeth, Daniel, Ann, John, Hiram, Charlotte, and Harrison. (Ref: KA 15:4, p. 242)

Jeremiah BROWN was an early Catholic settler to Pottinger's Creek in Kentucky with the "Maryland League" in 1785 from St. Mary's County. (Ref: KC:28, 30)

Elizabeth BROWN was born in Hardin County, Kentucky in 1824, Her ancestors were from Virginia and Maryland and were among the earliest settlers of Kentucky. She was married to Thomas McCORMACK who emigrated from Ireland in 1836. (Ref:KB 2:187)

Hugh BROWN and wife Sarah, of Jefferson County, Kentucky, heirs of Absalom BARNEY, late of Baltimore County, Maryland, conveyed to Thomas BARNEY their estate right and claim to lands of said Absalom BARNEY. (Ref: BCLR Liber WG #83, p. 45)

Caleb BROWN and wife Jemima of Madison County, Kentucky, conveyed land to Henry STEVENSON of Frederick County, Maryland on March 25, 1822 (Ref: BCLR Liber WG #70, p. 222).

BRUINGTON. The Bruingtons of Ellston Mills, Maryland moved to Breckinridge County, Kentucky in 1800. George BRUINGTON was born in 1778 and married Mary Ann BROWN in 1805 in Nelson County. His brother James migrated with him, as did their sister Elizabeth (1785-1872) who married (1) John BEAR in 1807 and (2) William WHEELER in 1817 (Ref: KA 12:1, p. 53).

BRUNER. Jacob BRUNER applied for a Revolutionary pension while residing in Boone County, Kentucky in 1821, age 62. He stated that he enlisted in 1777 for one year in Maryland at Fort Frederick under Capt. Samuel MOORE. He also served in 1778 or 1779 in the company of Capt. CRESAP in Maryland, as well as with a Company of Rangers in Pennsylvania. Henry DUGAN confirmed his statement. In 1823, Christian BRUNER and Elizabeth ROHRER, of Jessamine County, Kentucky, made oath that Jacob BRUNER served in the military as noted above. Jacob also stated that his wife (not named) was 66 and that she was a mother of 14 children. She "had been for the last 12 years unable to attend to her business due to a peculiar and

20

unusual weakness which had stricken her." His youngest daughter (not named) was then age 17. In 1851 in Hamilton County, Ohio, the children of Jacob BRUNER made oath of their relationship to him: Moses BRUNER, age 54; Solomon BRUNER, age 51; Simon BRUNER, age 49; Lydia ROWAN; Samuel BRUNER; and David BRUNER. Jacob BRUNER died in Boone County, Kentucky on February 14, 1845. He had received pension S35792 beginning November 15, 1823. Margaret BRUNER received pension W332, indicating she was a widow of a Jacob BRUNER (Ref: MRP:6; MRR:12; MS:7).

BRUNT. Chloe BRUNT, daughter of Peter BRUNT, was born in 1776 in Maryland and married on June 9, 1794 to William Henry SOUTH, who was born November 6, 1772 near Springfield, Kentucky. Their son, Henry Prator SOUTH, married Matilda Ann PARSON, of Nova Scotia, on February 22, 1853 (Ref: KA 11:1, p. 43).

BRYAN. Francis BRYAN and William BRYAN were among the early Catholic settlers on Hardin's Creek, Kentucky in 1785. They migrated there from southern Maryland (Ref: KC:28, 55).

BRYANT. William BRYANT (1792-1884) was a Private in Capt. WELLS Artillery Company, 22nd Regiment, Anne Arundel County in the War of 1812 in Maryland. (Ref: William Marine's The British Invasion of Maryland, 1812-1815, p. 232. Baltimore: Genealogical Publishing Co., 1977) William BRYANT moved to Nelson County, Kentucky and his son, Ben S. BRYANT, married Allie SPALDING (Ref: KB:145, 146).

BRYARLY. Samuel W. BRYARLY was born in Maryland in 1786 and married Margaret LOGAN, daughter of John LOGAN (died 1818) of Kentucky. She was born in Kentucky in 1788 and died in 1855. Their children were: Henry, 1815-1826; Elizabeth, born 1818; John, 1820-1832; Margaret Ann, 1822-1846, who married a HUDSON; Isabella Jane, 1824-1898, who married Nathaniel BUTTERFIELD and died in Iowa; and, Martha Mary, 1826-1847, who married a LUCKY (Ref: KBG 6:4, p. 157. Note: The Bryarly, or Briarly, family resided in Baltimore and Harford Counties, Maryland).

BUCKLEY. William BUCKLEY of Maryland married Permelia EATON of Kentucky in Fleming County, Kentucky prior to 1820. Their son, William BUCKLEY, was born November 12, 1820 and was in Missouri by 1866 (KM:60).

BUCKMAN. Joseph BUCKMAN, Harry BUCKMAN and William BUCKMAN were settlers on Cartwright's Creek, in (now) Washington County, Kentucky in 1788, and Ignatius BUCKMAN and Clement BUCKMAN settled at Rolling Fork before 1800. (Ref: KC:80, 110)

John Sims BUCKMAN was born August 21, 1791 in St. Mary's County, Maryland and married Elizabeth ROBARDS (or ROBERTS) in Kentucky on January 14, 1811. She was born February 8, 1795 and died March 3, 1868. John died May 5, 1865. They had 15 children, including Joseph R. BUCKMAN (born November 5, 1813) who married Martha S. SIMS. The Buckmans migrated to Monroe County, Missouri in 1836. (Ref: KA 7:1, p. 41; KA 10:1, p. 43).

BULLITT. This notice appeared in the Elizabeth-Town Advertiser on March 26, 1801: "William BULLITT, living in Moorfield, Virginia offers reward for negro fellow Isaac, 6 feet tall, who ran away from his son, Benjamin BULLITT, at Redstone Fort; was on his way to Kentucky; purchased of one HOGGONS, who lives on the Sugar lands near Mr. PETER's quarters." (Ref: WMNA 2:61).

BURCH. Walter BURCH was among the early Catholic settlers who migrated from St. Mary's County, Maryland to Nelson County, Kentucky in 1785 (Ref: KC:28)

Zachariah BURCH married Mildred ROBEY on December 26, 1787 in Charles County, Maryland. Source MRR:111 indicates he was born in 1757 and they married December 22, 1776. Zachariah received bounty land warrant 38846-160-55 for his military service in the Revolutionary War and subsequently migrated to Kentucky and Missouri. His widow received pension W9759. (Ref: LU 5:80)

Benjamin BURCH was a Sergeant in the 3rd Maryland Line in the Revolutionary War. He married in 1809 to Chloe -----, about 2 miles from Washington, D.C., by Rev. Joseph MESSENGER of Prince George's County, Maryland. Benjamin received bounty land warrant 108-160-55 and also applied for a pension in 1826 in Kentucky. He received a pension in 1827, and died December 17, 1830. His wife was 84 in 1855, and received pension W4137. (Ref: LU 5:78; MGS 4:43; MRP:6; KPR:1835; MRR:12)

John BURCH applied for pension in Barren County, Kentucky. He was born in Prince George's County, Maryland on January 18, 1759 and was taken by his father to Charles County, Maryland where he lived until age 19 or 20. In the second year of the war his father moved to Prince William County, Virginia and later to Fauquier County for 16 or 17 years. Then he moved to Amherst County for 16 years and then to Barren County, Kentucky. He served in both Maryland and Virginia. His wife Elizabeth -----, was born 1779 and stated she married John BURCH in Loudon County, Virginia in her 17th year. John died March 1, 1834 and had received a pension since March, 1831. Elizabeth received pension W5238 beginning March 4, 1848. She died November 13, 1850. Their children were: Robert D., born July 11, 1797; Margaret F., born June 21, 1799; Landon J., born August 9, 1801; Anne, born September 30, 1804; Fanny P., born December 19, 1806; William D., born October 9, 1809; and, John, born February 12, 1816. "Long John" BURCH (1759-1834) and wife Elizabeth BURCH (1779-1850) are buried in the Bales Graveyard on the W. E. BALES farm on the Burkesville Road, 7 miles from Glasgow, Barren County, Kentucky. (Ref: LU 5:79; MS:6; KCR:24; MRP:6)

Joseph BURCH was born in Maryland circa 1790 and migrated to Kentucky where a son, Romanus W. BURCH, was born in Meade County in 1825 (KB 1:198-199).

BURCHAM. Eleanor BURCHAM, daughter of David and Rebecca, of Pennsylvania, was born March 16, 1781 in Maryland and married William HAYS, Jr. (1788-1866) on November 21, 1797 in Kentucky. Eleanor HAYS died in Washington County, Kentucky on March 20, 1863. They had 13 children: William Hercules; Nancy; Mary Polly, married Berry LEWIS; Rebecca Vanvactor, married William G. SHORT; Hercules, married Anna Isabel RAY; Sally, married Joseph SHAUNTY; John J., married Susan STONE; Dr. Alfred B., married Belle -----; Teneriffe, died in infancy; Dr. Cyrus Wayne; David Randall, married Mary McMAKIN; Eleanor J., died in infancy; and, James Benjamin, married Sidney Anna NEAL. (Ref: Robert G. Lowry's book entitled Footprints: The Life Stories of Robert Graham Lowry and Susan Louise Thurman and Those of Their In-America Ancestors From Jamestown and Plymouth to the Present, 1620-1985, available at the Maryland Historical Society).

BURGESS. Joshua BURGESS was a Lieutenant in the 4th Maryland Line during the Revolutionary War and applied for a pension in 1826 in Mason County, Kentucky, which he received in 1830. (MRP:7; MGS 5:43; KPR:1835)

Capt. James B. BURGESS was born on January 26, 1800 and died on April 26, 1854. Catherine BURGESS, formerly McCALIB, originally ARMSTRONG, was born in Baltimore, Maryland in 1784 and died in Russellville, Kentucky on May 13, 1857. Both are buried in Maple Grove Cemetery in Logan County, Kentucky (Ref: KCR:282)

Henry D. BURGESS of Maryland had a son, Judge Cavon D. BURGESS, born November 5, 1833 in Mason County, Kentucky, and was in St. Joseph, Missouri by 1855. John D. BURGESS of Maryland married Lydia M. WISE of Virginia and son Thomas J. BURGESS was born June 15, 1828 in Mason County, Kentucky and was in Missouri by 1850, and J. Kate BURGESS was born March 12, 1830 in Mason County, Kentucky and was in Missouri by 1855. O.B. BURGESS was born August 15, 1820 in Mason County, Kentucky and was in Platte County, Missouri by 1864. H.G. BURGESS, son of O.B. BURGESS and P.D. KILGORE, was born October 13, 1851 in Mason County, Kentucky and was in Clinton County, Missouri by 1864 (Ref: KM:116).

BURNAM. Thomas BURNAM, a native of England, settled in Maryland near Georgetown (now Washington, D.C.) prior to the American Revolution. His son, John BURNAM, was born in Cecil County, Maryland and served in the Revolutionary War at the Battle of Guilford Courthouse in North Carolina. (Source DAR:103 shows a John BURNHAM, 1762-1831, who married Mary Ann FORT, and served in the Carolinas) John returned to Maryland and then moved to North Carolina before migrating to Madison County, Kentucky. His son, Thompson BURNAM, was born in Wake County, North Carolina on February 4, 1789 and moved with his father to Richmond, Kentucky. He married Lucinda FIELD, daughter of John FIELD of Culpeper County, Virginia, who moved to Bourbon County, Kentucky circa 1800. Thompson had these children: John Field BURNAM; Mary WILSON; Edmond H. BURNAM; Eugenia HUME; and, Curtis F. BURNAM (Ref: BCK:235).

BURRIS. Sarah BURRIS of Maryland married John SHOTWELL of New Jersey and their son Nathaniel SHOTWELL was born in Mason County, Kentucky on December 8, 1811. They were in Missouri by 1831 (Ref: KM:119).

BUTLER. John BUTLER was born in Maryland in 1769 and moved to Kentucky soon after the Revolutionary War and settled in the upper part of the State in the blue grass country where he was married. Soon thereafter he moved to Green County (now Adair) where he died in 1839. A son, Champness BUTLER, was born March 10, 1799 in Adair County, Kentucky. (Ref: KB 5:70)

Tobias H. BUTLER was born in Frederick County, Maryland on February 20, 1792 and was a soldier in the War of 1812. He married four times: (1) Elizabeth WALLER, daughter of Thomas WALLER, in Jefferson County, Kentucky on November 9, 1818; (2) Sally REED, daughter of William REED, in Jefferson County, Kentucky on June 4, 1826; (3) Sarah GOSS, daughter of Daniel GOSS, in Owen County, Indiana on March 6, 1828; and (4) Elizabeth RUSSELL in Jefferson County, Kentucky on November 3, 1856 (Ref: KA 14:3, p. 183).

BYRNE. Ignatius BYRNE was among the early Catholic settlers who migrated from St. Mary's County, Maryland and settled on Pottinger's Creek in (now) Washington County, Kentucky in 1785 (Ref: KC:28, 31).

CALMES. General Marquis CALMES applied for pension in Woodford County, Kentucky in 1832 (age 77) and subsequently received pension S12674. John MALONE, Thomas JONES and Solomon BISHOP all signed affidavits that they knew him in Maryland and Virginia during the Revolution. (Ref: MS:54)

Miss Nancy CALMES, daughter of Gen. Marquis CALMES, married Dr. William R. JENNINGS of Tennessee in February, 1825, in Woodford County, Kentucky (Ref: KYM:38).

CAMBRON. Henry CAMBRON was an early Catholic settler in Kentucky in 1788, and was accompanied by his father, Baptist CAMBRON. They were from Montgomery County, Maryland. Henry CAMBRON's son Charles C. CAMBRON wrote the following, in part, in 1878: "My father's name was Henry CAMBRON; that of my mother before her marriage, Margaret HARBIN. They removed to Kentucky from St. Mary's County, Maryland in 1790 or 1791. I was myself born in Kentucky on November 5, 1791. My parents were then living on Cartwright's Creek. I helped to build the old St. Rose Church in 1808. I was married on Jan. 17, 1817 by Rev. R. P. MILES." (Ref: KC:69-72)

Charles CAMBRON, son of Harry, married Margaret MONTGOMERY, daughter of Basil MONTGOMERY, and died June 27, 1863. Charles died January 10, 1881. They had eight children: Stephen H., William C., Christopher C., Martha A. McGILL, Margaret I., James R., Nicholas L., and one child died in infancy (Ref: KB 5:73).

CAMPBELL. John CAMPBELL was a Private in the Maryland Line and applied for a pension for his Revolutionary services in 1831 (age 73) in Scott County, Kentucky, and subsequently received pension S30915. (Ref: MRP:7; KPR:1835)

Matthew CAMPBELL of Pennsylvania married Dorothy MARTIN of Maryland in Harrison County, Kentucky by 1819 and their son, Colin M.

CAMPBELL, was born February 7, 1820. By 1826 they were in Missouri (Ref: KM:78).

CANADY. Charles CANADY appears in Floyd County, Kentucky and Andrew CANADY in Pike County, Kentucky in 1810. Ruth CANADY was also in Pike County. They possibly were in Cecil County, Maryland in 1800 (Ref: MGS 24:4, p. 371).

CARLISLE. Robert CARLISLE of Woodford County, Kentucky was murdered in February, 1828, on the U.S. Turnpike Road, two miles from Washington, Pennsylvania near the bridge over the Chartier Creek. He was on his way home from to Kentucky from Cumberland, Maryland with a runaway slave named Kit, who has been charged (Ref: NAW:18).

CARLTON. Edwin CARLTON of Maryland married Sarah MOURNIN of Maryland and subsequently moved to Virginia and Kentucky. A daughter Eliza CARLTON married Thomas FOSTER in Scott County, Kentucky and their son, Robert E. FOSTER, was born in Gallatin County near Napoleon, Kentucky in 1830 (Ref: KB 8:61).

CARPENTER. Squire C. CARPENTER married Elizabeth SMITH after 1810 in Kentucky; county not stated. Their marriage was proven through a Maryland Revolutionary War pension application; soldier's name not given (Ref: MRR:111).

CARRICO. Joseph CARRICO, Cornelius CARRICO, and Nathaniel CARRICO were among the early Catholic settlers to Kentucky who settled on Cartwright's Creek in (now) Washington County in 1788. (Ref: KC:80)

Vincent CARRICO of Charles County, Maryland married Susannah QUICK in Madison County, Kentucky on February 18, 1796 and their children were probably Asa, Marie, Elizabeth, and James. (Ref: KA 12:4, p. 216)

Vincent CARRICO, son of Thomas Ignatius CARRICO and Elizabeth KIRBY, was born circa 1773 in Montgomery County, Maryland and married Mary ELDER in Nelson County, Kentucky on January 27, 1807. Levi CARRICO married Harriet NEAL in 1803 in Washington County, Maryland and they also migrated to Nelson County, Kentucky. James CARRICO was born in Montgomery County, Maryland circa 1775 and died in Hardin County, Kentucky January 31, 1847. He married Elizabeth TROUTMAN, daughter of John Michael TROUTMAN and Rebecca BEARD of Bullitt County, Kentucky. Elizabeth was born in Frederick County, Maryland in 1778 and died in Kentucky in 1836. Mary CARRICO was born in Maryland and married Benjamin H. KERRICK, a Revolutionary War soldier, and moved to Nelson County, Kentucky. Priscilla CARRICO was born in Maryland and married James LUCKETT circa 1795 in Washington County, Maryland and subsequently moved to Nelson County, Kentucky. Cornelius CARRICO was born in 1772 in Charles County, Maryland and married first to Susanna SHANKS in 1806 in Nelson County, Kentucky and secondly to Theresa O'BRYAN in 1823 in Washington County, Kentucky. Bartholomew CARRICO, son of Peter CARRICO and Margaret GATES, was born circa 1745 in Charles County, Maryland and married Winifred PAGET circa 1766. They subsequently settled in Nelson County, Kentucky. Basil CARRICO, son of Peter and

Margaret, was born circa 1747 in Maryland and married in Montgomery County. They moved to Washington County, Kentucky between 1794 and 1806. Theresa CARRICO (1790-1858), daughter of Basil, was born in Maryland and died as Sister Theresa of The Sisters of Charity at Nazareth, Kentucky. She was one of the founders of the order in 1812. (Ref: Genealogy prepared by Homer E. Carrico in the Filson Club Quarterly, VOl. XXV (1951), pp. 217-252 and published in Genealogies of Kentucky Families (Baltimore: Genealogical Publishing Co., 1981, pp. 215-250).

CARRINGTON. Thomas CARRINGTON and Elizabeth CAYWOOD were married August 5, 1804 in Maryland. Elizabeth CARRINGTON and Stephen CAYWOOD married April 15, 1804 in Maryland. Thomas CARRINGTON married (2) Turzy Jane WILSON on April 18, 1847 in Indiana. Thomas CARRINGTON was born November 20, 1782. Elizabeth CAYWOOD was born February 27, 1786. Their children were born in Kentucky: Eleanor on March 6, 1805; Samuel on December 27, 1807; Milton on June 30, 1810; Lucinda on October 12, 1812; Augustus on February 17, 1816; Asa on December 29, 1818; Edmund on May 24, 1821; and Thomas Peary on May 24, 1824. The children of Thomas and Turzy born in Indiana were: John Press on March 19, 1848; Taylor on October 1, 1849; and, George on January 31, 1852. Turzy Jane CARRINGTON was born September 11, 1820 and died April 19, 1906. Stephen CAYWOOD died February 23, 1802. Linna UMSTARD died September 6, 1805. Sally CAYWOOD died December 26, 1799. Aquilla CAYWOOD died March 4, 1822. Samuel CARRINGTON, husband of Milla, died May 6, 1818. John Thomas McDONALD died June 20, 1825. Thomas CARRINGTON died November 28, 1874 (Ref: Carrington Bible record published in Maryland Historical and Genealogical Bulletin 18:4, pp. 69-70 (1947).

CARROLL. John CARROLL served in the Revolutionary War from Charles County, Maryland in 1776 and applied for a pension while residing in Jessamine County, Kentucky in 1832, age 78; received pension S30913 (Ref: MS:53, MRP:8. Note: The Carrolls of Maryland were very prominent in early Maryland and many of them have been well researched. See SRM:57-60).

CASEY. Archibald CASEY lived in Allegany County, Maryland and Kent County, Delaware prior to the Revolutionary War. He enlisted in Dover, Delaware in 1775 and after the war moved to Kentucky. He married Hannah -----, in Allegany County, Maryland on January 23, 1800. He applied for a pension in 1818 (age 75) in Harrison County, Kentucky and died April 22, 1815. His widow received pension W9381 (Ref: MS:46).

CASKEY. Joseph CASKEY applied for a Revolutionary pension in Christian County, Kentucky in 1829. He stated he served as a Sergeant in Pennsylvania and lived in Westmoreland County. Since the Revolution he has lived in Baltimore, Maryland two different times, then in Richmond, Virginia, then in Mason County and Pulaski County, Kentucky, and now in Christian County for the past 27 years (Ref: MS:32).

CASSELL. Abraham CASSELL was a son of Henry CASSELL of Hesse Cassel in Germany who came to America in early 1700's. Abram was born near

Frederick, Maryland on September 25, 1756 and married Catherine LINGENFELDER (1755-1847) on April 24, 1782. He served as a Lieutenant in the Revolutionary War in Frederick County, Maryland in 1776. He applied for a pension in 1833 (age 77) in Jessamine County, Kentucky and included this family record of his children: Mary, born February 17, 1782; John, January 10, 1785 - March 30, 1815; Elizabeth, July 1, 1787 - June 6, 1789; Infant, born and died 1790; Catarena, born September 21, 1791; Barbara, born August 15, 1794; Susannah, born November 22, 1798; and Thomas Jefferson born August 30, 1802. Abram CASSELL died May 26, 1844 and his 84 year old widow received pension W2916 on December 21, 1844. Youngest son Thomas Jefferson CASSELL was born in Fayette County, Kentucky and married Susan M. DANIEL, and their youngest son Benjamin F. CASSELL died at Gettysburg in the Civil War (Ref: MS:53; LU 6:78-79; BCK:302-303; MRP:8; KPR:1835; MRR:14).

CASSIDY. Michael CASSIDY was born October 22, 1755 in Dublin, Ireland. In 1767 he ran away from home and went to America as a cabin boy on the ship "Maryland Merchant". He was apprenticed by the ship's captain to Robert CRAYTON in Baltimore, Maryland. Michael CASSIDY entered the Revolutionary War and was present at the surrender of Cornwallis in 1781. In 1782 he migrated to Kentucky and settled at Strode's Station in Clark County, and then moved to Fleming County and established Cassidy's Station. He was 5'3" tall, weighed 170 pounds, and was an Indian fighter and Kentucky pioneer. He married Mary EVANS, daughter of Francis EVANS, on February 17, 1795 and they had ten children. Michael became a Judge and was Fleming County's first Senator in 1800. He died March 19, 1829. (Ref: BCK:623-625)

John CASSIDAY appeared in Breckinridge County, Kentucky between 1810 and 1820, probably from Maryland (Ref: KC:42).

CECIL. Augustine CECIL was born in St. Mary's County, Maryland and married Frances HAMMIT. He went to Kentucky by way of the Ohio River on a flatboat, leaving the river where Louisville now stands. He settled on Pottinger's Creek in Washington County. His son, Sylvester CECIL, married Hedric MEDLEY in Washington (now Marion) County and their children were: Thomas W. (born August 2, 1826), Ignatius C., and Annie S. (Ref: KB 5:80).

CHADD. Samuel CHADD was born in Frederick County, Maryland in 1754 and enlisted as a Private in the militia in 1776. He moved to Bourbon County, Kentucky in 1792 and then migrated to Harrison County, Kentucky where he applied for and received pension S16339 in 1832 (Ref: MS:46; RSK:89; MRR:14; KPR:1835).

CHANCE. Ann CHANCE (1799-1886), of Maryland, married and went West (husband's name not stated) and settled in Cincinnati, Ohio. She married (2) John HUDSON in 1820 in Kentucky. He died in 1825. Their son, Homer HUDSON, born in Covington, Kentucky on March 5, 1824, married Esther FOWLER (1826-1894), daughter of Edward FOWLER (Ref: BCK:258-259).

CHANEY. Sarah CHANEY was born in Maryland in 1772 and married Manasseh LYLES in Virginia in 1792. They migrated to Warren County, Kentucky where Manasseh died in 1810. A daughter, Nancy LYLES, married William BLACKWELL in 1810 in Warren County, Kentucky (Ref: KA 16:2, p. 114).

CHINOWITH, CHENOWETH. Nicholas CHINOWITH was born in Maryland and migrated to Washington County, Tennessee prior to 1812. His son, Archibald S. CHINOWITH, was born there on December 5, 1812 and moved to Barren County, Kentucky when very young. (Ref: KB 2:111) He married Malvina DENHAM, daughter of Isaac, on August 26, 1840. (Ref: Martha P. Reneau's Marriage Records of Barren County, Kentucky, 1799-1849, p. 43. Glasgow, Kentucky: Published by author, 1984) Archibald CHINOWITH died in Barren County on June 29, 1874. (Ref: KB 2:111)

John CHENOWETH married Mary BUSKIRK on March 11, 1793 in Shelby County, Kentucky (Ref: MRR:112).

CHRISTESON. Elisha CHRISTESON married Agnes DRAKE in Maryland and migrated to Adair County, Kentucky where their son Elijah J. CHRISTESON was born in 1819 and their son Robert L. CHRISTESON was born in 1823. They moved to Pulaski County, Missouri in 1829 (Ref: KM:10).

CHRISTOPHER. Elizabeth CHRISTOPHER of Maryland married William COLGAN of Virginia and they were apparently in Shelby County, Kentucky as early as 1800 (Ref: KB 9:25).

CISSELL. Ignatius CISSELL and his sons Rody, Ignatius, Joseph and James, were among the early Catholic settlers from Maryland to migrate to Pottinger's Creek, Kentucky in 1785. Robert CISSELL and Bernard CISSELL were also among this "Maryland League" from St. Mary's County, Maryland. (Ref: KC:28, 30)

Among the early Catholic settlers on Hardin's Creek, Kentucky were Matthew CISSELL, Zachariah CISSELL, Sylvester CISSELL and Jeremiah CISSELL, brothers, and all from St. Mary's County, Maryland. The brothers CECIL, of Cecilia College, Hardin County, were sons of Charles CECIL and grandsons of Matthew CISSELL, the elder. Charles and Matthew CISSELL, Jr. secured the passage of an act by the Kentucky legislature empowering them and all who bore the name in the State, to change the spelling from CISSELL to CECIL. It is not believed, however, that the change was adopted outside of the families of the brothers named. (Ref: KC:45-46)

John CISSELL was in Hardin's Creek in (now) Washington County, Kentucky by 1786 (Ref: KC:56).

CLARK. Ignatius CLARK was an early Catholic settler from St. Mary's County, Maryland who settled on Hardin's Creek in Kentucky circa 1786 where he married Aloysia HILL, daughter of Thomas HILL. Their son was Rev. Edward CLARK of the diocese of Louisville. (Ref: KC:54-55)

28

Joseph CLARK was an early Catholic settler with the "Maryland League" who went to Pottinger's Creek in Nelson County, Kentucky in 1785. His widow, Mary CLARK, died in 1863 at the age of 95. (Ref: KC:28, 30, 44)

There was also a Joseph CLARK on Cox's Creek in 1800, as was Clement CLARK and Richard CLARK, the latter being the father of Rev. William E. CLARK. (Ref: KC:114-131)

John CLARK appeared in Breckinridge County, Kentucky circa 1810-1820. (Ref: KC:142)

John C. CLARK, Sr., an Englishman who lived in Maryland, served in the Revolutionary War with Washington's Army, migrated to Kentucky and died in Butler County around 1830. His son, John C. CLARK, Jr., was born in Maryland in 1785 and served in the War of 1812. He died in Simpson County, Kentucky in 1879 at the age of 94, having resided briefly in Smith County, Tennessee in the 1820's. His wife was Benetee HUGHS (1789-1884) of Sumner County, Tennessee (Ref: KB 4:184)

Amos CLARK was born in Maryland and moved to Owen County, Kentucky. His daughter, Margaret CLARK, married R. H. SHIPP who was born in Bourbon County, Kentucky in 1797 and became a minister in the Baptist Church. (Ref: KB 8:148)

Clement CLARK was born in Maryland and was married by 1780 to Eleanor LILLY, daughter of Richard LILLY and Mary ELDER. He moved to Kentucky in 1788 and died in Nelson County in 1823. (MGS 16:2, p. 94)

Richard Barkley CLARK was born in Maryland in 1787, son of John CLARK of Virginia who moved to Maryland, married Elizabeth Ann BARKLEY and then moved to Kentucky. (Ref: MGS 25:1, p. 133)

Elijah CLARK applied for and received pension S37861 in Laurel County, Kentucky in 1831, age 81, stating he served as a Private in the Maryland Militia. (Ref: MRP:9; KPR:1835)

Mary BECKETT was born and married ----- CLARK in Maryland. They were in Bourbon County, Kentucky by 1812 when their son James CLARK was born. They moved to Missouri by 1855. (Ref: KM:22) They may have been from Prince George's County, Maryland because Henry CLARKE married Elizabeth BECKETT there in 1777 (Ref: MM-2:39).

CLARKE. John CLARKE was a Sergeant in the Maryland Line in the Revolutionary War and applied for and received pension S3158 in 1820 in Logan County, Kentucky, age 91 (Ref: MRP:9; RSK:111; KPR:1835; MRR:14).

CLARKSON. Knotley CLARKSON was an early Catholic settler from Maryland who migrated to Cartwright's Creek in (now) Washington County, Kentucky in 1788. His wife was Lucy EDELIN, a sister of Samuel, and they had three sons: Henry CLARKSON married Elizabeth WORLAND and their sons James and Sidney became Dominican priests;

Edward CLARKSON married a BUCKMAN; and, Lloyd CLARKSON married Elizabeth HAMILTON. Knotley CLARKSON had two daughters - one married a CONSTANTINE and one married a SUTCLIFFE (Ref: KC:78).

CLEAVER. Benjamin CLEAVER was born January 29, 1751 in Maryland and enlisted in 1774 in Tiger's Valley on the Monongahela River. In 1779 he moved to what is now Nelson County, Kentucky and then on to Grayson County, Kentucky in 1816. Benjamin CLEAVER applied for a pension in 1832 (age 81) and the affidavit of a fellow soldier named William CLEAVER (no relationship stated) was made in Grayson County in 1833, at which time William said he was 72 and had known Benjamin since he was a boy. Benjamin CLEAVER also received bounty land warrant 11029 in 1795. Charles C. CLEAVER was his administrator (Ref: MS:41-42; MRP:9; RSK:82).

CLEMENTS. The Clements family were early settlers from Maryland who settled in Nelson and Washington Counties, Kentucky: Thomas CLEMENTS was on Cartwright's Creek by 1785; John CLEMENTS was on Hardin's Creek by 1786. Austin CLEMENTS was on Cox's Creek by 1800. (Ref: KC:56, 80, 114)

William CLEMENTS married Winifred HARDY, daughter of Frederick HARDY who lived and died near Baltimore, Maryland. William served, as did his brother Charles CLEMENTS, in the Revolutionary War. William's son Charles O. CLEMENTS was born January 29, 1808 near Baltimore and married Susan PHILPOTT (1811- 1872), daughter of John S. PHILPOTT (1780-1839) of Maryland. They migrated to Nelson County, Kentucky, near Bardstown, and then on to Daviess County where Charles died December 29, 1879. (Ref: BCK:195)

This notice appeared in the Hagerstown Advertiser on May 8, 1807: "William CLEMENTS offers reward for negro man Frank, 5' 10", aged 25, who ran away when subscriber was at McConnel's Town, Pennsylvania, on his way to Kentucky. Deliver to Greenbury HOWARD, Montgomery County, Maryland, about 3 miles from Clarksburg." (Ref: WMNA 3:57).

CLYMER. The Clymer family originated on the Eastern Shore of Maryland in colonial days and migrated south and west to North Carolina and Ohio, primarily. Some, like Sara CLYMER who married Alexander McCLANAHAN, ended up in Tennessee and Kentucky (Ref: KPG 2:3, p. 162. Note: For a very detailed genealogy on this family see Anita Ockert's book entitled The Clymer Clan of Maryland, Delaware and Points West. (Vienna, Virginia: Published by author, 1987).

COCKRILL. Joseph COCKRILL married Nancy LUCAS of Maryland and they were in Fayette County, Kentucky by 1804 where their sons were born: Fielding, born April 10, 1804; Clinton, born April 10, 1810; and Felix G., born December 27, 1811. They migrated to Howard County, Missouri by 1819 (Ref: KM:55).

COFFMAN. Jacob COFFMAN applied for a Revolutionary pension while residing in Casey County, Kentucky in 1821, at age 60. He stated he enlisted in Maryland in 1777 or 1778. He also stated he married Chloe RICHARDS in Casey County, Kentucky on December 24, 1826.

Jacob COFFMAN made an affidavit in 1838 (age 75) that he knew Jacob HAVELY about 49 years and he first knew him near Emit's Town (Emmitsburg), Maryland. Jacob died June 2, 1840 and his widow Chloe subsequently filed for and received pension W6943 at age 58 on December 12, 1853 (Ref: MS:20; MRP:9; RSK:54; KPR:1835; MRR:112).

COLE. Benjamin COLE was born in Frederick, Maryland in 1750 and married Elizabeth LONG (born 1760) in Nelson County, Kentucky on November 15, 1784. Source MRR:112 states they married in Washington County, Maryland. Their children were: Sarah, born 1798; Ann, born 1804; and, James, born 1808. Benjamin COLE enlisted in 1778 in the German Regiment of the Maryland Line, served at Valley Forge, and was discharged in 1783. He applied for a pension in Mason County, Kentucky in 1818 and also received bounty land warrant 13441-1-60-55. (Ref: MS:63; LU 7:102)

"John A. BEAN and James IRELAND personally appeared in court and made oath that Benjamin COLE whose name is inscribed on the pension list of the Kentucky Agency departed this life July 12, 1832 at his residence in Mason County, and Elizabeth COLE, who has assigned the Power of Attorney to John A. BEAN, is the widow of the said Benjamin COLE." Elizabeth COLE was still alive on July 1, 1848. (Ref: Mason County, Kentucky Court Order Book M, p. 56, April Court, 1833, as published in Source KP:185)

John COLE was a Private in the Maryland Militia and applied for and received a pension in Barren County, Kentucky in 1831, age 81 (Ref: RSK:35, KPR:1835; MRR:15).

COMPTON. Edmund H. COMPTON (1759-1836) served in the Revolutionary War as a Lieutenant in the 1st Maryland Line and applied for a pension in 1826 while living in Marion County, Kentucky, receiving pension S17896 (Ref: MRP:10; RSK:117; KPR:1835; DAR:117; MRR:15).

CONNELLY. John CONNELLY, born 1755 in Maryland, married Elizabeth TURNER of Kentucky and a son, Sanford CONNELLY, was born January 8, 1815 in Madison County, Kentucky. By 1827 they were in Missouri (Ref: KM:106).

CONRAD. Isaac CONRAD of Maryland migrated to Kentucky and his son William CONRAD was born December 6, 1797. William lived in Harrison County, Kentucky and married Elizabeth BOYERS. A son, Isaac B. CONRAD, was born in Grant County, Kentucky on July 28, 1818 (Ref: KB 8:39).

COOK. Robert COOK (Irish) was an early settler from Maryland on Hardin's Creek in Kentucky circa 1786. (Ref: KC:54)

William COOK, Sr. was born in 1782 in (now) Howard County, Maryland. He moved with his family to Richmond, Virginia and from there, in 1819, to Columbus, Kentucky, having first purchased a stock of general merchandise in New Orleans. These goods were brought to Kentucky by a keeler and were the first ever sold at this point. His son, William COOK, Jr., was born April 27, 1815, married Sophia M. COBB of Lyon County, Kentucky and died in Columbus, Kentucky on September 27, 1872 (Ref: KB 6:141-142).

COOKENDORFER. Michael COOKENDORFER was a Fifer in the Maryland Militia during the Revolutionary War and applied for and received pension S30337 in 1831, age 84, in Pendleton County, Kentucky (Ref: RSK:140; MRP:10; KPR:1835).

COOMES. Francis COOMES was an already an old man when he went to Kentucky from Maryland and settled on Cox's Creek. He possibly was born prior to 1720 and he died in 1822 at the age of 102 or so and was buried in Fairfield, Kentucky in the cemetery of St. Michael. He had a son named Richard. (Ref: KC:114, 130)

Ignatius COOMES moved to Breckinridge County, Kentucky in 1800. His wife was Sarah LEWIS (widow), nee STUART, and their children were Walter, Linus, Francis and Matilda. Walter and Linus became priests. (Ref: KC:142)

William COOMES was a Catholic originally from Charles County in Maryland. He moved to the south branch of the Potomac River in Virginia and then in 1785 he migrated to Kentucky with his family and the HITE family, settling on Pottinger's Creek. (Ref: KC:25)

Charles COOMES was a Bardstown elder in 1820 (Ref: KC:142).

COOPER. William COOPER was born in Maryland in 1750 (or as early as 1734) and enlisted in Harford County, Maryland on July 15, 1776 and served in the 4th Maryland Line until 1779. (Ref: HCP:48-49) William was married to Mary HARRISON (1754-1838) in Frederick County, Maryland by a Presbyterian minister on January 20, 1780, and they moved to Ohio County, Kentucky around 1798. William COOPER applied for a pension in 1818. (Ref: MGS 5:2; KPR:1835) He died in Ohio County on January 3, 1836, and his widow applied for and received pension W8632 until her death on December 30, 1838. (Ref: MS:61, LU 8:46, MGS 24:1, p. 88, MGS 27:1, p. 89) Their daughter, Elizabeth COOPER, married Benjamin COX of Maryland on April 12, 1807, and they moved to Dubois County, Indiana. (Ref: MGS 24:1, p. 88)

Henry COOPER (1783-1863) and Weaver HOCKER (1748-1818) were early settlers from Maryland in Ohio County, Kentucky. Clarissa COOPER married Nicholas HOCKER. (Ref: KB 3:149)

Philip B. COOPER was born in Baltimore, Maryland in 1803 and was a son of Basil P. COOPER and Mary QUINLEY. Philip migrated to Kentucky around 1822 and worked as a traveling salesman. He wa also Master Commissioner of Marion County. (Ref: KB 5:90)

Joseph COOPER was a son of Arch COOPER and Mary RAMSAY of Maryland, and they went to Kentucky around 1800, settling in Clark County. Joseph married Priscilla BAXTER and their son, A. R. COOPER was born in 1821 in Clark County, Kentucky (Ref: KB 7:168).

CORBET. Jacob CORBET applied for a Revolutionary War pension in 1826 (age 68) while residing in Washington County, Kentucky. He stated he enlisted in 1777 at Port Tobacco in Charles County, Maryland under Capt. John STONE in the 1st Maryland Line. In his pension claim (S35852) he named his daughters Mary (age 20), Julia (age 20), James (age 18), and Eliza (age 13), but does not mention his wife's name (Ref: MS:56; RSK:163; MRR:15).

CORBIN. Nicholas CORBIN, of Bourbon County, Kentucky, one of the heirs of Abraham CORBIN, late of Baltimore County, Maryland, deceased, conveyed to Joshua MARSH of Baltimore County, part of "Valley of Jehosophat." (Ref: BCLR Liber WG #86, p. 252).

CORD. Neomy CORD, daughter of Jacob CORD and Elizabeth COOK, married John CORD on February 12, 1784 in Cecil County, Maryland. They migrated to Kentucky (now Fleming County) around 1794. Also, Jacob CORD and Mary Mitchell DONOVAN married in Mason County, Kentucky on November 16, 1791. Some Cord marriages in early Fleming County were: Patsey CORD, daughter of Milca CORD, to John DOYLE, April 10, 1811; Sally CORD to Samuel LEE, December 19, 1816; Carvel CORD to Polly BLAIR, daughter of Sarah BLAIR, January 27, 1819; Philip CORD, son of Jacob CORD, to Nancy GIVENS, May 18, 1819; Betsey CORD, daughter of JACOB CORD, to John JARVIS, December 20, 1820; William B. CORD to Elizabeth CAYWOOD, daughter of Erasmus CAYWOOD, November 27, 1823; William H. CORD to Rebecca TORRENCE, daughter of John TORRENCE, Oct. 23, 1823; John W. CORD to Creasy CAYWOOD, daughter of Erasmus CAYWOOD, February 24, 1824; and, Hannah Ann CORD, daughter of Zacheus CORD, to Isiah BENTLEY, August 29, 1824. (Ref: KA 7:4, pp. 192-194) Zacheus CORD was a Revolutionary soldier who resided in Fleming County, Kentucky in 1840. He was a Lieutenant and was blind in one eye (Ref: Ibid).

CORN. John CORN married Anne WILLIAMS after 1815 in Kentucky; county not stated. Their marriage was proven through a Maryland Revolutionary War pension application; soldier's name not stated (Ref: MRR:112).

COX. Benjamin COX was born in Maryland on May 16, 1783 and married Elizabeth COOPER, daughter of William and Mary, on April 12, 1807. Their children were: William Henry, born in 1816; Matilda, born in 1821; and, John M., born in 1826. They lived in Kentucky and Indiana. Elizabeth COX died in Dubois County on April 10, 1868. (Ref: MGS 24:1, p. 88)

James COX was a Revolutionary soldier in Maryland and went to Ohio County, Kentucky in 1801. His son, Thomas J. COX, was born there on February 25, 1811 and married Marinda LEACH (1807-1859), daughter of William. (Ref: KB 3:131)

Isaac COX, Gabriel COX, and Friend COX moved from Maryland circa 1750 and settled in Frederick (now Hampshire) County, Virginia. Only Isaac's children moved to Kentucky. They were: James, John, Isaac, David, Gabriel, George, Nancy, Ann, Polly, Joseph, Jonathan, and Benjamin. Isaac COX (c1716-1783) married Susannah TOMLINSON and died in Nelson County, Kentucky. Benjamin COX was the founder of Cox's Station on Cox's Creek. (A history was prepared by Evelyn C. Adams entitled "The Coxes of Cox's Creek, Kentucky" and was published in the Filson Club Quarterly, Vol. XXII (1948), pp. 75-103, and in Genealogies of Kentucky Families, pp. 442-470 (Baltimore: Genealogical Publishing Co., 1981).

COY. Christopher COY married Elizabeth -----, on April 15, 1773 probably in Worcester County, Maryland. He enlisted in the 4th Maryland Line in 1779, became a Corporal, and was discharged August 12, 1783. They migrated to Kentucky and Illinois, and had seven children, including Anna SMITH, born 1777, and John COY, born 1796 (Ref: LU 8:76; Pension W9798; Archives of Maryland, Vol. 18, pp. 419, 509, 530).

CRABB. Jeremiah CRABB was born September 17, 1769 in Frederick County, Maryland. Although too young to bear arms and fight in the Revolutionary War, he still served as a prisoner guard. A tanner by trade, he migrated to Kentucky in 1796 and settled first in Nelson County, and later in Shelby County. His wife, Eleanor Williamson COMPTON (September 4, 1774 - December 26, 1851) was a daughter of John and Elizabeth COMPTON. Jeremiah's children were: Elizabeth Compton CRABB married James CARTER; Stephen Drane CRABB, born April, 1802, married Nancy B. POSTON (1802-1888) in 1823; Jeremiah CRABB Jr. married (1) Emily POSTON, and (2) Lucy DAWSON, and (3) ----- BAKER; Samuel Compton CRABB married Hemia THOMPSON; Priscilla Sprigg CRABB married Richard YOUNG; and, Alexander Compton CRABB married (1) Sarah BARNETT and (2) Lucy B. REES. Jeremiah CRABB died March 21, 1840 (Ref: BCK:304-306; KB 7:170).

CRADY. David CRADY (c1762-c1845) was the son of John CRADY of Ireland who immigrated to Maryland in 1759 and settled on a tract called "Hibernia" near the wagon road from Baltimore Town to Conowago. David CRADY served as a Fifer and Private with the Maryland Troops during the Revolutionary War from August 1, 1780 to November 15, 1783. He migrated to Nelson County, Kentucky, and married Polly EDLIN on December 31, 1789. They had twelve children: Jenney CRADY married Sharp SPENCER in 1809; Thomas CRADY married Margaret COY in 1815; John CRADY married Elizabeth COY in 1818; Catherine CRADY married Stephen GREENWELL in 1817; William CRADY married Keturah TUCKER in 1821 and Nancy DEWITT in 1829; James CRADY married Polly COY in 1826; Richard CRADY married Nancy MILLER in 1834 and Amanda RUST in 1837; Felix CRADY married Emily -----, in 1851; Polly CRADY, married Zadock BROWN and Mr. ASH; Sharp CRADY married Letticia ATHERTON in 1834; Keziah CRADY married Richard EDLIN in 1832; and, Sarah CRADY married Aaron DEAVER in 1835. The estate of David CRADY was administered in LaRue County, Kentucky in 1868 (Information from "David Crady, Kentucky Pioneer" by Evelyn Adams, 1947, and available at the Maryland Historical Society Library).

CRAIL. James CRAIL was born in 1787 in Maryland and married (1) Sara GREENSTREET on February 12, 1824 in Green County, Kentucky, and (2) Emily -----. A son, Calvin CRAIL, was born in 1826, and a son Jason CRAIL (born 1828) married Elizabeth MURRAY in 1863 in Macon County, Missouri (Ref: KA 8:3, p. 157).

CRAWFORD. Alexander B. CRAWFORD of Maryland married Charlotte RIGGS in Nicholas County, Kentucky and their son, Alexander B. CRAWFORD, was born in March, 1824 in Nicholas County. By 1859 they were in Missouri (KM:133).

CRAYCROFT. Thomas CRAYCROFT was among the early Catholic settlers from Maryland to Cartwright's Creek in (now) Washington County, Kentucky in 1785 (Ref: KC:80).

CREAGER. Christian CREAGER died in Frederick County, Maryland in 1768. Valentine CREAGER was born in Berks County, Pennsylvania in 1734 and died in Washington County, Kentucky circa 1810. Daniel A. CREAGER was born in 1794 and died in 1848 in Hardin County, Kentucky. (Ref: MMG 3:2, p. 95)

Elizabeth CREAGER, born in Frederick County, Maryland, in 1769, married Jacob LINK (born 1762) and migrated to Washington County, Kentucky in 1797 (Ref: KB 5:110).

CROOKE. Absalom CROOKE married Mary Ann POFFER circa 1755. A son, Zachariah CROOKE, was born circa 1760 in St. Mary's County, Maryland and served in the Revolutionary War. He died after 1800 in Madison County, Kentucky (Ref: MMG 4:1).

CROSSLEY. Mary CROSSLEY was born near Hagerstown, Maryland. Her father and brother served in the Revolutionary War. She married Patrick McELWEE (of Ireland) and migrated to Brown County, Ohio, where daughter Mary McELWEE was born. Their descendants moved to Lewis County, Kentucky (Ref: BCK:248).

CROWNOVER. Ann CROWNOVER married John KENNETT and migrated from Maryland. They were among the earliest settlers on Rolling Fork in Kentucky circa 1785 (Ref: KB 5:285).

CULLUM. Francis CULLUM (born 1723 in Maryland) migrated to Kentucky and his descendants settled in Estill and Clark Counties between 1790 and 1830 (Ref: KPG 1:3, p. 46).

CULVER. Benjamin CULVER of Bullitt County, Kentucky, by the power of attorney he granted to Thomas JEFFERY in 1804, conveyed part of "Culver's Entrance" to Elisha GREENLAND of Harford County, Maryland on March 16, 1814 (Ref: HCLR Liber HD #Y, p. 109).

CUNNINGHAM. Robert CUNNINGHAM and wife Nancy BEALE migrated to Kentucky in 1796 and settled near the present site of the City of Lebanon. Their daughter, Ellen CUNNINGHAM, married George A. BRICKEN in Marion County (Ref: KB 5:62).

DAILEY. Bennett DAILY (DALY) was living in Washington County, Kentucky when he applied for pension in 1832, age 75. He enlisted in St. Mary's County, Maryland in April, 1777, and served in Pennsylvania during the Revolution. Afterwards, he returned to Maryland for 10 or 12 years and then migrated to Kentucky around 1787. Mary ALVEY (age 70 in 1833) stated that she knew Bennett

DAILEY in St. Mary's County and she moved to Kentucky about 2 years after him. Randall HOSKINS stated in 1833 that he had lived in Charles County, Maryland about 5 or 6 miles from Bennett DAILEY and they had served in the same company during the Revolutionary War. Bennett DAILEY, in Marion County, Kentucky, received pension S30980 (Ref: MS:57; RSK:117).

DALE. John Postley DALE, son of James DALE and Margaret READ of Worcester County, Maryland, was born circa 1785. The Dales subsequently moved to Kentucky (Ref: MGS 24:4, p.369).

DALLAM. The Dallams were prominent in colonial Harford County, Maryland and several members moved to Kentucky. Francis Matthews DALLAM, son of William DALLAM and grandson of Richard DALLAM and Elizabeth MARTIN, married Martha Cassandra SMITH. Their son, Nathan Smith DALLAM, was born December 19, 1782 in Harford County and married Sarah HICKS (born 1792 in Richmond, Virginia) in 1807 in Winchester, Clark County, Kentucky. They moved to Hopkinsville, Kentucky where Nathan DALLAM became Clerk of the Court and served in the Legislature. They moved to Princeton, Kentucky circa 1825 where Nathan died on June 1, 1837. Their children were James Lawrence, Mary Frances, Maria, Francis Henry, Jane Marian, Charles B., William J., Edward Winston, Lucien Clay (born May 17, 1829) and Virginia Josephine. (Ref: BCK:3-4)

Richard DALLAM "of Kentucky but now in Harford County, Maryland" conveyed land to Benjamin RICHARDSON and Grace SHAW of Harford County on February 21, 1807. (Ref: HCLR Liber HD #T, pp. 142-143)

Richard DALLAM of Logan County, Kentucky conveyed part of "The Woodyard" to William ALLEN of Harford County, Maryland on April 8, 1814, in presence of Richard B. DALLAM and John DALLAM. (Ref: HCLR Liber HD #Y, pp. 154-155)

Richard B. DALLAM of Butler County, Kentucky appointed William ALLEN and Ebenezer ALLEN of Harford County, Maryland to be his attorneys to convey Lot No. 12 in Havre de Grace, Maryland to Daniel GILDEA on March 27, 1814. (Ref: HCLR Liber HD #Y, pp. 123-124) Richard Boothby DALLAM of Butler County, Kentucky conveyed to John DALLAM of Harford County, Maryland, parts of "Fanny's Inheritance," "Palmer's Point" and "Palmer's Neglect" on August 29, 1810. (Ref: HCLR Liber HD #V, pp. 450-452)

William S. DALLAM of Fayette County, Kentucky conveyed a lot in Havre de Grace, Maryland to William ALLEN of Harford County on October 5, 1813 (Ref: HCLR Liber DH #X, pp. 343-344; HCP:57; BCF:157).

DANNELL. The following notice appeared in the Washington Spy newspaper on October 26, 1791: "Laurence PROTZMAN, Hagerstown, forewarns persons from taking assignments on bonds given by him to Robert DANNELL of Kentucky." (Ref: WMNA 1:33).

DANT. John Baptist DANT, Joseph DANT and James DANT were among the Catholics who migrated from St. Mary's County, Maryland to Washington County, Kentucky in 1785, settling on Pottinger's Creek. (Ref: KC:28, 31)

J. W. DANT was born May 7, 1820 in (now) Marion County, Kentucky, a son of John B. DANT (1799-1881) and Mary J. SMITH, daughter of Samuel SMITH who went to Kentucky from Maryland circa 1800. John B. DANT was a son of Joseph DANT (died 1833) who married Malinda SHIRKLES in Maryland and migrated to Loretto, Kentucky (Ref: KB 5:98).

DAUGHADAY. Rev. Thomas DAUGHADAY (born circa 1815) was a Methodist circuit rider in western Tennessee and Kentucky. He married Elizabeth CLOAR, and two of their children, John Thomas DAUGHADAY and Sarah Catherine SHORT, lived and died in Graves County, Kentucky. (Ref: KA 4:1, p. 36) The Daughadays were from Baltimore County, Maryland (Ref: SRM:87).

DAVENPORT. Adrian DAVENPORT applied for a Revolutionary War pension in Fayette County, Kentucky in 1818, age 60. He had two children living with him (Barbary Ann, age 8, and Abram, age 6) and his wife (unnamed), age 49. Adrian enlisted in 1776 in Maryland for three years in the Rifle Regiment of Col. Moses RAWLINGS. The regiment was later transferred to the 11th Virginia Line. Adrian received a pension (S35874) for his services. (Ref: MS:34; MRR:17; KPR:1835)

John Robert DAVENPORT was born circa 1796 and married in Ohio County, Kentucky on November 13, 1817 to Catherine WISE, born 1800 in Pipe Creek, Maryland. John died on May 23, 1828 and Catherine died on August 6, 1850 in Ohio County, Kentucky. Their children were: William P.DAVENPORT, born 1818; Robert S. DAVENPORT, born 1822; Merideth DAVENPORT; Philip DAVENPORT; and, Thomas DAVENPORT (Ref: KPG 1:3, p. 45).

DAVID. Michael DAVID was born in 1763 in Frederick County, Maryland and served in the Revolutionary War in Shenandoah County, Virginia in 1780 under Capt. CROOKSHANKS. He applied for and received pension S12729 in 1832 (age 69) in Mason County, Kentucky. Marshall KEY and Charles WARD verified his service. Michael DAVID died on June 3, 1833 and his wife, Celia DAVID, was then still living (Ref: MS:64; KP:182; Mason County, Kentucky Court Order Book M, pp. 25, 111).

DAVIDSON. Samuel DAVIDSON (1784-c1855) was born in Virginia and married Margaret PATTON of Maryland on July 21, 1806 in Fayette County, Kentucky. They lived in Clark, Gallatin and Owen Counties. Their children were: William P. DAVIDSON; Jane SANDERS; Elizabeth GRAHAM; and, Joicy MOORE. Margaret DAVIDSON died in 1842 (Ref: KA 12:1, pp. 24-27).

DAVIS. Charles DAVIS was born circa 1740 in Maryland and married Sarah MORELAND on May 11, 1762 in Charles County. (Ref: MM-1:47) Their son Isaac DAVIS was born in 1766 in Maryland and married Margaret McSWAIN on July 2, 1813 in Madison County, Kentucky. (Ref: KA 16:3, p. 178)

Another Charles DAVIS of Maryland married Elizabeth CARTER and their son Isaac P. DAVIS was born in 1826 in Madison County. They were in Montgomery County, Missouri by 1834. (Ref: KM:107)

Clarissa DAVIS, daughter of Daniel DAVIS of Salisbury, Maryland, married Henry BELL (born 1808 in Georgetown, Delaware) and moved to Lexington, Kentucky, where their son, D. D. BELL (1849-1892) married Sydney S. SAYRE. (Ref: BCK:120-123)

Forrest DAVIS applied for a Revolutionary War pension in Hardin County, Kentucky in 1832, age 70, stating that he enlisted in 1780 at Fort Frederick, Maryland. Benjamin GRAY of Warrick County, Indiana stated he resided in Montgomery County, Maryland in 1780 and knew Forrest DAVIS. Lodowick DAVIS of Warrick County, Indiana also said he was acquainted with Forrest DAVIS who served with him in Maryland in 1781. (Ref: MS:43-44; KPR:1835; MRR:17)

James DAVIS (1751-1826) married Florence BLACKWOOD of Maryland, a daughter of Samuel BLACKWOOD and Sarah RUSSELL. They lived in Virginia before settling on 1,000 acres (granted in 1783) on Flat Creek in Fayette County, Kentucky. (Ref: KA 2:2, p. 37)

Francis DAVIS (1722-1779) died testate in Frederick County, Maryland, naming his children: Ruth WELSH, Mary Ann DAVIS, Rezin DAVIS, Matthias DAVIS, Samuel DAVIS, Zachariah DAVIS, Thomas DAVIS, Lucy DAVIS, and Nancy DAVIS. Katherine -----, was his second wife; his first wife was Anne HAMMOND. Matthias DAVIS married Rachel MAYNARD in 1788 in Frederick County, Maryland and moved to Lewis County, Kentucky, where he died in 1852. (Ref: KA 8:1, pp. 10-11)

Phanuel DAVIS (born 1786 in Virginia) was a tailor's son from Hagerstown, Maryland. He married Jane WOOD in 1807 in Kentucky (possibly Hart County) and they subsequently moved to Jennings County, Indiana. (Ref: KA 8:2, p. 97)

Samuel D. DAVIS was a Private in the Maryland Militia and applied for and received pension S34730 in 1831 (age 71) in Gallatin County, Kentucky. (Ref: MRP:11; RSK:77; KPR:1835)

Hillery DAVIS was born in 1817 in (now) Marion County, Kentucky, a son of Nathaniel DAVIS and Dolly MILLS. His grandfather was a native of Maryland and his father was born in Kentucky, migrating to Hickman County in 1824 where he died in 1844 (Ref: KB 6:142).

DAWSON. Caleb D. DAWSON (April 10, 1808, Maryland - May 5, 1891, Kentucky) married Caroline MOODY (1815-1872) and both are buried in Bucksville Cemetery in Logan County, Kentucky. (Ref: KCR:278)

William C. DAWSON (1791-1845), son of Revolutionary soldier Robert D. DAWSON of Montgomery County, Maryland, married Mary DARBY and moved to Logan County, Kentucky in 1810. Their son, George C. DAWSON, was born April 6, 1815. (Ref: KB 4:187)

Anak DAWSON was an early settler in Allen County, Kentucky. He was a son of George DAWSON and Hannah ASBURY of Maryland. They migrated to Adair County, Kentucky about 1790. Anak migrated to Allen County and then Simpson County, Kentucky. He married Nancy CHAPMAN and a son James M. DAWSON was born in Scottsville, Kentucky on June 28, 1823 (Ref: KB 4:187-188).

DEAN. John DEAN was born in Maryland in 1763 and served in the Revolutionary War in Bedford County, Pennsylvania. He served from 1779 to 1782 in the militia and married Jane ----- (born 1762) on January 2, 1785. They moved to Gallatin County, Kentucky in 1810. He applied for a pension while residing there in 1833, age 71, and died on March 5, 1841. (Ref: MS:30; KB 8:49)

Another John DEAN was born in 1757 or 1759 in Dorchester County, Maryland and also served in the Revolutionary War. He married Mary LLOYD and their daughter Elizabeth DEAN (1794-1864) married in 1813 to Chesley VEST in Henry County, Kentucky. (Ref: KA 12:3, January, 1977, p. 165; MRR:18)

Capt. William DEAN was a native of Maryland who settled on the Kentucky River circa 1780, about eight miles from Carrollton where he was a Captain in the State Militia. His daughter, Mary A. DEAN, married Thomas BAILEY of Carroll County, Kentucky (Ref: KB 8:6).

DEAVER. William DEAVER was born in Harford County, Maryland in 1756/1757 and enlisted in 1778 in the 3rd Maryland Line. He applied for a pension while residing in Mason County, Kentucky in 1820 (age 64), stating that his wife (unnamed) was age 38 and they had eight children: William, age 17; Deborah, age 15; Elizabeth, age 13; George, age 10; Rebecca, age 8; Micajah, age 7; Delila, age 5; and, Mary Ann, age 2. He apparently had applied earlier in 1818 in Scioto County, Ohio and transferred to Kentucky in 1822, having received pension S12754. In 1890 Rose ROSENER inquired from Indiana to see if she could get her grandfather's pension (Ref: MS:64; MGS 6:3; KPR:1835. Source MRR:18 states he was born in 1761 and was a prisoner during the Revolutionary War).

DEBRULAR. John DEBRULAR was born in 1751 or 1752 and enlisted in Harford County, Maryland in Capt. Alexander Lawson SMITH's Company. He served three years with Col. Moses RAWLINGS in the Maryland Line and was discharged August 9, 1779. John applied for a pension in Bourbon County, Kentucky in 1818. In 1820 his wife (unnamed) was age 71 and unable to take care of herself, and their daughter Mary (age 31) was living with them. John received pension S35890 (Ref: MS:9-10; RSK:41; KPR:1835; MRR:18; HCP:61-62).

DEVINE. William DEVINE (born 1766/67) enlisted in Calvert County, Maryland in 1782 and served three years under Capt. James SOMERVILL. He married Mary HARRIS on February 2, 1799 in Mason County, Kentucky and they had one child, Thomas. In 1832 William applied for a pension. He died August 6, 1846, and his wife died April 9, 1849 in Maysville, Kentucky (Ref: MS:63; LU 9:101; RSK: 119; KPR:1835; MRR:18).

DICKERSON. Solomon DICKERSON was born in 1754 and enlisted in the Revolution in Montgomery County, Maryland in 1777. He migrated thereafter to Berkeley County, Virginia and Perry County, North Carolina, and then to Virginia and Kentucky. He applied for and received pension S30990 in 1832 in Monroe County, Kentucky (Ref: MS:62; RSK:126; MRP:12; KPR:1835; MRR:18).

DIMMITT. Richard DIMMITT, born in 1760 in Baltimore County, Maryland, married Rebecca MERRYMAN, daughter of Joseph and Mary MERRYMAN, on December 6, 1783. Soon thereafter they moved to Bourbon County, Kentucky. He died testate on June 4, 1827. Some of his children moved to Ohio, Indiana and Missouri (Ref: KM:23; MGS 27:2, pp. 240-242).

DITTO. Abraham DITTO of Baltimore County, Maryland married Martha FORCE of Maryland and a son, Joseph DITTO, was born July 12, 1824 in Shelby County, Kentucky, later settling in Missouri. Another son, William DITTO, was born August 30, 1810, in Shelby County, Kentucky. (Ref: KM:147; KB 7:174)

Nancy ADAMS (1800-1872) of Maryland, married William DITTO, of Williamson County, Tennessee (died 1835) and descendants settled in Hickman County, Kentucky. The Nicholas Day AMOS family also married into the Ditto family (Ref: KB 6:143).

DOLAN. James DOLAN was one of the early Catholic settlers from St. Mary's County, Maryland who settled at Rolling Fork in Washington County, Kentucky prior to 1800 (Ref: KC:110).

DONOVAN. Alexander DONOVAN was born December 10, 1780 in Maryland and married Hannah WHIPPS on February 9, 1806. He died in Mason County, Kentucky on December 7, 1846. He may have been related to Peter DONOVAN (born in 1748 in Ireland) who served in Col. EWING's Battalion in 1776 in Harford County, Maryland (Ref: KA 10:1, p. 51; HCP:65).

DORA. John DORA came to Maryland from England and settled in Somerset County. He had five sons in the Revolutionary War, two of who were never heard from since, namely Jesse DORA and Benjamin DORA. John's son, Ferdinand DORA, born May 13, 1758, went to Kentucky and settled in Bracken County. He married Nancy BEAUCHAMP, and their son, William DORA, born September 6, 1802, married Elizabeth MORRIS. Ferdinand DORA died January 24, 1830 and Nancy DORA died January 10, 1840 (Ref: BCK:87-88).

DORAN. Thomas DORAN, Nicholas DORAN and Francis DORAN of Washington County, Kentucky appointed Edward DORAN of Harford County, Maryland their attorney on October 5, 1801 to settle their interests in the estate of Margaret DORAN, deceased, and of Patrick DORAN, deceased. (Ref: HCLR HD #Q, pp. 28-30)

Francis DORAN of Washington County conveyed his rights, interest and title to "Manto Santo" to Edward DORAN and Philip DORAN of Harford County, Maryland on April 17, 1812 (Ref: HCLR Liber HD #X, pp. 356-357).

DORCH. William DORCH was a Private in the Maryland Line in the Revolutionary War and received a pension in 1818, age 74, in Lewis County, Kentucky (Ref: KPR:1835. Source MRR:18 states he enlisted in Virginia and served in Maryland).

DORSEY. The Dorsey family was very prominent in colonial Maryland. Edward DORSEY and wife Susanna had migrated to Jefferson County, Kentucky and subsequently sold part of "John's Industry" and "Lawrence's Pleasant Valley" to Jacob TEANOR on February 9, 1804 in Baltimore County, Maryland (Ref: BCLR Liber WG #81, p. 149)

Leaven DORSEY enlisted in Baltimore in 1777 and while home visiting his sick mother, Cornwallis surrendered, although Source MRR:18 states he deserted. Leaven DORSEY migrated to Jefferson County, Kentucky and in 1833 he applied for a pension, age 78 (Ref: MS:52; MRP:13; AAG II:7-218).

DOUGLASS. William DOUGLASS was born in 1755 in Maryland and migrated to Boyle County, Kentucky by 1819. His son, General Joseph B. DOUGLASS, was born there on November 12, 1819. The family was in Menifee County, Missouri by 1827 (Ref: KM:30, 121).

DOWDEN. Clementius DOWDEN enlisted in Montgomery County, Maryland in 1779 or 1780 and served under Capt. Thomas BELL. In 1780 he moved to Washington County, Pennsylvania and in 1781 enlisted under Capt. Edward RICHARDSON. In 1782 he was drafted under Col. George VANLANDINGHAM, and in 1783 he was Orderly Sergeant for Col. John MARSHALL. Clementius DOWDEN was born on January 11, 1762 in Prince George's County, Maryland and applied for and received pension S30995 in Bourbon County, Kentucky in 1832. A friend, Robert M. JOHNSON, wrote the Commissioner of Pensions in 1833, asking him to quickly process the application as Dowden wanted to to go Illinois. (Ref: MS:9; MRP:13; RSK:42)

James DOWDEN was born in 1757 in St. Mary's County, Maryland and enlisted in 1779 in Montgomery County, Virginia. After the war he lived in Virginia and then migrated first to Bourbon County, Kentucky and then Madison County, Kentucky where he received pension S30996 in 1833, at age 77 (Ref: MS:57; MRR:19).

DOWLING. James DOWLING served as a Private, Corporal, and Sergeant in the 2nd and 7th Maryland Lines from 1777 to 1780, and was pensioned as an Invalid in 1803. He died on May 8, 1831 in Washington County, Kentucky (Ref: KPR:1835; MRR:19; Archives of Maryland, Vol. 18, pp. 101, 201).

DOWNEY. Francis DOWNEY was a Private in the Maryland Militia and pensioned in Scott County, Kentucky in 1831 at age 88. (Ref: KPR: 1835)

John DOWNEY was born October 3, 1755 in Frederick County, Maryland and served in the Revolutionary War from Bedford County, Pennsylvania for 12 months. He served under Capt. John NELSON and Lt. William OLDHAM in 1776, and received pension S1195 in Henry County, Kentucky at age 77. John migrated to Kentucky in 1790 to Woodford and Scott County. His wife was Mary -----, and their known children were: Andrew DOWNEY, married Calley YORK; William DOWNEY; James DOWNEY; Mrs. Philip JACKSON; and, Mrs. John PERKINS. (Ref: MS:48; KA 5:1, p. 44)

Thomas DOWNEY was born in Frederick County, Maryland in 1754 and enlisted February 10, 1776 under Capt. John NELSON in the 4th Pennsylvania Line. He received pension S35895 in Ohio on May 16, 1818 and subsequently moved to Henry County, Kentucky (Ref: MS:48).

DOWNING. Benjamin DOWNING was born in Ireland (or possibly Wales), but of English parents. He emigrated to Maryland prior to the Revolutionary War and settled in Frederick County. He married Sarah GRAY (born November 17, 1754 in Maryland) and migrated to Convington, Kentucky circa 1794, later settling in Green County, where he was killed during the manufacture of powder. His widow moved to Allen County and then Barren County, now Monroe County. A son, Benjamin DOWNING, Jr., was born April 9 or 17, 1789 in Maryland and married Isabella CAMPBELL in Kentucky. Other children were: Rachel DOWNING; Sarah DOWNING; Sophia DOWNING, born March 31, 1782, married Benjamin PRIGMORE in 1802; James DOWNING; Elizabeth DOWNING married Joseph KINCAID; and, Nancy DOWNING married Sylvester HALL, moved to Missouri circa 1819 where she died in 1827. (Ref: MGS 24:3, p. 260; KB:2, pp. 14, 15, 50)

Francis DOWNING married Henrietta -----, circa 1775 (a son, John DOWNING, was born October 10, 1775) and he served in the Revolutionary War from Montgomery County, Maryland. They had six children and settled in Kentucky, but the place and year were not stated in the record. Henrietta DOWNING received pension W8674. (Ref: LU 10:45)

Samuel DOWNING was a Private in the Maryland Line and pensioned in 1819 in Barren County, Kentucky (Ref: KPR:1835; MRR:19).

DOWNS. John ("Uncle Johnny") DOWNS was among the early Catholic settlers from St. Mary's County, Maryland who settled on Pottingers Creek, Kentucky in 1785. He died at age 104 during the 1860's. (Ref: KC:44)

Benjamin DOWNS was also from Maryland and settled in Nelson County, Kentucky where he was a farmer and distiller, as was his son James DOWNS. (Ref: KB 7:175)

Michael DOWNS married Margaret LEWIS in Montgomery County, Maryland in 1781. He died in March, 1789 and she married John McCAW who died in January, 1805. Margaret McCAW applied for a pension in Gallatin County, Kentucky in 1838, based on Michael DOWNS' service, but she was rejected (R6614) in spite of statements by James REMINGTON and Alexander LEWIS of Harrison County, Kentucky, both of whom said they had known "the pensioner" Michael DOWNS in Montgomery County, Maryland (Ref: MS:40).

42

DOYLE. John DOYLE was born in Maryland circa 1782 and moved to Kentucky in the 1800's with stepfather William H. LAYTON. (Ref: KA 14:1, p. 44)

Dr. H. George DOYLE of Louisville was married to Mary Ann Elizabeth TODD, daughter of late William TODD, Esq., of Lexington, on April 24, 1821 by Rev. BLYTHE. (Ref: NAW:36)

One John DOYLE was born in 1748 and was a Private in the Maryland Line (Ref: MRR:19).

DRANE. Anthony DRANE was born in 1766 in Maryland and married Catharine SCOTT on March 29, 1792 in Prince George's County. She was born in 1775 and died August 11, 1855. He died October 30, 1839 and both are buried in Drane Cemetery in Barren County, Kentucky. Their children were: Richard K. S. DRANE; Martha DRANE, married Benjamin LEVELL; Sarah DRANE, married Hubbard DUFF, although Franklin Gorin's The Times of Long Ago, p. 132 (Louisville, Kentucky: John P. Morton Co., 1929) states Sallie DRANE was a daughter of Thomas DRANE, and Hubbard DUFF was a son of John DUFF; Judson Scott DRANE, married Louisiana CLAYTON; Anthony DRANE, Jr., married Frances SETTLE; Margaret S. S. DRANE; Sabrina S. DRANE; and, Thomas J. DRANE, married Mary WILLIAMS. (Ref: KA 14:4, p. 242) The following are buried in the Drane-Trabue Cemetery, Barren County, Kentucky: Anthony DRANE, 1766-1830; Catherine DRANE, 1775-1855; Sabrina DRANE, 1805-1837; Richard S.DRANE, 1799-1834; Margaret S.DRANE, 1811-1830; Frederick DRANE, 18??-1854; Richard K. S. DRANE, 1850-1860; Lou DRANE, 1826-1894; Z. Taylor DRANE, 1845-1864; John R. DRANE, 1829-1874; Anthony DRANE, 1803-1878; Francis DRANE, born 1804; Mollie F. DRANE, 1882-1897; and, James L. DRANE, born and died 1872. (Ref: Barren County, Kentucky Cemetery Records, Vol. I, by Eva C. Peden, pp. 44-45, Glasgow, KY: Published by Author, 1976)

Stephen DRANE was born in 1768 in Prince George's County, Maryland, married Priscilla Sprague CRABB, and migrated to Shelby County, Kentucky circa 1801. A son, Capt. Stephen T. DRANE, was born in 1808 (Ref: KB 7:175).

DRURY. Hilary DRURY and Ignatius DRURY were among the early Catholic settlers from St. Mary's County, Maryland who moved to Cox's Creek, Kentucky by 1800, and Charles DRURY was an elder in Bardstown in 1820. (Ref: KC: 63, 114)

Elizabeth DRURY (born circa 1788 in Emmitsburg, Maryland, parents not known) moved to Nelson County, Kentucky where she married on August 1, 1814 to Aloysius Lewis BROWN, who was born January 18, 1793 in Bladensburg, Maryland. His sister, Monica BROWN, married Barnaby REYNOLDS (cousin), son of John REYNOLDS and Ann FRENCH, on July 6, 1813. (Ref: KPG 2:3, p. 161)

Leonard DRURY was born in 1759 and served in the Maryland Militia in the Revolutionary War (Ref: MRR:19).

DUCKER. John DUCKER was a Revolutionary soldier from either Maryland or Virginia who was alive in 1840, age 81 in Kenton County, Kentucky and receiving a pension. He married Mary HARDESTY and their daughter Nancy DUCKER married May 4, 1813 to Stephen RICH, of Lancaster County, Pennsylvania, in Covington, Kentucky (Ref: KB 8:134; RSK:103).

DUCKETT. Thomas DUCKETT, son of Jacob and Sarah DUCKETT, was born November 24, 1744 in Prince George's County, Maryland. He married Mary ODELL and died in Newberry District, S.C. in 1824, testate. They had twelve children, one of whom, John DUCKETT, was born July 30, 1779 in South Carolina and in 1807 married his cousin Charity WHITTEN. In 1808 they went to Warren County, Kentucky where they joined the Whittens (Ref: KA 9:2, p. 86; KA 4:4, pp. 182-184).

DUDDERAR. Conrad DUDDERAR was a son of George P. DUDDERAR who emigrated to Philadelphia from Germany in 1722. Conrad moved to Frederick County, Maryland and married and raised a family. They moved circa 1798 to Lincoln County, Kentucky. Their children Catherine, Conrad and William were born in Maryland, and children Samuel, Margaret, Elizabeth, John and Polly Ann were born in Kentucky. Conrad DUDDERAR, eldest son of Samuel, was born in 1793, married Catherine RUFFNER and had James (born 1820), Margaret, Samuel, Mary Ann, and Catherine. (Ref: KB 5:103-104)

John DUDDEROW, born in 1758, was a Musician in the Revolution (Ref: MRR:19).

DUER. Macey DUER of Baltimore, Maryland migrated in an early day to Robertson County, Tennessee where he was massacred by Indians soon after his arrival, date unknown. His son, John H. DUER, married Mary A. E. BIGBY and had 12 children, including C. L. DUER who settled initially in Livingston County, Kentucky. The Duers later settled in Caldwell and Simpson Counties, Kentucky (Ref: KB 4:8).

DUGAN. Hugh DUGAN applied for a pension in Campbell County, Kentucky in 1834 stating he was 50 (sic) years old and that he had enlisted in 1792 (sic) under Capt. William LEWIS in the 3rd Maryland Line and served under General WAYNE against the Indians at the rapids of the Miami River, now in Ohio. He left the service in 1795 and resided near Hagerstown, Maryland. His pension was rejected (R3107) since he had no proof of service in the Revolutionary War (Ref: MS:20).

DUKE. John DUKE was born in Maryland in 1773 and migrated to Ohio County, Kentucky where his son Thomas was born in 1807. (Ref: KB 3:135) John DUKE had a daughter, Frances DUKE, who married George W. BOOKER (Ref: KB 4:176).

DULEY. Enoch DULEY was born two miles from Georgetown, Maryland on December 28, 1773 and his wife Polly RAY was born in northern Maryland in June, 1778. Both were of Welsh descent. About 1792 they migrated to Scott County, Kentucky and about a year later returned to Maryland and brought his father's father to Kentucky. In 1815 he moved to Livingston County where he died in 1864. Enoch's son, T. R. DULEY, was born in Scott County on March 19, 1807 (Ref: KB 4:114).

DUNBAR. Charles BUCKMAN married a DUNBAR and migrated early (no date given) to Marion County, Kentucky (Ref: KB 5:252).

DUNHAM. Timothy DUNHAM was born in 1775 in Maryland and married in 1802 to Mary HARRIS, daughter of James HARRIS and Ann McKINNEY, in Warren County, Kentucky. Timothy and Mary DUNHAM died in Lafayette County, Missouri circa 1855 (Ref: KPG 2:4, p. 236; KBG 7:3, p. 102).

DUNN. Augustine DUNN married Ellen ALDRIDGE in Maryland and migrated to Kentucky circa 1800. Their son John A. DUNN was born in Maryland and married Margaret BRIGHT, born 1795 in Lincoln County, Kentucky, a daughter of Henry BRIGHT. John's son, Henry B. DUNN, was born February 23, 1824 in Garrard County, Kentucky (Ref: KB 2:51).

DUNNINGTON. William DUNNINGTON was a Private in the Maryland Line in the Revolutionary War and applied for a pension in 1818 (age 84) in Logan County, Kentucky. (Ref: KPR:1835) His widow, Martha LOYD, stated she married William DUNNINGTON on June 7, 1828 in Calloway County, and she was age 70 in 1856. His daughter, Ann LYNCH, was age 62 in 1853. William died in the 1830's and Martha then married John A. SWINEY on March 7, 1842. She subsequently received pension W27409 (Ref: LU 10:71).

DURBIN. Nicholas DURBIN, Sr. was born circa 1778 in Maryland and married Margaret BROWN, daughter of Joshua BROWN and Honor DURBIN, in 1798 in Madison County, Kentucky. She was born circa 1783 in Maryland died October 8, 1855 in Grayson County. He died May 17, 1822 in Hardin County, Kentucky. Their children were Isabella, Mary, Ann, Margaret, Thomas, Emily, Marjorie, Nicholas Jr., Celia, and Dominic. (Ref: KPG 2:3, p. 239)

John D. DURBIN was born circa 1769 in Maryland and was a pioneer settler at Sun Fish in Edmonson County, Kentucky. His father was Christopher DURBIN, Sr., born 1741. John D. married Patience LOGSDON and died April 8, 1793 in Madison County, Kentucky. Their children were Christopher, Joseph, John, Elisha J., Rebecca, Nicholas, Richard, Nancy, Robert A., and Margaret (Ref: KPG 1:4, p. 52; KPG 2:2, p. 101).

DUVALL. Gabriel DUVALL, Sr. was born in 1787 in Annapolis, Maryland and in 1790 removed with his mother to Kentucky, where he died August 1, 1827. He was a farmer and cooper. His father Miles DUVALL was a privateer in the Revolutionary War and afterwards a coast trader supposedly killed in 1787 by pirates. He was a son of Hugh DUVALL, a French Huguenot. Gabriel DUVALL, Sr. married Mary GRABLE (1792-1869) and their children were Cyrus G., Joseph, Thomas, Gabriel and Louisiana. (Ref: KB 5:107)

John DUVALL was born in 1784 in Maryland, moved to Scott County, Kentucky, was a Colonel in the War of 1812, and served in the legislature in 1827. He married Jennie BRANHAM and their children were Thomas; Alvin died 1893; Elizabeth; William P.; Burbridge; Edward; Annie married William G. SIMPSON; Martha; John Jr.; and Willina married Howard TODD. John DUVALL, Sr. died in 1859. (Ref: BCK:501-502)

Thomas DUVALL was born in Maryland and married Hannah DAVIS of Kentucky. A son Thomas was born October 31, 1823 in Hardin County, Kentucky and they were in Missouri by 1854 (Ref: KM:75)

The Duvalls were prominent in Annapolis, Anne Arundel County, Maryland and information can be found about them in many sources, including J. Warfield's Founders of Anne Arundel and Howard Counties, and Harry W. Newman's Anne Arundel Gentry, Volumes I and II, which are available at the Maryland Historical Society Library in Baltimore.

DYER. George DYER was born in 1753 in Prince George's County, Maryland and died in 1827 in Henry County, Virginia. He married Rachel DALTON and lived in Virginia after the Revolutionary War. Some of their children later moved to Kentucky, Iowa and Missouri. (Ref: MGS 14:2, p. 27) George DYER was a Private in the Maryland Line, 1778 to 1783. (Ref: Maryland Archives, Vol. 18, pp. 328, 443, 543)

Jonathan DYER was an Invalid soldier in the Maryland Line (Ref: MRR:19).

EARICKSON. Judge James EARICKSON of Maryland married Rebecca MALONE of Maryland in Jefferson County, Kentucky. A son Richard EARICKSON was born July 4, 1803. Peregreen EARICKSON of Maryland married Laraine STUCKY of Kentucky and a son William L. EARICKSON was born May 10, 1816. By 1819 they were in Chariton County, Missouri (Ref: KM:86).

EASTENHOUSER. Conrad EASTENHOUSER was born in Germany in May, 1755, came to America in 1776, deserted the German army in 1779 and joined the U.S. Army in Hanover County, Virginia in 1780. He lived in Washington County, Maryland until 1801 when he moved to Jessamine County, Kentucky. He applied for a pension (R3199) in 1832, but it was rejected, probably due to lack of sufficient proof of service (Ref: MS:53).

EATON. William EATON was born circa 1773 in Maryland and married Nancy Ann BRYAN on May 19, 1793 in the German Reformed Church of Frederick, Maryland. A son John was born May 12, 1794 and died young. Afterwards, William moved to Virginia or North Carolina before migrating to Gallatin County, Kentucky where he died in 1817 (Information contributed by Robert Ewing of Nampa, Idaho, in 1988).

EDELIN. Joseph EDELIN was among the early Catholic settlers from St. Mary's County, Maryland who settled in Washington County, Kentucky in 1795. Some of his children were born in Maryland and others in Kentucky: Cloe; Teresa; Peggy; Elisa; Lewis; Lucy;

Benedict; James; George; Helen; and Leonard, 1800-1865, married Sarah BRUCE of Lincoln County, Kentucky and their eight children were Sarah A., William B., Mary C., James H., Lucy R., Leonard G., George T., and Robert H. By trade Leonard was a hatter. Benedict and George migrated to Missouri. (Ref: KC:28, 31 and KB 5:107-108)

John EDELIN and Zachariah EDELIN also migrated from Maryland and settled in Kentucky on Cartwright's Creek in (now) Washington County circa 1785 (Ref: KC:80).

EDLEMAN. Leonard EDLEMAN was born in Hagerstown, Maryland in 1761 and enlisted in the Revolutionary War in Washington County, Maryland in March, 1781. After the war he moved to Green County, Tennessee and from there to Bourbon County, Kentucky in 1817. In 1824 to moved to Rush County, Indiana where he applied for and received pension S30397 in 1832. He transferred his pension from Indiana to Harrison County, Kentucky in April, 1840 (Ref: MS:46).

EDWARDS. Josiah EDWARDS of St. Mary's County, Maryland moved to Marion County, Kentucky prior to 1800 (wife unknown) with children Elkamah, Josiah, John, Stouton, Joseph, Hezekiah, Henry, and Ann. James F. EDWARDS, son of Josiah, Jr., was born in Kentucky in 1813 and married in 1844 to Martha WALSTON. (Ref: KB 5:109)

Ninian EDWARDS was born in March, 1775, in Montgomery County, Maryland and was sent by his father to Nelson County, Kentucky in 1794 to care for his landed estate. His father settled in Kentucky in 1800. Ninian was elected to the House of Representatives in Kentucky in 1796 and moved to Russellville, Logan County, Kentucky in 1798 where he served as Judge from 1804 to 1807. In 1808 he was Chief Justice of Kentucky and in 1809 was appointed Governor of the Illinois Territory by President James Madison. In 1818 he became a U.S. Senator and in 1824 he was appointed Minister to Mexico but declined. In 1826 he was elected Governor of Illinois, and died July 20, 1833 at Belleville in St. Clair County, Illinois. (Ref: BCK:314)

Benjamin EDWARDS was born in Stafford County, Virginia on August 12, 1752 or 1753 and served as a Lieutenant in the Revolutionary War. He died November 13, 1826 in Todd County, Kentucky. His wife Margaret BEALL was born in October, 1756 in Montgomery County, Maryland and died July 20, 1826 in Elkton, Kentucky. Their son Elisha EDWARDS was born May 11, 1781 in Maryland and died October 13, 1823 in Kentucky. His wife Martha (1792-1854) and other Edwards family members are buried in Edwards Cemetery at Edwards Hall in Elkton, Logan County, Kentucky (Ref: KCR:360; DAR:215).

ELDER. The Elders of Maryland were a prominent family in St. Mary's County and in Nelson County, Kentucky. Thomas ELDER (1748-1832) migrated to Kentucky in 1799 from his farm in Frederick County, Maryland, having married in 1771 to Elizabeth SPALDING, a sister of Basil SPALDING, Esquire, of Charles County, Maryland. Their children were as follows: Annie or Nancy ELDER, born July 1, 1772, single, died in Bardstown, Kentucky, March 25, 1842; Basil Spalding ELDER, born October 29, 1773, married Elizabeth SNOWDEN, died in

Baltimore, Feb. 20, 1860; Catharine ELDER, born March 7, 1776, married Joseph GARDINER, Esq. of Nelson Couunty, Kentucky, died March 7, 1866; William Pius ELDER, born May 4, 1778 and died in Baltimore, August 22, 1799; Clementina ELDER, born June 16, 1780, married Richard CLARK, died in Nelson County, Kentucky on August 21, 1851; Ignatius ELDER, born July 31, 1782, married Monica GREENWELL; Theresa ELDER, born March 1, 1785, died unmarried in Kentucky, December 19, 1816; Thomas Richard ELDER, born June 14, 1789, married Caroline CLEMENTS, died July 11, 1835; Christiana ELDER, born October 30, 1791, married John B. WIGHT; Mary Elizabeth ELDER, born May 15, 1794, married John JARBOE; and, Maria M. ELDER, born April 29, 1791; married John HORRELL. James ELDER (1761-1845) was the first Catholic of his name to migrate to Kentucky. Born in Frederick County, Maryland, his father was Guy ELDER and his grandfather was William ELDER. In 1791 James moved to Kentucky (having been shortly before married to Ann RICHARDS, a non-Catholic) and settled on Hardin's Creek. William ELDER (1757-c1822) came to Kentucky a few months after his brother James in 1791. He moved to Breckinridge (now Meade County) in 1804, and his sons were: Arnold ELDER, died 1830; William ELDER, died 1854; Samuel ELDER, died 1843; and, John ELDER, died 1876; his daughters were Mrs. Peter JARBOE, Mrs. Peter BRUNER, and Mrs. Walter READ. (Ref: KC:117-128). Additional information on the Elder family is available in the DAR Library in Washington, D.C.).

ELDRIDGE. James ELDRIDGE married Elizabeth WILLIAMS after 1800 in Kentucky; county not stated. Their marriage was proven through a Maryland Revolutionary War pension application; soldier's name not stated (Ref: MRR:113).

ELLIOTT. William ELLIOTT (born 1743 in Baltimore County, now Harford County, Maryland) married Kerenhappuck JOHNSON and subsequently conveyed land on Deer Creek to their son William ELLIOTT Jr., of Wilkes County, North Carolina. He later sold it to Edward ELLIOTT in 1793 who in turn sold it to Thomas ELLIOTT in 1795. These Elliotts may have gone to Fleming County, Kentucky where the had land in 1816 and 1827 before moving on to Indiana. (Ref: KA 7:2, p. 103)

In 1785 Stephen ELLIOTT was among the Maryland League of Catholics who settled on Pottinger's Creek in (now) Washington County, Kentucky (Ref: KC:28).

ELLIS. John ELLIS of Maryland moved with his parents to Virginia and about 1785 migrated to Fayette County, Kentucky where he married Elizabeth CHAPMAN. He also served with General Wayne and in 1802 located on Peter's Creek in Barren County, Kentucky where he built the first mill south of Glasgow. His son William was born in 1795 in Fayette County and later was Deputy Sheriiff and Colonel in the State Militia in Barren County. (Ref: KB 2:114)

Isaac ELLIS was born in Frederick County, Maryland October 29, 1752 and served in the Revolution in Washington County, Pennsylvania. He migrated to Jefferson County, Kentucky from Frederick County, Maryland in 1784. In 1791 he moved to Shelby County, Kentucky and

48

in 1829 to Owen County, Kentucky. His widow Anne applied for and
received pension W10013 in 1836 (age 74), stating they were married
in 1779 in Pennsylvania. She later moved to Lincoln County,
Missouri to live with her son in 1846. (Ref: MS:60)

Samuel ELLIS was born April 9, 1762 in Montgomery County, Maryland
and served in the Revolutionary War in 1778 in Rowan County, North
Carolina. He lived in Surry County and Buck County, North Carolina
and Jefferson County, Tennessee before moving to Cumberland County,
Kentucky in 1826 and Russell County, Kentucky in 1832. In 1843 he
applied for a pension in Ray County, Missouri (wife deceased and
two daughters and a son are mentioned unnamed) and he received
pension S30400. (Ref: MS:1)

On October 6, 1802, Joseph ELLIS and wife Eleanora of Kentucky
conveyed part of a tract called "Ellis Folly" in Baltimore County,
Maryland to John GORSUCH, of Thomas (Ref: BCLR Liber WG #73, p.
610).

ESMENARD. Caroline E. ESMENARD of Baltimore, Maryland married Dr.
G.R.A. BROWNE of Virginia (died 1834) and their son, Capt. Stanley
BROWNE, was born in Breckinridge County, Kentucky on February 10,
1820 and later moved to Paducah, Kentucky (Ref: KB 6:176).

EVANS. John Cheshire EVANS was born April 10, 1798 and moved from
Maryland to Kentucky in May, 1799 with his father, a soldier of the
Revolutionary War who died in the Spring of 1800 in Jefferson County. John Cheshire EVANS married Miss HALL on September 27, 1821 and
died in Chicago on December 24, 1872. His wife died on July 4, 1884
in Bullitt County, Kentucky (Ref: KB 5:18).

FAIRBAINE, FAIRBAIRN. Maria Eliza FAIRBAINE (FAIRBAIRN), wrote her
will on February 14, 1828 in Baltimore County, Maryland and left
land in Kentucky, included in the City of Louisville, to her
children: John Hamton FAIRBAINE, Daniel Henry FAIRBAINE, Elizabeth
Ann FAIRBAINE, Mary Muston FAIRBAINE and Frances FAIRBAINE. The
witnesses to her will were N. H. RIDGELY, Gerald T. HOPKINS and
Samuel D. TOY. When probated on March 18, 1828, her executors were
Luke TIERMAN and Isaac C. LEE (Ref: Abstracts of the Wills of
Baltimore County, 1827-1831, Vol. 13, by Annie W. Burns, and available at the Maryland Historical Society Library).

FAIRLEIGH. William FAIRLEIGH (1797-1865), son of Andrew FAIRLEIGH
of Maryland, was an early settler in Hardin County, Kentucky and
when Meade County was organized in 1832 he became county and
circuit clerk continuously until his death. He married Elizabeth
ENLOW and had at least two sons, Thomas B. FAIRLEIGH and James L.
FAIRLEIGH (Ref: KB 9:47).

FALLIN. William FALLIN was born in Maryland in 1805 and he and wife
Jane had six children: Mary, Eliza, Emerine, Laura, Cordelia and
Penelope. They later resided in Bracken County, Kentucky (Ref: KBG
8:1, p. 34).

FARQUHER. James FARQUHER allegedly served in the American Revolution in Maryland from 1776 to 1779, married Betsey JACK on February 15, 1798, and died January 3, 1829. Joseph ELSTON of Henry County, Kentucky stated he had known James FARQUHER since 1808 and referred to him as a pensioner, but Betsey's pension claim (R3445) was rejected. Robert FARQUHER was a son of James and the record states he appointed John T. NELLY of D.C. his attorney; nothing further. (Ref: MS:50) James FARQUHER was a Private in the Maryland Militia and a Revolutionary War pensioner (according to Source MRR:21).

FENWICK. Thomas FENWICK, Cornelius FENWICK and Henry FENWICK were among the early Catholic settlers on Cartwright's Creek in Nelson County, Kentucky circa 1785.(Ref: KC:80) A native of St. Mary's County, Maryland, Cornelius FENWICK served in the U.S. Navy as a sailor and was once a prisoner. He died in Franklin County, Kentucky at the age of 94. His daughter, Mary FENWICK, married Jacob COX and moved to Franklin County in 1800 and died in 1878. (Ref: KB 7:40)

William FENWICK was born in St. Mary's County, Maryland in 1757 and served in the Revolutionary War in 1776 under Capt. Allen THOMAS in 1776. Later, as the owner of two vessels, he was pressed into service at the time of Lafayette's muster in Baltimore and transported provisions from Baltimore to Yorktown on his boat "Fair Wind" until 1781. He moved to Franklin County, Kentucky in 1790 and applied for and received pension S16381 in 1831. He died June 18, 1833 in Franklin County (Ref: MS:38, RSK:75, KPR:1835, MRR:21).

FIELD. Wilfred FIELD was among the early Catholic settlers from St. Mary's County, Maryland to settle on Cartwright's Creek in (now) Washington County, Kentucky circa 1785 (Ref: KC:80).

FIELDER. George FIELDER applied for a Revolutionary War pension in Washington County, Kentucky at age 74 (in 1819), and stated he was discharged in Frederick, Maryland, having served in the Virginia line. He received pension S35935 in 1820 and died on December 5, 1825 (Ref: MS:56 and RSK:163).

FIELDS. Joseph FIELDS served in the Revolutionary War for three years under Capt. John SMITH in the Maryland Line. He may have married Nancy NOLAND and had six children: Tusey, Joseph, Thomas, Elizabeth, George and Nancy. He applied for a pension on August 12, 1822 (age 66) in Washington County, Kentucky and subsequently received pension S35933, which he transferred to Indiana and then back to Kentucky in 1828. He may have died in Nelson County, Kentucky in 1844 (Ref: MS:56; RSK:164; KPR:1835; KA 4:2, p. 97; KA 7:2, p. 103)

John FIELDS of Maryland married Elizabeth WISEHEART of Kentucky and son, Henry H. FIELDS, was born November 6, 1822 in Washington County, Kentucky. They were in Missouri by 1855 (Ref: KM:159).

FIFER. Jacob FIFER was born in 1754 and was a Private in the Maryland Militia and/or German Regiment. He applied for and received a pension in 1831 in Nicholas County, Kentucky. (Ref: RSK:135,

KPR:1835, MRR:21) His widow Katherine's claim (R2534) was rejected? (according to Source MRP:15).

FINNELL. Alexander FINNELL married in March, 1821 to Mrs. Catharine MITCHELL, relict of J. MITCHELL, deceased, and daughter of Samuel HANSON, Esq., formerly of Maryland, but now of Kentucky, all of Clover Hill, Shenandoah County, Virginia (Ref: NAW:54).

FISHER. David FISHER, Sr. was born in Maryland circa 1785 and married Mary LOTSPIEK in Fayette County, Kentucky prior to 1807. They had at least three sons: John Wesley FISHER, born 1810; David FISHER Jr.; and, James FISHER, born 1826. They were in Shelby County, Illinois by mid-1830's (Ref: KA 13:4, p. 216; KA 14:4, p. 244)

James E. FISHER was born circa 1795 in Harford County, Maryland and married Oct. 22, 1821 in Pennsylvania to Margaret Jane E. BOYD, possibly a daughter of Thomas and Elizabeth BOYD. Their children were all born in Maryland: Mary, Thomas John, Cooper B., Sarah, John and James. James FISHER served in the War of 1812 and moved to Campbell County, Kentucky and then Kenton County, Kentucky where he died on May 14, 1852 (Ref: MGS 14:2, p. 27).

FITZGERALD. Benjamin FITZGERALD stated he was age 65 in 1818 when he applied for a Revolutionary War pension in Mason County, Kentucky. He enlisted from Montgomery County, Maryland on February 11, 1777, served as a Private, Corporal and later a Quartermaster Sergeant under Capt. John COATS, and was discharged from Col. John GUNBY's 7th Maryland Line at Fredericktown, Maryland. In court in 1820, he stated that his wife was lame and very old and his property was worth only $25. He subsequently received pension S35931 (Ref: MGS 5:2; KP:175-176; RSK:115; KPR:1835; MRR:21; Mason County, Kentucky Court Order Book B, 1820, p. 135).

FITZHUGH. Samuel T. FITZHUGH of Kentucky married Miss Eliza M. FITZHUGH of Baltimore, Maryland in January, 1823 (Ref: NAW:61).

FITZPATRICK. Hugh FITZPATRICK was among the early Catholic settlers from St. Mary's County, Maryland who settled on Cartwright's Creek in Kentucky circa 1785 (Ref: KC:80).

FOGLE. Robert H. FOGLE was born May 1, 1788 in Maryland and migrated with his parents in 1792 to Washington (now) Marion County, Kentucky. His father was ----- FOGLE and his mother was Sarah HAMMETT. Robert later became the first Postmaster of Lebanon, Kentucky, and moved to Daviess County in 1849. His first wife was Rachel SHUTTLEWORTH (died 1860) and their children were Ebenezer, McDowell (born 1815), Sallie Ann, and Mary. His second wife was Sallie NEWBOLD and their children were Catherine and Rachel (Ref: BCK:296-298).

FORD. Charles FORD and wife Sarah, of Bourbon County, Kentucky conveyed land on September 26, 1807, in Baltimore County, Maryland to Rebecca FORD and Lloyd FORD as tenants in common land which was willed to Charles by his late father (not named), part of "Gist's Search." (Ref: BCLR Liber WG #95, p. 53)

William FORD was born in Montgomery County, Maryland on March 5, 1763 and served in the Revolutionary War in 1781 under Capt. John NICHOLS as a Private in the militia. He applied for and received pension S31034 in 1831 while residing in Caldwell County, Kentucky (Ref: MS:23; KCR:82; KPR:1835, MRR:22).

FOREMAN. Joseph FOREMAN migrated from Maryland to Nelson County, Kentucky prior to 1800 and daughter Nancy FOREMAN married Martin YEWELL in 1809. Their children were: Lavina, married Edward NALL; Harrison; Nancy, married James H. BROWN; Elizabeth, married James McGEEHEE; Joseph; Rebecca; Morgan R.; Vardaman; Bemia; and, Isabel (Ref: KB 5:310; Foreman-Farman- Forman Genealogy compiled by Elbert Eli Farman in 1911, and available at the Maryland Historical Society Library in Baltimore).

FORREST. Zepheniah FORREST of Maryland settled between Rolling Fork and Lebanon, Kentucky circa 1800 (Ref: KC:111).

FORSTER. Thomas FORSTER of Pennsylvania married Catharine HARBAUGH (of Pennylvania or Maryland) on October 16, 1793 in Fayette County, Pennsylvania and died August 27, 1849 in Ray County, Missouri. She was born January 24, 1776 and died on June 24, 1857 in Edgar County, Illinois. Their children were born in Kentucky: Nancy, born circa 1796 in Bullitt County, Kentucky; Hannah, born November 17, 1798 in Kentucky, married Jesse ESAREY in 1822 and died in 1879; Arthur, born February 28, 1801 in Muhlenburg County, Kentucky, married (1) Nancy ESAREY (2) Phebe SMITH (3) Mary Ann PATRIDGE and Arthur died April 25, 1875 in Edgar County, Illinois; John married Eve RHODES 1828; Christina, 1811-1895, married Jonathan PATTERSON; Elizabeth, born 1818, married Thomas RHODES; Margaret, married John HOUSE; and, Lelia (Ref: KPG 1:3, p. 54).

FORT. Peter FORT (1746-1819) married Mary Taylor (born 1750) and was possibly related to the FOURTS (FORTS) of Ten Mile Run, New Jersey. Peter FORT appeared in the 1776 census of Harford County, Maryland (Susquehannah Hundred), with his wife and these children: Nancy FORT, born 1771, married Benjamin JAMES; Frances FORT, born 1773; Dority FORT, born 1775, married John CRAWFORD; and, two other children were born later: David Andrew FORT, married Sally WYATT in Kentucky; and Margaret FORT, married David HOWARD. Peter FORT is also listed in the 1783 Tax List of Harford County, Maryland in the Broad Creek Hundred. He moved to Kentucky circa 1790 and died in Mt. Sterling. His son David moved on to Missouri circa 1810 (Ref: MGS 25:2, p. 208; MGS 26:1, 2; MRR:22; Gaius M. Brumbaugh's Maryland Records: Colonial, Church and Revolutional, Vol. II, p. 176 (Baltimore: Genealogical Publishing Co., 1985 repr.; originally published in Lancaster, Pennslvania in 1928).

FORWOOD. William FORWOOD, son of Samuel FORWOOD (deceased in 1808), late of Jefferson County, Kentucky, now of Harford County, Maryland, conveyed several tracts of land to John GRINDALL of Harford County on October 8, 1808 (Ref: HCLR Liber HD #T, pp. 278-281).

52

FOSTER. Isaac FOSTER of Maryland was an early pioneer in Kentucky. His daughter Sarah M. FOSTER married Erastus B. BAINBRIDGE (born December 1, 1801) of Fayette County, Kentucky; their son Eusebius C. BAINBRIDGE was born in Owen County on November 14, 1828 (Ref: KB 8:8).

FOULK. Thomas D. FOULK married Cassandra SMITH circa 1805 in Kentucky; county not stated. Their marriage was proven through a Maryland Revolutionary War pension application; soldier's name not stated (Ref: MRR:114).

FRANTZ. David FRANTZ was born August 30, 1810 in Alsace, Germany and came to America in 1829. He was a journeyman tanner in Baltimore, Maryland until 1831 when he walked to Cincinnati, Ohio. He married Christina STAEBLER (born 1805 in Wurtemberg, Germany, a daughter of Jonathan STAEBLER) and moved to Louisville, Kentucky in 1847 (Ref: BCK:90-91).

FRAZIER. Alexander FRAZIER, son of Andrew FRAZIER of Maryland, a soldier of the Revolutionary War, was born in Shelby County, Kentucky in 1793. He married Rosann PIERCE, a daughter of Absalom PIERCE and Diademia WEBB of Kentucky, and their children were Andrew J., Absalom P., Alfred, Allen L. (died in Civil War), Gilbert H., Ann A., Elvira, and John W. FRAZIER. They later settled Ohio County, Kentucky, and were possibly related to Elisha L. FRAZIER of Shelby County (Ref: KB 3:141; KB 7:180).

FREELAND. John FREELAND was born in 1762 and served in the Revolutionary War as a Privateer in Baltimore, Maryland at age 17. He stated he served on vessels owned by Sterrett and Yellott, and sailed to places like St. Thomas, Guadalupe and Cuba. He was captured by the British and robbed. They set him and other prisoners ashore in New Jersey. He returned to Baltimore to find that peace had been declared. He applied for a pension while residing in Fleming County, Kentucky in 1832 (age 70) and stated he was born in Prince George's County, Maryland and had resided in Kentucky for 22 years. His application (R3773) was rejected according to Source MS:37, but not according to Source MRR:22. Joseph FREELAND of Calvert County, Maryland set free his negro man named Thomas in Mason County, Kentucky in 1817. Thomas paid one cent for his freedom. Witnessed by R. J. WHEATLEY, James CHAMBERS and William SUTHERLAND (Ref: KA 3:2, p. 55, and Mason County, Kentucky Deed Book R, 1817, p. 103).

FRENCH. Ignatius FRENCH was among the early Catholics who settled with the Maryland League of St. Mary's County in Nelson County, Kentucky circa 1785 (Ref: KC:28).

FRIAR. The following appeared in the Frederick Town Herald newspaper on October 17, 1803: "Greenbury HOWARD, Trustee, appointed by Walter FRIAR, residing in Kentucky, to sell tract whereon he formerly lived in Montgomery County, Maryland, 140 acres, 4 miles from Clarksburg. Christian LEAMAN living thereon will show the land." (Ref: WMNA 3:15).

FROMAN. John FROMAN of Maryland migrated to Spencer County, Kentucky and his daughter Mary married Nathan CAIN. She died at age 83, but no birth year was given. Their son Enoch CAIN was born December 5, 1831 in Kentucky (Ref: KB 7:160).

FROST. Katie FROST of Frostburg, Maryland, married William DORRIS of New Jersey and whose father Samuel FROST moved to Maryland after marrying Miss HUEY and then moved to North Carolina. Their daughter Katie DORRIS married Drew EDWARDS (born 1801) who had moved with his family from Virginia to Sumner County, Tennessee in 1814 and then to Simpson County, Kentucky (Ref: KB 4:191).

FUGATE. Edward FUGATE, possibly a son of Edward FUGATE who died in 1785 and Elizabeth BACON of Baltimore County, Maryland, died in Mason County, Kentucky by 1805 and his widow Cassandra married John LAWS in Bourbon County, Kentucky in 1807. Edward FUGATE has three daughters, Sarah, Priscilla and Nancy, each of whom married --- McKENNEY and migrated to Butler County, Kentucky (Ref: KA 16:1, p. 48).

FUNK. The following appeared in the Elizabethtown Advertiser newspaper (Maryland) on October 4, 1798: "To Susanna FUNK from Commonwealth of Kentucky-----You are commanded to appear before the Justices of our Court of Quarter Sessions for the County of Jefferson at Louisville to answer the complaint of John FUNK, your husband, for openly living in adultery with another man, in the state of Maryland and for desertion and refusal to come with him from the said state of Maryland to this state and show cause why the contract of marriage shall not be dissolved-----Worden POPE, Clerk." (Ref: WMNA 1:78).

GADD. Thomas GADD was born in 1760 and was a Private in the Maryland Militia in the Revolutionary War. He applied for a pension in 1831 in Rockcastle County, Kentucky (Ref: MRR:22; RSK:136; KPR: 1835).

GAITHER. Some members of the Gaither family migrated early to Kentucky from Anne Arundel County, Maryland. Jeremiah GAITHER (1762-1815) moved to North Carolina and after his death his widow and family moved to Woodford County, Kentucky. Others, like John Franklin GAITHER and Wiley GAITHER, went to Grayson County, Kentucky from Iredell County, North Carolina. John Rogers GAITHER (1752-1825) was in Nelson County, Kentucky by 1780 (on land granted for his services in the Revolution) and in 1796 that part of Nelson became Bullitt County and the only Gaithers in the 1800 tax list were John Roger GAITHER and Cornelius GAITHER. Dr. Nathan GAITHER (1788-1862), son of Captain Basil GAITHER and Margaret WATKINS, was an Assistant Surgeon in the Kentucky Volunteers during the War of 1812, and died in Columbia, Kentucky in 1862. Lureene W. WATKINS of Davies County, Kentucky, wrote to her brother Thomas W. WATKINS of Ellicott Mills, Maryland on July 2, 1820 that John GAITHER, nephew of Uncle Basil GAITHER, married Rebecca BELL two weeks ago and they went to Missouri. These are just a few of the Gaithers who lived on tracts with names like "Bite the Biter" and "Left Out" in

Anne Arundel County, Maryland and who subsequently moved to North Carolina, Tennessee and Kentucky circa 1800 (AAG I:59-148).

GALLIHAN. Clement GALLIHAN was an early Catholic settler on Cartwright's Creek in Nelson County, Kentucky circa 1785, having migrated from St. Mary's County, Maryland (Ref: KC:80).

GANNON. James GANNON of Maryland settled on Hardin's Creek in Nelson County, Kentucky prior to 1800. Elizabeth GANNON, a daughter of James, married John GRAVES. Their descendants settled Marion County, Kentucky (Ref: KC:54).

GARDINER. Clement GARDINER was born in 1748 most likely in St. Mary's County, Maryland and married Henrietta BOONE. He was a leader in the settlement of the Cox's Creek settlement in Kentucky circa 1792. Their children were as follows: Joseph GARDINER, married Winifred HAMILTON in Maryland; Polly GARDINER, married Benedict SMITH in Maryland; Theodore GARDINER, married Miss RAPIER in Kentucky; Harry GARDINER; Francis GARDINER, married Ann SMITH in Kentucky; Ellen GARDINER, married Thomas MILES in Kentucky; Ignatius GARDINER, moved to Louisiana; and, Ann GARDINER, married Edward JENKINS in Kentucky (Ref: KC:114-117).

GARRISON. Samuel GARRISON apparently served in the North Carolina Militia during the Revolutionary War and was then discharged in Frederick County, Maryland on January 12, 1782 according to his pension application in Warren County, Kentucky in 1832. He received pension S31049 (Ref: MS:54; RSK:162).

GATES. Elisha GATES of Maryland was a Bardstown, Kentucky elder in 1820 and for many years his house was the church station for the Catholics in his neighborhood (Ref: KC:63).

GAU. William GAU, a teacher from Maryland, was an early Catholic settler on Cartwright's Creek in Nelson County, Kentucky circa 1785 (Ref: KC:80).

GAUGH. Ignatius GAUGH enlisted in the Revolutionary War in St. Mary's County, Maryland where he lived and served for two years under Capt. THOMAS. In 1777 he served at Annapolis under Capt. William CAMPBELL and was discharged in May, 1778 due to ill health. At that time he lived in the east end of the county, about 20 miles from the courthouse. A resident of Breckenridge County, Kentucky, in 1832, he applied for a pension before Cornelius GAUGH, Justice of the Peace. Anne HOWARD (age 90) and Susan MONTGOMERY (age 80) stated they were sisters of Ignatius GAUGH in Nelson County, Kentucky in 1833. He received pension S1205 (Ref: MS:16).

GEIGER. Jacob GEIGER of Kentucky and Miss Eliza GEIGER of Baltimore City were married in November, 1821, at Funkstown, Maryland by Rev. B. KURTZ (Ref: NAW:38).

GEOGHAN, GEOGHEGAN. John GEOGHEGAN applied for a pension for Revolutionary War service while residing in Nicholas County, Kentucky in 1818, age 63. He was born March 23, 1755 in Baltimore County,

Maryland and his family in 1818 consisted of his wife (unnamed, age 56) and daughter (also unnamed) age 18. Fellow soldier S. SMITH made affidavit in Baltimore in 1818 that he had known John since childhood and in the army. John GEOGHAN was an Ensign in the Maryland Line and died February 20, 1826 in Kentucky (Ref: MS:60; RSK:134; KPR:1835; MRR:23).

GETTINGS, GITTINGS. McKenzie GETTINGS was among the early Catholic settlers from St. Mary's County, Maryland who went to Cartwright's Creek in (now) Washington County, Kentucky circa 1785 (Ref: KC:80).

GIDDINGS. George GIDDINGS was born in Maryland in October, 1776, possibly a son of John GIDDINGS (born 1732) who moved from Ipswich, Massachusetts to Maryland before 1756. George moved to Kentucky prior to 1800 and died in 1854 in Monroe County, Missouri (Ref: MGS 26:4, p. 445).

GILBERT. The Gilberts were a prominent family in colonial Baltimore County (now Harford County), Maryland. Aquilla GILBERT, son of Gervais and Mary, was born February 23, 1727 and married Elizabeth BUTLER on January 17, 1749. They moved to Madison County, Kentucky circa 1780 and settled initially on Muddy Creek. Later, they moved to Jessamine County where Acquilla GILBERT died testate in February, 1807. (Ref: Will Book A.P. 113, Jessamine County, Kentucky) In his will he named only his children Michael (Micha) GILBERT, Benjamin GILBERT, Samuel GILBERT, and Martha GILBERT. Not named are his sons Isaac GILBERT (who had six children) and Charles GILBERT, who had moved to Logan County, Kentucky. Benjamin GILBERT, son of Aquilla, died testate in 1814 in Jessamine County, Kentucky, naming son Isaac GILBERT, daughter Polly GILBERT, daughter-in-law Eleanor GILBERT (formerly WELCH, and wife of deceased son Ezekiel GILBERT), and son-in-law William SIMPKINS (husband of his deceased daughter Fanny GILBERT) and Mary GILBERT, wife of Benjamin, deceased. (Ref: Will Book B, p. 82, Jessamine County, Kentucky) Some of these Gilberts moved to St. Charles County, Missouri and Pike County, Missouri. Charles GILBERT was born March 21, 1756 in Baltimore County, Maryland and taken as a small child to Virginia. In 1777 he moved to Surry County, North Caorlina and enlisted in the Revolutionary War in Wilkes County, North Carolina in 1779, serving under Capt. MARTIN in Col. CLEVELAND's Regiment. After the war he moved to Franklin County, Georgia and Grainger County, Tennessee and Dickson County, Tennessee and Graves County, Kentucky. He applied for and received pension S31057 in 1833, stating that he also served in the Maryland Militia (Ref: MS:41; RSK:81; KPR:1835. Not listed in Source MRR:23)

Samuel GILBERT was born February 10, 1752 in Baltimore County, Maryland, a son of Jarvis GILBERT and Elizabeth PRESTON. He lived in Georgia and by 1795 he was in Madison County, Kentucky, at which time he had been granted a power of attorney and had acquired 1,313 acres on Muddy Creek by virtue of land office treasury warrant 11042 and a survey dated February 6, 1797. (Ref: Deed Book C, p. 488, Madison County)

Samuel GILBERT, Jr. married Jane DINWIDDIE on August 29, 1807, and William P. GILBERT married Polly MAUPIN on July 19, 1826 in Madison County, Kentucky; both were sons of Samuel GILBERT. Micah GILBERT was a Methodist Preacher in 1803 in Madison County, Kentucky, and a Justice of the Peace in 1804. In 1806 he was Inspector of Tobacco at Goggins Tobacco Gatehouse. Jonathan GILBERT was admitted to practice law on November 3, 1790 in Madison County, Kentucky. Some early Gilbert marriages in Madison County were: Sarah GILBERT to Peter TURNER in 1803; Polly GILBERT to John STEWART in 1809; Aquilla GILBERT to Jane STEWART in 1811; Hannah GILBERT to James THOMAS in 1812; Elizabeth GILBERT to William BENNETT in 1812; Benjamin GILBERT to Rhoda HENRY in 1819; and, Aquilla GILBERT to Mary BAKER in 1825. Also, in Jessamine County, Kentucky, a deed was recorded in 1824 that involved Charles GILBERT of Logan County, Kentucky, Isaac GILBERT of Madison County, Kentucky, Samuel GILBERT of Pike County, Kentucky and Micah GILBERT of Clermont County, Ohio, Elizabeth SNOW of Clermont County, Ohio, and Benjamin NICHOLSON of Henry County, Kentucky, heirs of Benjamin GILBERT. (Ref: Deed Book H, page 3, January 2, 1824)

There are many other Gilberts in Kentucky who trace their ancestry to Maryland from the above mentioned families. Information has been researched and documented over the years by several researchers, including Henry C. Peden, Jr., Esther Gilbert Hannon, Jon H. Livezey, Edna E. Briggs, William W. Finney, Joseph L. Hughes, Richard B. Miller, John M. Robinson, and Robert W. Barnes. Another excellent research compilation has been privately published by Fonda G. Marcum who traces the Gilberts back to England and, in addition to many of the aforementioned Kentucky Gilberts, she writes about Samuel GILBERT and wife Martha WEBSTER who migrated from Baltimore County, Maryland to Bedford County, Virginia in 1757. Samuel died in 1776 and some of his children, namely Samuel GILBERT, Michael GILBERT, and Mary WELCH, moved to Kentucky. Around 1795 another son, John Webster GILBERT, a Captain in the Revolutionary War, moved to Kentucky also. (Ref: Fonda Marcum's Gilbert and Allied Lines, pp. 220-240, 1986, n.p.) John Webster GILBERT was born December 27, 1738 in Baltimore County, Maryland and moved to first to Bedford County, Virginia and then Lincoln County, Kentucky in 1794. His first wife was Rebecca and his children were James, Rachel, John Wesley, Isham, Sally and Patsy. (Ref: KBG 8:1, p. 42, Spring, 1981, and information from S. Wallace Gilbert of Birmingham, Alabama)

Amos GILBERT married Sarah MAGRUDER before 1814 in Kentucky; county not stated. Their marriage was proven through a Maryland Revolutionary War pension application; soldier's name not stated (Ref: MRR:114).

GILTNER, GILDNER. The Giltner family came to America from Amsterdam, Germany. Bennett GILTNER, son of John, settled initially in New York and then in Maryland. John GILTNER was born in Maryland and went to Bourbon County, Kentucky after the Revolutionary War. His son, Abraham GILTNER, lived at Bryan's Station and married Katherine LIGHTER, daughter of Henry LIGHTER. Their son, John GILTNER, was born March 4, 1797 in Bourbon County, Kentucky and died March 14, 1863. His son, Professor William Spencer GILTNER, was born May 18, 1827 and married Elizabeth RAINES, daughter of Ayelette RAINES, in 1856 (Ref: BCK, pp. 527-528).

GIST. The Gist family was a very prominent family in early Maryland history, notably the famous General Mordecai GIST of the Maryland Line during the Revolutionary War. The Gist family also migrated to South Carolina as well as Kentucky. One Mordecai GIST of Frederick County, Maryland married in Lexington, Kentucky on February 19, 1806 to Patsy CLARKE of Clarke County, Kentucky (Ref: KYM:8; SRM: 131).

GLASS. Joseph GLASS married Miss Elizabeth WIRE in Fleming County, Kentucky on November 12, 1822 (Ref: NAW:60).

GLOVER. On September 29, 1804, Samuel GLOVER, now of Baltimore County, Maryland, but a resident of Kentucky, sold part of tract "John's Mistake" and tract "John's Chance" to John O'DONNELL (Ref: BCLR Liber WG #83, p. 206).

GOODMAN. Dr. John GOODMAN was born in Frankfort, Kentucky on July 22, 1837, a son of John GOODMAN and Jane WINTERS. John GOODMAN, the father, was born in Germany and migrated to Kentucky in 1801 and settled in Lexington. Jane WINTERS, the mother, was a native of Maryland (Ref: KB 9:60).

GOODRUM. Wilfred GOODRUM was among the early Catholic settlers to migrate from St. Mary's COunty, Maryland to Hardin's Creek, Kentucky circa 1786 (Ref: KC:56).

GOODSON. William GOODSON was born in Frederick County, Maryland in 1759 and moved with his family to Botetourt County, Virginia at age 2. He enlisted in the Revolutionary War in Virginia in 1776 and after the war he migrated to Montgomery County, Tennessee and then to Cumberland County, Kentucky in 1800. He applied for a pension in 1833 and did receive pension S30440 (Ref: MS:32).

GOOTEE. Joseph W. GOOTEE died testate in 1810 in Washington County, Kentucky and was probably born in Dorchester County, Maryland. His wife was Sarah BRAMBLE (Ref: MGS 20:2, p. 171).

GORE. Notley GORE was born in Maryland on June 10, 1755 and migrated to North Carolina where he served in the Revolution in the Camden District. He was a Sergeant in 1777 under Capt. James PEDIGREW for ten months. He later moved to Green County and Lawrence County, Kentucky. He received pension S31070 for his services. (Ref: MS:48)

Thomas Weston GORE was born in Boyle County, Kentucky on September 29, 1819, a son of Christian GORE, a native of Reisterstown, Baltimore County, Maryland. Christian was born in Baltimore County on April 11, 1788 and moved to Mercer County, Kentucky in 1811 and located on 1,000 acres of land purchased by his father on Glenn's Creek near Harrodsburg. His father, Jacob GORE, was born in Baltimore County, Maryland and served in the Revolutionary War.

58

His grandfather, Michael GORE, was also from Baltimore County and a son of Christian GORE, a noted officer in the Prussian Army who settled in Lehigh Valley, Pennsylvania (Ref: KB 5:127).

GRAHAM. Nelson JOLLY of Londonderry, Ireland, came to Bucks County, Pennsylvania in 1755 with his father (unnamed) who served under John Paul JONES and died in battle. Nelson married a Miss GRAHAM in Maryland and they went to Kentucky around 1780. They settled near Hardinsburg in 1790. He died in 1819 in Breckinridge County. Their son, Nelson JOLLY, was born on February 20, 1786 in Hines Fort near Elizabethtown, Kentucky and married Barbara BARR. Their son, John B. JOLLY, was born in 1815 and married Rachel HARDIN, 1817-1893 (Ref: BCK:309).

GRAVES. John B. GRAVES was born in Maryland in 1776 and married Catherine THOMISON of Scotland. They migrated to Franklin County, Kentucky in 1814 where their son William L. GRAVES was born. He was in Missouri by 1831. (Ref: KM:63)

Dr. W. S. GRAVES was born on August 28, 1820 in Marion County, Kentucky. His father (name not given) was born in St. Mary's County, Maryland on November 15, 1783 and his mother (also of St. Mary's) was born in 1793. They went to Washington County, Kentucky around 1795 and were married. The father died in 1844 and the mother in 1866 (Ref: KB 4:42).

GRAY. Jonas GRAY was born circa 1768 in Maryland and was in Nelson County, Kentucky by October 19, 1789 at which time he married Hannah SWANK of Pennsylvania, daughter of Rev. John SWANK. Their daughter Elizabeth GRAY married William MORGAN of Virginia on December 24, 1814 in Hardin County, Kentucky. Jonas GRAY died in 1837, leaving a wife and eleven children. (Ref: KA 5:3, January, 1970, p. 165)

Patrick L. GRAY was born in Baltimore, Maruland in 1800, a son of James L. GRAY who died in the War of 1812. One James GRAY is listed in the 27th Regiment of Baltimore in 1814. (Ref: William Marine's The British Invasion of Maryland, 1812-1815, p. 302 (Baltimore: Genealogical Publishing Co., 1977 reprint; originally published in 1913) Patrick GRAY moved to Nelson County, Kentucky in 1820 and to Hardin County in 1841. He married Mary HOWLETT (born 1798 in Baltimore and died in 1861) and their son Lynch GRAY was born on May 28, 1828 in Nelson County, Kentucky. Patrick L. GRAY died in 1854. (Ref: BCK:96)

William GRAY was born in St. Mary's County, Maryland on August 23, 1755 and served in the Revolution in 1776 in Chester County, Pennsylvania and in 1781 in Rockbridge County, Virginia. He applied for and received pension S2253 in Montgomery County, Kentucky in 1832, having lived also in Warren County, Ohio (Ref: RCK:128; MS:57).

GREATHOUSE. Samuel GREATHOUSE was born in 1768 in Maryland, moved to northern Kentucky and married a cousin, Susannah GREATHOUSE, and migrated to Warren County, Kentucky in 1799. Their son, Josiah

GREATHOUSE, married Sarah Jane MARRS (Ref: KA 16:2, October, 1980, p. 117).

GREEN. Paul GREEN enlisted in the Revolution in Annapolis, Maryland in 1777 and served to 1780. He applied for and received pension S10767 in 1832 (age 69) in Woodford County, Kentucky. (Ref: MS:54; MRR:23; RCK:170; KPR:1835)

Benjamin GREEN and Leonard GREEN were among the early Catholic settlers from St. Mary's County, Maryland to settle on Hardin's Creek, Kentucky circa 1786. (Ref: KC:56)

Leven E. GREEN was born in Breckinridge County, Kentucky on January 17, 1819. His father, Isaac GREEN, was born either in Pennsylvania or Maryland and he migrated to Nelson County, Kentucky with them when only nine years old. Isaac's father was Leven GREEN. (Ref: KB 1:178)

Adam BEATTY came to Mason County, Kentucky from Frederick, Maryland as early as 1802 (born May 10, 1777 in Maryland) and married Sally GREEN, eldest daughter of Capt. John GREEN of Maryland on July 2, 1804. John GREEN migrated to Kentucky just a few years before Judge Adam BEATTY. (Ref: KB 5:3)

Ellen GREEN married Edward BEAVEN in St. Mary's County, Maryland prior to 1796 (when their son Charles was born; he died in 1869) and then migrated to Marion County, Kentucky (Ref: KB 5:50).

GREENUP. John GREENUP married Elizabeth WITTEN in Maryland and moved to southwest Virginia circa 1766 and then to Wayne County, Kentucky in the early 1800's. (Ref: KPG 2:2, April, 1990, p. 100)

Sallie GREENUP of Maryland married William BURT of Virginia and their son Franklin BURT was born in Scott County, Kentucky on March 17, 1809. By 1835 they were in Missouri (Ref: KM:143).

GREENWELL. Bennett GREENWELL was born December 7, 1761 in St. Mary's County, Maryland and served in the Revolutionary War under Capt. Thomas GREENWELL. (Many Greenwells served in the St. Mary's County Militia, but Bennett GREENWELL served in Montgomery County, according to Maryland Militia in the Revolutionary War, by S. Eugene Clements and F. Edward Wright, pp. 201, 214 (Silver Spring, Maryland: Family Line Publications, 1987) Bennett GREENWELL married and moved to Scott County, Kentucky in 1795, settling on the South Fork of Elkhorn Creek. His second wife, Mary Allouisa, was born in 1784 and died in 1842. Bennett died on July 12, 1838 and left heirs: Wilfred GREENWELL, 1788-1857; Susannah MANNING; Benedict GREENWELL, 1790-1875, married Mariah GOUGH; Ann MILLS, 1794-1856, wife of James MILLS; Elizabeth JONES; Clare JACKSON; James GREENWELL; Augustine M. GREENWELL; Robert GREENWELL; Juliana TWYMAN, wife of Stephen T. TWYMAN; and, Catherine GREENWELL, 1820-1848. Bennett GREENWELL received a pension for his military service. (Ref: RCK:150; MRR:24; KPR:1835; KA 6:1, October, 1970, p. 48)

Jeremiah GREENWELL of St. Mary's County, Maryland, married Susan WILLIAMS (or WILLIAMSON) and they were among the early Catholic settlers on Pottinger's Creek in Nelson County, Kentucky circa 1786. Their son James GREENWELL was born in 1790 and married Mary GURNETT (GURNEY) who was a daughter of Patrick GURNETT (GURNEY) of Ireland and Ann TEAR, daughter of John TEAR and Frances FARTHING of St. Mary's County, Maryland. These families later moved to Louisiana. (Ref: KA 16:1, July, 1980, p. 61)

John GREENWELL was born October 2, 1760 and enlisted in 1781 in St. Mary's County, Maryland under Capt.Samuel JUNIPER and Col. Richard BARNES. His brother, Richard GREENWELL, was born in 1767 and made an affidavit in 1834 when John applied for a pension. John was on the East Tennessee Roll of Pensioners in 1834 (Pension S31076) and later transferred to Greensburg in Green County, Kentucky. He said he had moved to Kentucky in 1798 and had lived in Green County for 32 years (Ref: MS:43).

GREENWOOD. Joseph GREENWOOD was born in Delaware or Maryland in 1755 and was raised in Kent County, Delaware. He enlisted in 1776 in Sussex County, Delaware under Capt. Nathan ADAMS, and subsequently was drafted on the Maryland side of the line in 1777 as a substitute. After the Revolution he moved to North Carolina for twelve years and then to Kentucky for six years, Tennessee for six years, Alabama for twenty years and then to Calloway County, Kentucky in 1829. In 1832 he applied and received pension S13225 (Ref: MS:24; RCK:51; MRR:24).

GREER. Stephen GREER, son of George GREER and Ann JONES, was born in Baltimore, Maryland in August, 1749 and married Ruth ANDERSON on April 25, 1771. Their children were: Rachel GREER, born February 10, 1772, married Nathan WORLEY; Elizabeth GREER, born January 29, 1774, married John CALDWELL; Nancy GREER, born February 11, 1776, married Stephen EVANS; James GREER, born August 14, 1778, married Elizabeth MOTHERSHEAD; Elisha GREER, born November 3, 1781; John GREER and Aaron GREER, twins, born January 28, 1786; Moses GREER, born January 1, 1789; and, Joshua GREER, born July 6, 1792. Stephen GREER may have lived in Greenbrier County Virginia before migrating to Fayette County, Kentucky circa 1790. He is also mentioned in the will of Caleb WORLEY and may have signed his name "Spencer GREEN." He died in Scott County, Kentucky in December, 1798 (Ref: KA 3:3, January, 1968, p. 136).

GRIDER. John GRIDER was born July 13, 1755 in Maryland and moved with his father when a small boy to Caroline County, Virginia and then to Burke County, North Carolina. John enlisted in the Revolutionary War in March, 1778 in Burke County, North Carolina and married Isabel BLAIR in 1781. In 1811 they moved to Adair County, Kentucky and he died in Henderson County, Tennessee on October 3, 1838. His widow received pension W358 (Ref: Beverly England's Revolutionary War Soldiers from Adair, Green, Russell, and Taylor Counties in Kentucky, pp. 17-18 (Columbia, Kentucky: Printing Creations, Inc., 1989).

GRIFFITH. Joshua GRIFFITH, son of Henry GRIFFITH (1720-1794) and Ruth HAMMOND (1733-1782) was born March 25, 1764 in Anne Arundel County, Maryland and migrated to Kentucky circa 1811 and died in Owensboro on November 29, 1845. (BCK:160-162)

The Griffiths were prominent in Maryland and additional information can be found in Robert H. McIntire's Annapolis Maryland Families (Baltimore: Gateway Press, Inc., 1980), and Harry Wright Newman's Anne Arundel Gentry, Vol. I, (Annapolis: Published by Author, 1970, and reprinted by Family Line Publications, Westminster, Maryland (1990).

GROSH. In 1743 John Conrad GROSH and his family immigrated from Mayence on the Rhine in Germany to Frederick, Maryland. His eldest daughter Mary Dorothea GROSH (born 1739) married William BEATTY, Jr. and his eldest son Peter GROSH married Mary CHARLTON. In Kentucky, Peter's daughters Eleanor GROSH married Thomas HART, Sophia GROSH married Edward Porter CLAY, and Catherine GROSH married John W. HUNT of Fayette County (Ref: KB 5:2).

HADEN. George W. HADEN was born in Washington County, Maryland on December 6, 1813, the eldest of two children born to Joseph HADEN and Ellen THOMAS. When only six months old he was carried on horseback from Maryland to Logan County, Kentucky where his parents lived for four years and then moved on to Todd County, Kentucky where they lived for three years. They then returned to Maryland where his father died. After four years, George returned with his mother to Logan County, Kentucky. In 1837 he moved to Muhlenberg County (Ref: KB 3:93).

HAGAN. The Hagans were among the early Catholic settlers to move from St. Mary's County, Maryland to Pottinger's Creek in Nelson County, Kentucky circa 1785. Monica HAGAN was a widow when she moved to Kentucky with Ignatius HAGAN and Randal HAGAN, and settled with her three sons, Clement HAGAN and James HAGAN and Edward HAGAN, near New Hope. Clem HAGAN married Millie MILES of Virginia. Their son, Sidney HAGAN, was born in 1800 in Kentucky and married Miss Nancy CECIL, daughter of James CECIL and Nancy HAMMETT of Cecil County, Maryland. James HAGAN was born in 1754 and was a Private in the Maryland Line. He applied for a pension in 1818 and died in Nelson County, Kentucky, December 30, 1829. (Ref: MRR:25)

Raphael HAGAN was born in 1744 and was a Corporal in the Revolutionary War in Maryland, married Rebecca LAVIELLE and had seven children: Thomas HAGAN; Basil HAGAN; Sylvester HAGAN; Joseph HAGAN; Elizabeth HAGAN, who married Joseph MITCHELL; Susan HAGAN, who married Philip AUD; and, Theresa HAGAN, who married John LILLY. Polly HAGAN married Leonard MATTINGLY, an early settler from St. Mary's County, Maryland who moved to (now) Marion County, Kentucky. Two of their sons were Dr. William E. MATTINGLY and Benjamin F. MATTINGLY (Ref: KC:28, 31, 114, 130; KB 5:133, 199, 200; RCK:132; KPR:1835; MRR:25).

HAGER. James HAGER was a surveyor between 1791 and 1799 in Rolling Fork, Nelson County, Kentucky, having migrated there from St.

Mary's County, Maryland. Jonathan D. HAGER married Sallie SPRINGLE in Lexington, Kentucky on June 17, 1830. His parents had migrated from Hagerstown, Maryland to Woodford County, Kentucky (Ref: KC: 110, 111; KB 7:130; NAW:121).

HAINES. Catherine HAINES was a daughter of Michael HAINES of Baltimore County, Maryland, who moved to Mercer County, Kentucky and died there in 1821. Catherine HAINES married Christian GORE and had three children: James GORE, born on November 5, 1812 and married a Miss CASEY in 1847; Thomas W. GORE, died childless; and, Sarah GORE (Ref: KB 5:127).

HALL. John HALL was born in Anne Arundel County, Maryland on December 9, 1758 and moved at an early age to Prince George's County where he enlisted in the Revolutionary War in September, 1776. In the Fall of 1779 he moved to Caswell County, North Carolina and resided there until 1800 when he moved to Patrick County, Virginia. In 1801 he moved to Wayne County, Kentucky and in 1832 he moved to Russell County, Kentucky. He was also a Private in the North Carolina Line, receiving pension S1210 in 1833. (Ref: RCK:147; MRR:25; and Beverly England's Revolutionary Soldiers from Adair, Green, Russell and Taylor Counties in Kentucky, p. 42 (Columbia, Kentucky: Printing Creations, 1987)

Justus J. HALL was born in Bourbon County, Kentucky on January 18, 1813, a son of Joshua H. HALL and Mary BEASMAN of Maryland who moved to Kentucky in 1796. Joshua H. HALL was a son of James HALL and Sarah BURK of Maryland, who went to Kentucky in 1800. Squire HALL, a son of Squire HALL and Joanna ROBARDS, was born in Henry County, Kentucky on December 25, 1823. Squire HALL was a merchant in Baltimore, Maryland but after migrating to Kentucky he became a farmer in Henry County and then Shelby County. His son, William M. HALL, was born in Baltimore on May 31, 1816. Squire migrated to Kentucky between 1816 and 1823, the birth years of his sons so noted (Ref: KB 7:186).

HAMBLEN. The Hamblens were in America by 1750 and lived in Maryland, Virginia, Kentucky, Indiana, Illinois and Missouri. Refer to "The Hamblen and Allied Families" by A. Porter HAMBLEN (as advertised for sale in the Maryland Genealogical Society Bulletin, 26:3, p. 322, Summer, 1985).

HAMILTON. The Hamilton family was among the early Catholic settlers from St. Mary's County, Maryland who migrated to Cartwright's Creek, Kentucky circa 1785 and Rolling Fork, Kentucky circa 1791. At the head of this colony was Leonard HAMILTON who was the maternal grandfather of the Archbishop SPALDING of Baltimore and the Very Rev. Benedict J. SPALDING of Louisville. (Ref: KC:110)

Other early Hamiltons were Clement HAMILTON who died in 1851 at age 80 (and his widow who died in 1863, age 92), Samuel HAMILTON, Walter HAMILTON, and Hoskins HAMILTON. In 1878, one year before his death in 1879 at age 90, Alexander HAMILTON wrote that he was born in Maryland and brought to Kentucky at age eight by his father in 1797 and settled in Washington County about six miles north of

Springfield. Alexander HAMILTON's father was Thomas HAMILTON. Alexander married Harriett EDELEN and their son Richard HAMILTON was born in Washington County, Kentucky on December 29, 1811. Alexander's sister Mary HAMILTON was married to Clement HILL, son of Thomas HILL, in 1798. (Ref: KC:71, 80, 110, 111, and KB:5, pp. 91, 133, 151, 266)

John HAMILTON was born in Baltimore County, Maryland, November 1, 1765 and entered in the Revolutionary War in Bedford County, Pennsylvania, having also lived in Northumberland County, Pennsylvania prior to the Revolution. He married Deborah PERKINS in Perry County, Pennsylvania on June 3, 1788, and moved to Monroe County and then Bracken County, Kentucky. Their children were: Elizabeth, born August 16, 1790; William, born March 16, 1792; John, born August 25, 1794; Polly HAMILTON, born March 6, 1798; and Jean HAMILTON, born October 6, 1799. On October 21, 1833 John HAMILTON applied for and received a pension. His widow subsequently received pension W1759, having applied in 1849 while residing in Bracken County, Kentucky (Ref: MS:14; RCK:44; MRR:25).

HAMMITT. Frances HAMMITT married Augustine CECIL in St. Mary's County, Maryland and they went to Kentucky by way of the Ohio River on a flatboat, landing where Louisville now stands. They settled on Pottinger's Creek in Washington County, Kentucky, and were members of the Catholic Church. Sylvester CECIL, son of Augustine, married Hedric MEDLEY and his son, Thomas W. CECIL, was born August 2, 1826 (Ref: KB 5:80, 133).

HAMMOND. William HAMMOND was born on August 22, 1792 in Maryland and moved with his parents to Logan (now Simpson) County, Kentucky in childhood. He was a soldier in the War of 1812, fought at the Battle of Taladega, and later served as captain of militia and died on July 24, 1837. William's father was Thomas HAMMOND, 1762-1847, a Revolutionary War soldier from Maryland. William's son Vincent R. HAMMOND was born August 1, 1820 in the south of Simpson County, Kentucky and married Sarah M. LESTER on December 19, 1844. Their children were: Mary V. HAMMOND, married a NEWMAN; William R., married Martha V. SNIDER, daughter of Charles SNIDER and Pamelia A. J. PEDEN; John C.HAMMOND; Amanda V. HAMMOND, married a BRYANT; Olivia A. HAMMOND, married a RIEVES; James M. HAMMOND; Vincent M. HAMMOND, Jr.; and, Robert L. HAMMOND (Ref: KB 4:200; MRR:26)

The Hammond family was prominent in colonial Baltimore County (Ref: BCF:297-299; AAG I:187-292).

HANNON. William HANNON applied for a pension in Greenup County, Kentucky on October 13, 1842, stating he enlisted in 1777 at the age of 16 in Charles County, Maryland, serving under Col. DENT. Gabriel HANNON, age 52, stated his father, William HANNON, and Charles RIGGS had served together in the war with the military between St. Mary's and Potomac Rivers. Joseph SHELTON stated he heard the mother of his wife, Sarah RIGGS, stated that William HANNON served in the Revolution. Mary HANNON, age 77, stated she had been acquainted with William HANNON since he was age 25 and until he died; no date given. Subsequently, Mary HANNON (widow of

William) reported they had sons Gabriel HANNON and Jefferson HANNON, and they had grandchildren named Lucy P. HANNON, William HANNON, Mary HANNON, Perry HANNON, ELizabeth HANNON, Gabriel HANNON, America HANNON, Isabelle HANNON, John T. HANNON, and Catharine HANNON. It appears this pension application was rejected (R4579) according to Source MS:42 (but he is listed as a pensioner in Source MRR:25).

HARDESTY. Benjamin HARDESTY and family migrated to Kentucky from Maryland circa 1784. He died in Bourbon County in 1818, leaving 11 children. A son, Benjamin HARDESTY, married Mary SAGESER of Fayette County, Kentucky. They had 13 children, one of whom was also named Benjamin HARDESTY, 1825-1900. He married Matilda ROBINSON on February 20, 1851. Most of their descendants lived in Henry County, Kentucky and their family Bible record, which covers birth and deaths over the span of 1830 to 1936, was contributed by Mrs. George Miles BOWLES of Pleasureville, Kentucky (and published in KA 3:2, October, 1967, p. 78)

Edward HARDESTY (1788-1865) was born in Maryland in 1788 and married Susan Ann YATES (1795-1863) in Springfield, Kentucky. He enlisted in Capt. PETERSON's Company, 7th Regiment, Kentucky Infantry Volunteer Militia, on August 23, 1812 and was discharged on August 10, 1814. Edward and Susan both died in Monroe County, Missouri. Their son, Felix HARDESTY (1824-1910) married Elizabeth Katherine GERTIN (1834-1897) circa 1852 at Indian Creek Missouri (Ref: General Society of the War of 1812 Register, p. 51, published by the National Society in 1972).

HARDIN. Ben HARDIN was born in Washington County, Kentucky on November 15, 1818. His father, Warren HARDIN, was born on November 30, 1786, on the boundary of Pennsylvania and Maryland in the portion which was assigned by Mason and Dixon to Pennsylvania. He was an officer in the War of 1812 and a son of Ben HARDIN of Virginia. In 1790 they were among the first settlers in (now) Washington County, Kentucky. Warren HARDIN married in 1813 to Eliza CALHOUN, daughter of Dr. Parker CALHOUN of Scott County, Kentucky (Ref: KB 1:203).

HARDING. Vachel HARDING was born in 1762 in Montgomery County, Maryland. He enlisted in March, 1778 in the company of Capt. John H. NICHOLAS and became a Sergeant. (Ref: MRR:25) Vachel applied for a pension on April 5, 1834 in Jefferson County, Kentucky. Pensioners Amos GOODWIN, James DAY and William MERRIWEATHER verified his services. He married Mary -----, in 1798 and after Vachel died on May 11, 1837, she received pension W1601, stating she was age 68. The record also mentions that a Vachel HARDING married Mary PARKER on July 20, 1850 in Frederick County, Maryland, and Sarah HURLEY, an acquaintance, aged 64, was in attendance (Ref: MS:51; KPR:1835).

HARDISTY. John HARDISTY and George HARDISTY were among the early Catholic settlers who migrated from St. Mary's County, Maryland to Hardin's Creek, Kentucky circa 1785. George's sons were James,

George, Richard, Cornelius and Benjamin, and their children settled Marion County (Ref: KC:55-56).

HARGAN, HARGIN. Michael HARGIN was born in 1752/55 and enlisted in Hagerstown, Maryland in 1776 in Capt. John Nelson's Rifle Company and served in the 1st Pennsylvania Line until discharged, April 1, 1777. He married Elizabeth WALLINGSFORD in 1791 or 1794. He applied for a pension in Hardin County, Kentucky on September 19, 1818 and was on the Kentucky Pension Rolls in 1835. His widow also received pension W8906. Another source states Michael HARGAN was born in 1752 in Ireland and came to America at age 16, settling first in New York, where he served in the Continental Army and then moved to Maryland and married Mary WELLINGFORD. They then moved to Virginia and in 1790 they went to Rolling Fork in Nelson County, Kentucky. Michael died in December, 1840. His youngest son, Daniel HARGAN, was born on December 25, 1804 and married Susan MIDDLETON (Ref: MS:45; RSK:87; KB 1:23; MRR:26).

HARKINS. Daniel HARKINS was in Bardstown, Kentucky by 1820, and was a descendant of the Marylanders who migrated to that area circa 1785 (Ref: KC:63).

HARLAN. James HARLAN was a Revolutionary War soldier from the Eastern Shore of Maryland. His son, Eli HARLAN, was born in 1793 and later migrated to Kentucky. Eli was in the War of 1812. He married Nancy CASEL (born 1797) and their son, Samuel F. HARLAN, was born in Louisville (Ref: KB 9:64).

HARRINGTON. Anthony HARRINGTON was born in 1762 in Talbot County, Maryland and served in the Revolutionary War in 1778 in Talbot County. He was a Marine in the Naval Service. He applied for and received pension S31108 in Madison County, Kentucky in 1832 (Ref: MS:57; RSK:115; KPR:1835; MRR:26).

HARRIS. Josiah HARRIS was a Captain in the Revolutionary War and died at the Battle of Cowpens. His son, Josiah (#2) moved from Maryland and settled near Elizabethtown, Kentucky after 1810. Josiah HARRIS (#3), son of Josiah and grandson of Josiah, was born April 26, 1810 in Maryland died married Sallie Wiles KING (1820--1878), daughter of Milton KING (1801-1884) of Virginia, in 1839 in Kentucky. Josiah died in Louisville, Kentucky on August 6, 1865. His son, Josiah (#4) was born in Adair County, Kentucky on November 14, 1840. (Ref: BCK:103)

Thomas HARRIS was born in Somerset County, Maryland on May 26, 1755 and resided in Newport, Maryland over 27 years. He married Nancy WOOLLEN prior to 1794 in Scott County, Kentucky. (Ref: MRR:115) He also served in Capt. Joseph COHAN's Company as 2nd Sergeant in 1781 and afterward moved to Campbell County, Kentucky where he applied for and received pension S4686. (Ref: RSK:189; MS:17-18; MRR:26)

James WOOD of Virginia and Elizabeth HARRIS of Maryland were married in Mercer County, Kentucky in 1813. She migrated to Kentucky with her parents in 1808 (Ref: KB 5:307).

HARRISON. James O. HARRISON, attorney at law, married Miss Margaretta ROSS in August, 1830 in Lexington, Kentucky. (Ref: NAW:121)

Zephaniah HARRISON, brother of President William Henry HARRISON, was a resident of Frederick, Maryland, and his son, William H. HARRISON, was born there in 1818 and died in Cincinnati, Ohio in 1866. William's son, Charles Leonard HARRISON, died in Bellevue, Kentucky in 1888 (Ref: BCK:101-102).

HARROD. The first settlement in Kentucky was Harrodsburg in 1774 and there is a Maryland and Pennsylvania connection to the Harrod family. Elizabeth HARROD, daughter of John HARROD and Sarah MOORE, married Benjamin DAVIS, a cousin of Anthony WAYNE and possibly a son of Garah DAVIS of Frederick County, Maryland who died in 1764. Elizabeth and Benjamin DAVIS were in Rostrovar Township in Cumberland County, Pennsylvania in 1775 when James HARROD conveyed land "near Contukey River" to Benjamin DAVIS. On October 18, 1776 Benjamin DAVIS sold some land in Lincoln County, Kentucky to William HARROD. The second wife of John HARROD was Sarah MOORE, who was possibly a daughter of James MOORE and Frances GAY of Baltimore County, Maryland. (Ref: Harrod Family Genealogy compiled by Bernice L. Swainson, published in the Filson Club Quarterly, Vol. XXXII (1958), pp. 107-131, 256-284; and in Genealogies of Kentucky Families, pp. 584-638, Baltimore: Genealogical Publishing Co., 1981).

HART. Colonel Thomas HART "died on 22nd day of this month, in Lexington, Kentucky, after a severe illness, in the 77th year of his age. He was for many years a citizen of this town, and one of the most active promoters of its increase and prosperity." Hagerstown Advertiser, July 22, 1808 (Ref: WMNA 3:69).

HARVEY. Gwillielmus HARVEY was born June 6, 1787 in Harford County, Maryland. Her parents moved to Kentucky and settled in Logan County circa 1800. She married Robert W. TEMPLE on March 3, 1808 and had ten children. One, William M. TEMPLE, was born in 1829 in Todd County and moved to Warren County. Gwillielmus TEMPLE died October 16, 1858 (Ref: KB 2:219).

HATHAWAY. Capt. John HATHAWAY of Baltimore married Miss Tabitha Ann S. JACKSON of Alexandria in Lexington, Kentucky on May 17, 1818 (Ref: KYM:18).

HATLER. Michael HATLER was born in 1760 near Baltimore, Maryland. His father, Sebastian HATLER, moved to Culpeper County, Virginia and Michael enlisted in 1778 or 1779 in the Company of Ensign Richard HICKMAN as a substitute for John NORMAN, and also served for three months on his own draft shortly thereafter. The family moved to Abington, Virginia and then Allen County, Kentucky. Michael applied for and received pension S31117 in 1832 (Ref: MS:4, RSK:32).

HAVELY, HEFLEY. Jacob HAVELY was born circa 1758 in Frederick County, Maryland and married Elizabeth -----, in 1788. Their children in 1838 were: John HAVELY, age 50; Susanna STARNS, age 47; Rhody ELLIS, age 45 or 46; Frederick HAVELY, age 43 or 44; Mary RUSSELL, age 42; Jacob HAVELY, age 40; and, George and Henry HAVELY, age 34. George HAVELY married Catherine GOOD, daughter of Joseph. Jacob HAVELY moved to Lincoln County, Kentucky circa 1814, and then to Casey County, having applied for a pension in 1818. He died December 22, 1833 and his widow received pension W8902 in 1838, at age 69. Jacob COFFMAN also stated he knew them in Emmitsburg, Maryland 48 or 49 years ago. By 1843 Elizabeth HAVELY was in Mercer County, Kentucky (Ref: MS:21; MRR:26).

HAWES. The 1790 Census lists Peter HAWES in Washington County, Maryland, and by 1798 he had bought land in Jefferson County, Kentucky. His will (February, 1821) names his wife Hannah HAWES and these children: Benjamin D. HAWES married Elizabeth ROACH; Sarah HAWES, married John MAPLE; John HAWES, married Nancy BAXTER; Peggy HAWES, married Daniel EBY; Mary HAWES, married Hiram MALOTT; Elizabeth HAWES, married George FINLEY; Sybella HAWES, married Henry THORN; Hannah HAWES, married George SEEBOLT; and, Rebecca HAWES, married Peter OMER (Ref: KA 12:1, 1976, p. 45).

HAWKINS. Aaron W. HAWKINS was born in Maryland on March 3, 1791 or 1793 and married Elizabeth A. MADDOX (born 1796 in Virginia) on November 17, 1814. Their children were John Alexander HAWKINS, Mahala Jane McCRAY, Ruhama Marietta HARBERT, Lucy Ann MONTGOMERY, Amanda Melvina GRAVES, Abiah CHAMBERLAIN, Upton Wilson HAWKINS, Joseph E. HAWKINS, and Dr. James D. HAWKINS. Aaron HAWKINS moved to Daviess County, Kentucky in 1820 and died in Ohio County, Kentucky on January 21, 1864. (Ref: KPG 1:2, April, 1979, page 60, and KB 3:146)

Giles HAWKINS was born on March 15, 1755 in Frederick County, Maryland, and he lived in Bedford County, Virginia in 1776, Botetourt County, Virginia in 1781, and Franklin County, Kentucky in 1789. He was a Revolutionary War pensioner (1833) and died in Jessamine County, Kentucky in 1841. His sons were John, George and Thomas HAWKINS. (Ref: KA 5:4, April, 1970, p. 29; RSK:102)

Gregory Farmer HAWKINS was christened in 1734, St. George's Parish, Baltimore County (now Harford County), Maryland, a son of Thomas HAWKINS and Elizabeth FARMER. He may have married Elizabeth MATSON of Pennsylvania and their children were: John, born 1760; James, born 1764; Robert, born 1766; Ruth, born 1768; Christiana, born 1770; Gregory Farmer, born 1772; Elizabeth, born 1775; and, William, born 1779. Most of his sons were in Montgomery County, Kentucky by 1810 and appear in that census (Ref: KA 5:2, October, 1969, p. 106).

HAYDEN. There were a number of Haydens who migrated in 1785 from St. Mary's County, Maryland to Nelson County, Kentucky. Basil HAYDEN was a leader of this Maryland Catholic League who settled on Hardin's Creek, Rolling Fork and Cartwright's Creek. William HAYDEN was another of these early settlers. His son, Thomas HAYDEN, migrated to Graves County, Kentucky in the 1830's and died in 1849. William HAYDEN and Wilfred HAYDEN and Bennet HAYDEN were on Cartwright's Creek circa 1785. Basil HAYDEN and James HAYDEN and William HAYDEN and John HAYDEN (a surveyor) were on Rolling Fork by 1791. Clement HAYDEN and Joseph HAYDEN were on Hardin's Creek by 1790. Edward HAYDEN, whose wife was Mary McMANUS, settled near Bardstown, Kentucky, and had a son, Charles HAYDEN. Edward HAYDEN was one of the principal purveyors for the army of defense under General Jackson in the War of 1812. Lewis HAYDEN was also in Bardstown by 1820. (Ref: KC:29, 55, 56, 62, 63, 80, 110, 111; KA 4:1, July, 1968, p. 35; KPG 2:3, July, 1980, p. 241; KB 5:77).

HAYES. Jesse HAYES of Maryland served seven years in the Revolutionary War and died in Maury County, Tennessee. His son, Aaron HAYES, was born in North Carolina and in 1799 moved to Barren County, now Monroe County, Kentucky, where he was a blacksmith. He died July 15, 1854. His wife was Hannah HOWARD, daughter of Obadiah HOWARD and Priscilla BREED of Union District, South Carolina. Christopher HAYES, son of Aaron HAYES, was born near Tompkinsville, now in Monroe County, Kentucky, on April 18, 1811 (Ref: KB 2:58).

HAYS. Thomas HAYS was born May 10, 1762 in Montgomery County, Maryland. He enlisted under Capt. Richard SMITH for two months in 1775, under Capt. Thomas SPRIGG for 2 months in 1777, and under Capt. Enos CAMPBELL for nine months in 1778. He moved to Bourbon County, Kentucky in 1801 where, in 1833, he applied for and received pension S31110 for his Revolutionary War services. Joshua IRVIN, Andrew CODUSKY, James BARNETT (all of Kentucky) and Benjamin WILLETT (of Maryland) gave testimony in support of his claim in the Revolution (Ref: MS:10; KPR:1835; MRR:16).

HEAD. Polly HEAD (born in Maryland in 1777) married Benjamin CLARK (born in Virginia in 1777) and their son, J. S. CLARK, was born May 8, 1813 in Washington County, Kentucky. He was in Missouri by 1866. (Ref: KM:159)

In 1790 Frank HEAD, who was of English descent, went to Kentucky from Maryland and settled near New Haven in Nelson County. His children were Nancy HUTCHENS, Pollie BROWN, Caroline HUMPHREY, Elizabeth HUMPHREY, and William HEAD. (Ref: KB:24)

Francis HEAD, who died at age 80 (no date given), married Miss WILLETT and both were natives of Pottinger's Creek in Nelson County, Kentucky. Francis' parents were of Scotch descent and were among the first settlers from Maryland to settle in Nelson County. Richard HEAD (1818-1858), a son of Francis, married Ann C. MEADLEY, a daughter of Ignatius MEADLEY (1777-1852) who went to Hardin's Creek, Kentucky from Maryland prior to 1800. Their descendants settled in Marion County, Kentucky (Ref: KB:145).

HEADINGTON. Elizabeth HEADINGTON (1773-1840) was born in Baltimore County, Maryland, a daughter of Zebulon HEADINGTON (1740-1839) of Virginia. Zebulon HEADINGTON married first to Elizabeth LEMMON on March 31, 1771, and second to Sarah BOSLEY on December 11, 1781 in Baltimore, Maryland. He moved to Kentucky in 1785, later settling in Harrison County. Zebulon HEADINGTON was a Revolutionary War soldier. (Ref: HCP:126; DAR:318; MM-1:83; and, Dawn B. Smith's Baltimore County Marriage Licenses, 1777-1798, p. 87 (Westminster, Maryland: Family Line Publications, 1989)

Andrew WARD (1770-1842) of Virginia married Elizabeth HEADINGTON and their son, Andrew Harrison WARD, born January 3, 1815, was a Congressman from Harrison County, Kentucky (Ref: BCK:29-30).

HEADLY. James HEADLY, Sr. of Ireland (1770-c1850) married Elizabeth PATTERSON of Maryland and their children were Polly SHIVRY, James HEADLY, Jr., William HEADLY, Elizabeth ELMORE, Samuel HEADLY, John HEADLY, Rebecca DUNN, Francis HEADLY, Marshall HEADLY, Nancy FARRA, and Alexander HEADLY. In 1799 or 1800, James HEADLY, Jr. (1792--1884) moved to Fayette County, Kentucky with his parents. James married Melinda ATCHINSON (1801-1841), daughter of Hamilton, and their children were Hamilton Atchinson HEADLY, James HEADLY, George HEADLY, and William HEADLY (Ref: KB 5:146).

HEETER. George HEETER was born in 1751 in Frederick County, Maryland. He enlisted under Capt. SPEIGER in the Maryland Militia in 1776 and fought in the Battle of White Plains. After the war he lived in Montgomery County, Maryland and from there he migrated to Allen County, Kentucky. He applied for and received pension S16410 in 1833 (Ref: MS:5; RSK:32; KPR:1835; MRR:27).

HELPHINSTINE. When William LAYTON made application for a Revolutionary War pension in Fleming County, Kentucky in 1832, William HELPHINSTONE stated that he had heard Layton and his father, Philip HELPHINSTONE (who was a pensioner), talk over experiences in the war. (Ref: MS:60) This Philip HELPHINSTONE was a pensioner who died October 14, 1831 in Fleming County, Kentucky, about age 87. (Ref: RSK:70)

It appears that the Helphinstones were from Virginia, but it should be noted that one David HELPHINSTONE married Lydia HAMBLETON in Baltimore County in 1791 (Ref: MM-1:68).

HENDERSON. Benjamin HENDERSON was born on January 1 1758 in Accomac County, Virginia and enlisted in the Revolutionary War in Worcester County, Maryland in 1776. He also lived in Somerset County, Maryland before returning to Accomac County and then migrating to Bracken County, Kentucky. He applied for and received pension S31119 in 1833 (Ref: MS:14; MRR:27. Note: Source RSK:44 states he was in the North Carolina militia)

"Miss Jane CALENDAR, lately of Baltimore, married in May, 1822, to Mr. HENDERSON, of the Lexington Theater." (Ref: KYM:30).

HENNIS. Benjamin HENNIS was born in 1760 in Montgomery County, Maryland and entered the service for three years on April 1, 1777 in the 7th Maryland Line under Col. John GUNBY and Lt. John Coates JONES. He fought in the Battles of Brandywine and Monmouth, and was discharged at Morristown, New Jersey on March 31, 1780. He moved to Fleming County, Kentucky where he applied for and received pension S35402 in 1820. In his application he stated his property value was $151.25 and he had a wife (not named), age 57, "who was entirely helpless," and daughters: Dorcas, age 25; Sarah, age 18; Charity, age 14; and, Angelina, age 10 (Ref: MS:10; KBG 7:1, Spring, 1980, p. 10; MS:34-35; RSK:70; KPR:1835; MRR:27).

HERBERT. Jeremiah HERBERT was born in 1763 and was a Private in the Maryland Militia and he later moved to Washington County, Kentucky. He received a pension and Mary, his widow, later received pension W9061 (Ref: RSK:164, MS:56; KPR:1835; MRR:27).

HERRINGTON. John HERRINGTON was born in 1715 in England and came to Maryland in 1730, allegedly one of thirty students either kidnapped or enticed on board a ship that set sail for America. His son, Gideon HERRINGTON, was born in Maryland in 1745. Merrick HERRINGTON, son of Gideon, was born in Maryland in 1771 and married Mary MAHANEY, who was born in 1773 in Maryland. Gideon moved with his family to North Carolina in 1775. James W. HERRINGTON, son of Merrick HERRINGTON, was born in 1802 and in 1803 they moved to Allen County, Kentucky. Merrick died in Simpson County in 1840 and his wife died in 1841 (Ref: KB 4:203; MGS 16:4, November, 1975, p. 222.
Note: Herrington and Harrington families lived on Maryland's Eastern Shore in the counties of Kent, Caroline, Talbot and Queen Anne).

HESSON. John HESSON was born in Maryland circa 1781 and moved to Kentucky circa 1806 and later moved to Spencer County, Indiana. His wife Sarah -----, was born in Virginia in 1791. Their children were: Benjamin HESSON, born May 29, 1807 in Kentucky; John HESSON, Jr., born 1813 in Kentucky; Alfred HESSON, born 1828 in Kentucky; Gideon S. HESSON, born 1822; Margaret BRAND; Nancy TOOLY; Elizabeth WOOD; and, Samuel HESSON (Ref: Information from Jack P. Freeman of Harvey, Louisiana, in KPG 1:4, October, 1977, p. 60).

HIATT, HYATT. Shadrach HIATT was born in 1749 in St. Mary's County, Maryland and enlisted in the Revolutionary War in 1776. He moved to Montgomery County, Kentucky in 1825, where he applied for and received pension S13361 (Ref: MS:58; MRR:27; RSK:128.
Note: The Hiatt and Hyatt families lived in Prince George's, Anne Arundel, and St. Mary's Counties).

HIGDON. Peter HIGDON and Thomas HIGDON were early Catholic settlers from Maryland who settled on Cartwright's Creek and Cox's Creek in Washington County, Kentucky between 1785 and 1800. (Ref: KC:80, 114)

James HIGDON was born in Maryland where he married Elizabeth VINSON. They migrated to Washington County, Kentucky in 1806 and then to Grayson County in 1807. He died in 1833 and she died in 1850. Their son, Augustine HIGDON, was born in Maryland July 23, 1803 and married Theresa ROBY on February 12, 1828 in Kentucky. (Ref: KB 1:179-180)

Joseph HIGDON was born in Charles County, Maryland on July 18, 1759 and served as a Corporal in the Revolutionary War from Montgomery County, Maryland, having entered the service in June, 1781. In 1784 he moved to North Carolina for 13 years and then to Tennessee. In 1801 he moved to Barren County, Kentucky. Joseph married Margaret HALBROOK (born February 17, 1766) on April 5, 1786 and their children were: Gabriel, born February 5, 1787; John, born August 8, 1788; Mary, born February 12, 1790; Susannah, born October 11, 1791; Jane, born August 30, 1793; Hays, born June 22, 1795; Rebecca, born March 17, 1797; Ishmael, born December 10, 1798; Joseph, born October 10, 1800; Margaret, born September 23, 1802; Thomas HIGDON, born August 4, 1804; Enoch E., born May 5, 1806; and, Sarah, born March 1, 1810. Joseph HIGDON applied for and received a pension based on service in the Virginia cavalry according to Source RSK:36, yet Sources MS:6-7 and MRR:27 state he was a Private and Corporal in the Maryland Line. Widow Margaret HIGDON also received a pension (1840).

HIGGINSON, HIGGERSON. George T. HIGGINSON was born in Ireland in 1762 and married Mary STOCKWELL in 1769 in Maryland. He died in Henderson County, Kentucky in 1820 and his will named these children: James, Polly, John Kidd, George C., Whiteside, Rebecca, Hinchliffe, Franklin, Jefferson, Hull, Elizabeth, Sarah, Madison, and Washington. (Ref: Information from JoAnn McGhee of Foristell, Missouri, in KPG 2:3, July, 1980, p. 163)

Jefferson HIGGERSON (or HICKERSON) was born in Kentucky in 1812 and married Nancy Ann BISHOP (born in Indiana in 1812) and they were in Perry County, Tennessee by 1860 (Ref: Information from Willie Mae Wetz of Austin, Texas, in KPG 2:4, October, 1980, p. 237).

HIGHFILL, HIGHFIELD. Jeremiah HIGHFILL of Charles County, Maryland, married Sabra -----, and their children born in Maryland between 1774 and 1789 were: Ann INLOW, Jeremiah HIGHFILL, Leonard HIGHFILL, and Sarah DENNIS. Jeremiah moved to Fayette County, Kentucky in 1789 and his children later settled in Woodford County (Ref: KA 3:3, January, 1968, p. 138. Note: Highfields were also from St. Mary's County).

HILL. "At the beginning of the year 1787, Thomas HILL and Philip MILES, brothers-in-law, living up to that time near Leonardtown, St. Mary's County, Maryland, arranged with each other to remove with their families to Kentucky. Their idea at the time was to settle on Pottinger's Creek whither had previously gone quite a number of their friends and neighbors. Their proposed journey was begun in February and toward the end of March, on the very day they expected to make landing above the falls of the Ohio, their boat was fired on by Indians with fatal effect. A negro belonging to Thomas HILL was killed, as were also all the horses on the boat, and Hill himself was seriously wounded by the passage of a one-ounce ball through both of his thighs. This happened at a point then and still known as Eighteen Mile Island, its distance above Louisville being just so many miles. Happily for the remainder of the emigrants, the boat was carried by the current beyond gun-shot range of the lurking savages, and by night they were safely housed in Louisville." (Ref: KC:68-70, KB 5:22)

The Hills and Miles party remained in Bardstown for about a year, but Thomas stayed longer due to his wounds. Harry HILL, an older son of Thomas, purchased farms in 1788 on Pottinger's Creek. In the Spring of 1789, Thomas HILL purchased land on Cartwright's Creek near Mr. CAMBRON. His youngest son, Clement HILL (born 1776), was with him at this time. Clement subsequently married Mary HAMILTON in 1798. He died in Lebanon, Kentucky in 1832 (Ref: KC:70-73) Thomas HILL, the father, had emigrated to the United States from England and settled in St. Mary's County, Maryland where he married in 1754 to Rebecca MILES (Ref: KC:72-73)

William HILL, another son of Thomas, served in the War of 1812 and died of dysentery after the Battle of Lake Erie (Ref: KB 5:22.

Note: The Hills were devout Catholics in Maryland and Kentucky. Additional information on the Thomas HILL family is in Source KB 5:150-152).

HINES. Jane HINES was born in Maryland and married in Wayne County, Kentucky to Joel BOND, a native of Maryland, or the Carolinas. Their children were: Benjamin; William; Joel; Elizabeth; Lewis G.; Margaret; and, Stephen W. BOND, born about 1820 in Wayne County, Kentucky. Joel and Jane BOND migrated to Missouri as early as 1835 and died in Millard County prior to the Civil War (Ref: KB 1:167).

HINTON. Vachel (Vitchel) HINTON was a native of Maryland and served in the Revolutionary War in Washington County, Pennsylvania. Sources differ as to when he went to Kentucky. One states he went to Kentucky before 1786, married Nancy ROY, had 13 children, and died in Fleming County, Kentucky between 1821 and 1825. (Ref: KA 2:1, July 1966, page 32) Another source states he went to Kentucky from Maryland in 1791 with Richard MATTINGLY, settled on Long Lick (now in Breckinridge County) and lived to be over 100 years old. He married twice. By his first wife he had Polly, Ann, Ellen, and another daughter known in religion as Sister Gabriella. By his second wife he had John, Sarah, Austin, Ezechiel, Joseph, Allan, William, Catherine, and Nancy (Ref: KC:141).

HITCHCOCK. Joshua HITCHCOCK was born in 1742 in Baltimore County, Maryland where he lived until a grown man, at which time he moved to Guilford County, North Carolina. He may have served in the Revolutionary War in Baltimore County because his pension application states he was drafted a second time in Guilford County, North Carolina. After the war he moved to Floyd County, Kentucky, then to Whitley County for three or four years, and back to Floyd County. Joshua applied for and received pension S31126 in 1833 in Floyd County, Kentucky (Ref: MS:39; RSK:73).

HITE. Abraham HITE and Isaac HITE migrated from Maryland to Nelson County, Kentucky circa 1774 with the COOMES family. (Ref: KC:25) Abraham HITE wrote his will on March 20, 1787 (probated February 2, 1790 in Jefferson County, Kentucky) and named his wife Rebecca and children Isaac HITE, Abraham HITE, Joseph HITE, and Hannah VANMETRE; also named John HITE and William HITE, sons of his brother Joseph, and Thomas VANMETRE, son of Hannah VANMETRE. He also mentions a lawsuit that his father Joseph HITE had against Lord FAIRFAX. Isaac HITE wrote his will on February 8, 1794 (probated March 4, 1794 in Jefferson County, Kentucky), naming his wife Harriet and children: Rebecca Vanmeter HITE, Elizabeth Rigby HITE, and Jacob Hite (all under age); also mentioned Abraham HITE, deceased (Rebecca HITE, legatee), and "partners" Isaac HITE, Rebecca HITE, Abraham HITE, Jr., and Joseph HITE. Rebecca HITE, being in poor health, wrote her will on April 21, 109 (probated June 12, 1809 in Jefferson County, Kentucky), naming her sons Abraham HITE and Joseph HITE, and mentioned Jacob HITE, son of Isaac HITE, and Isaac HITE (sic), son of Harriet BRIDGFORD (sic) (Ref: National Genealogical Society Quarterly, October, 1917, Vol. 6, No. 3, p. 54).

HOCKER. Joseph HOCKER was born October 29, 1786 near Ellicott Mills, Maryland and married Elizabeth DUNN (born September 3, 1794 in Maryland) on January 24, 1811 near Bryantsville, Gerard County, Kentucky. Their children were: Ben D. HOCKER, born February 12, 1812; Samuel HOCKER, born April 8, 1814; Richard W. HOCKER, born January 15, 1816; Margareta HOCKER, born April 8, 1818; Tilman HOCKER, born July 18, 1820; James M. HOCKER, born June 28, 1822; Dorcas HOCKER, born May 24, 1824; Mary HOCKER, born June 7, 1826; Sarah Myers HOCKER, born May 31, 1828; Isaiah Dunn HOCKER, born April 30, 1830; William Dunn HOCKER, born February 26, 1832; Nannie Barnes HOCKER, born in 1834; and, Gabriella HOCKER, born July 3, 1836. Joseph HOCKER is buried in Lincoln County, Kentucky. (Ref: KP:208)

Nicholas HOCKER wrote his will on July 21, 1812 (probated March 8, 1813 in Lincoln County, Kentucky, Liber E, p. 78) naming his wife Sarah HOCKER and children: Philip HOCKER; Alfred HOCKER; Nicholas HOCKER; George HOCKER; Margaret DUNN, wife of Benjamin DUNN; Mary CLEMENTS; and, Dorcas HOCKER, wife of Philip HOCKER. (Ref: KP:204)

Samuel HOCKER wrote his will on December 6, 1813 (probated in 1815 in Lincoln County, Kentucky, Liber G, p. 17), naming his wife Nancy HOCKER and children: Joseph HOCKER; John HOCKER; Richard Weaver HOCKER; Philip HOCKER; Jacob HOCKER, deceased, had daughter named Nancy; Polly HOCKER; Nancy HOCKER; and, Betsy Helen HOCKER. (Ref: KP:204)

William HOCKER and Sarah ALLNUTT of Maryland were in Lincoln County, Kentucky by 1811. Son, Larkin HOCKER, was born November 20, 1811, and son, William HOCKER, was born September 8, 1814. They were in Missouri by 1824. Philip S. HOCKER (of Maryland) and Amanda DUNCAN (of Virginia) were in Lincoln County, Kentucky prior to 1840 and they were in Holt County, Missouri by 1866. John HOCKER was in Monroe County, Missouri by 1830. (Ref: KM:98)

George B. HOCKER was born in Ohio County, Kentucky in 1832, a son of Nicholas HOCKER and Clarissa COOPER, both from Maryland. They were members of the Methodist Church. Richard P. HOCKER was born in Ohio County, Kentucky in 1845, a son of A. R. HOCKER and Susan M. BARRETT who migrated from eastern Maryland to Kentucky circa 1792. Henry D. HOCKER, another son of Nicholas HOCKER and Clarissa COOPER, was born in Ohio County, Kentucky. Nicholas HOCKER's father was Weaver HOCKER (1748-1818) and Clarissa COOPER's father was Henry COOPER (1783-1863), all natives of Maryland (Ref: KB 3:149).

HODGKINS. Samuel HODGKINS was born in Cumberland County, Pennsylvania on June 6, 1757. He moved with his father to Harford County, Maryland, and served in the Revolutionary War in Capt. Bennett BUSSEY's Company in 1776. After the war he went to Pittsburgh, Pennsylvania and then to Lexington, Kentucky. In 1798 he moved to Brown County, Ohio where he died October 13, 1845 and was buried in the Burgett-Purdum Cemetery (Ref: KA 2:4, 1967, p. 167; HCP:113; MRR:27).

HOGAN. William HOGAN was a Captain in the War of 1812 in Maryland. His wife, Mary E. DRURY, was also from Maryland and both settled in Nelson County, Kentucky circa 1810, and they were married January 4, 1814. Their daughter, Mary A., married John H. RODMAN in Washington County, Kentucky. Capt. William HOGAN kept a hotel in Fredericksburg, Kentucky. His parents were from Ireland (Ref: KB 5:249-250).

HOGGINS. Solomon HOGGINS migrated from Maryland to Bourbon County, Kentucky prior to 1797. They had eight children of whom these four are known: William HOGGINS, born in 1797 and married Mary McDANIEL in Gallatin County; James HOGGINS, married Mary HILL and was a Gallatin County magistrate and farmer; Wesley HOGGINS, born May 16, 1810 and married Rebecca SHAWAN in 1836; and a daughter, Delia HOGGINS, married a KIRBY in Warsaw, Kentucky (Ref: KB 8:83-84).

HOLLAND. John HOLLAND, whose father emigrated to Maryland from England, was born in Baltimore, Maryland and married Sarah JONES. Their eldest son, George B. HOLLAND, was born on May 26, 1806 in Wellsburg, Virginia and married Rebecca FRENCH, born in 1808 in Ohio, a daughter of Samuel FRENCH of Pennsylvania. George's son, William Allison HOLLAND, was born in 1825 in Edinburg, Indiana and the family later moved to Henry County, Kentucky. (Ref: BCK:585-586)

Asa HOLLAND, Sr. was born in Montgomery County, Maryland on February 13, 1780 and married Nancy WARD in Maryland. Asa learned the stonemason's trade in early life, and moved to Pickaway County, Ohio in 1830. He moved to Simpson County, Kentucky in 1831 and died there on November 29, 1852. His wife Nancy (daughter of Joseph WARD of Harper's Ferry, West Virginia) died on April 2, 1864. Her parents were murdered by one of their servants in Harper's Ferry and their house was burned over them. Joel J. HOLLAND, born 1807, a son of Asa HOLLAND, Sr. and Mary WARD, lived in Simpson County, Kentucky (Ref: KB 4:206).

HOLMAN. William HOLMAN was born circa 1767 in Kent County, Maryland and married Polly FOSTER in Franklin County, Kentucky on June 2, 1801. Their son, William HOLMAN II, was born February 4, 1809 in

Henry County, Kentucky and married Sarah HAWTHORNE in 1829. In the 1830 census William HOLMAN I and William HOLMAN II were in Ripley County, Indiana, and in 1860 William HOLMAN II was in Ballard County, Kentucky (Ref: KA 12:2, October, 1976, p. 105).

HOOVER. Moses HOOVER was born in Maryland and became a Preacher. He died in the pulpit, as he often said he had expected to, in his sixtieth year, stricken with apoplexy. His daughter Mary HOOVER, was born in Jessamine County, Kentucky circa 1800, and married Jacob RHORER prior to 1825. Their son, Henry RHORER, was born December 24, 1825. Mary Hoover RHORER died July 2, 1851. Jacob RHORER was born in Maryland on August 8, 1794 and migrated with his parents to Kentucky in 1795. He died September 19, 1871. Another son, Thomas J. RHORER, was born on January 17, 1833 in Jessamine County, Kentucky (Ref: KM:90; KB 7:95).

HOPKINS. Samuel HOPKINS was born in 1711 in Somerset County, Maryland. His son John HOPKINS had a son Ezekiel HOPKINS who inherited land located in Sussex County, Delaware. He sold the land in 1778 and in 1779 moved to Yohogania County, Virginia. Ezekiel HOPKINS moved to Fayette County, Kentucky in 1792 and lived in Bourbon County, Kentucky from 1796 to 1819 (Ref: KA 2:3, January, 1967, p. 122).

HORN. Aaron HORN was born in Betterton, Kent County, Maryland in 1762. By 1778 he was in Washington County, Virginia, where he served in the Revolutionary War. His brother was Matthias HORN. In 1834 Aaron HORN applied for a pension while residing in Estill County, Kentucky, but it was rejected (R5525) according to Source MS:57. However, Source RSK:70 states that Matthias HORN was a pensioner as he had served in the Virginia Line. His pension was granted on December 11, 1832, at age 72 (Ref: RSK:64).

HOSKINS. Randall HOSKINS was born in Maryland in 1758 and enlisted in June, 1778, in the 1st Maryland Regiment. He subsequently moved to Washington County, Kentucky where he applied for and received a pension S36584 for his services. (Ref: MS:56; KPR:1835; MRR:28) Pension Resolution 41 in 1828 was granted in behalf of one Randall HOSKINS, alias HASKINS, as a Private, entitling him to half yearly payments in Washington County, Kentucky (Ref: MGS 5:53).

HOSKINSON. Charles HOSKINSON was born in Frederick County, MAryland in 1759 and served in the Revolutionary War. In 1832 he applied for and received a pension S30493 while living in Breckinridge County, Kentucky. A clergyman named David HOSKINSON made an affidavit as to his character and service (Ref: MS:15; RSK:46; KPR:1835; MRR:28).

HOUSE. William HOUSE was born in Maryland and migrated to Hancock County, Kentucky in an early day, and settled on the Ohio River south of Troy. His son, Benoni HOUSE (1808-1849) married Hannah A. LEWIS (1811-1881) of Kentucky, who married Dr. F. LEWIS after Benoni died (Ref: KB 1:7).

HOWARD. The Howard family was a very prominent one early in Maryland history and information about this important family is readily available at the Maryland Historical Society in Baltimore, Maryland. As for the Howards who went westward to Kentucky in those early pioneer days, there was Edward HOWARD who was among the Catholic emigrants who traveled to Bardstown, Kentucky from St. Mary's County, Maryland circa 1785 and settled on Cartwright's Creek and Poplar Neck. Richard HOWARD, Charles HOWARD, John HOWARD and James HOWARD were also in Kentucky by 1786, settling on Hardin's Creek. (Ref: KC:68-80)

Susan HOWARD married Charles BOONE and they left Maryland for Nelson County, Kentucky in 1798 and later settled in LaRue County. (Ref: KB 5:26, 242)

John HOWARD was born in Frederick County, Maryland in 1760 and enlisted in the 2nd Maryland Regiment under Capt. Archibald ANDERSON on February 25, 1778. He married Margaret STATIONS in 1784 in Montgomery County, Maryland and their children were: Henry HOWARD, John HOWARD, Jr., Richard HOWARD, Maria(?) JOHNSON, Howard HOWARD, and Cynthiana REED. John HOWARD migrated to Mason County, Kentucky circa 1792 and applied for a pension in 1818, which he received (Ref: MS:64; MGS 5:54; RSK:118; KPR:1835; MRR:28) John HOWARD died January 18, 1835 and his wife died December 24, 1848. (Ref: MS:64)

Benjamin HOWARD was born in Frederick County, Maryland on September 6, 1755, enlisted in Rowan County, North Carolina in 1777, and served in the Virginia cavalry. He moved to Madison County, Kentucky in 1787 and applied for and received pension S31138 in 1833 for his service (Ref: MS:57, RSK:115)

The following notice appeared in the Fredericktown Chronicle on February 21, 1787: "About 12 families who are willing to move to the Kentucky country may hear of good encouragement by applying to N. HOWARD." (Ref: WMNA 1:7).

HOWE. John HOWE was born in 1755 and enlisted in Harford County, Maryland for three years on July 22, 1776, serving under Capt. Alexander Lawson SMITH in Rawlings Regiment during the Revolution-ary War. He applied for a pension under the Act of 1818 for his services as a Sergeant, and received the pension on Hardin County, Kentucky. His application, and that of his widow (pension W10113) contains the following genealogical data: John HOWE and Rachel PINDELL were married on July 26 or 27, 1782 by a Baptist Preacher named SAYLOR at Cat Fish Camp, Washington County, Pennsylvania. They lived in Red Stone, Pennsylvania and Jefferson County, Kentucky and Shelby County, Kentucky and Hardin County, Kentucky, where John died May 16, 1830. Affidavit of John CRAWFORD in Crawford County, Indiana in 1847 states that he knew the Howes when they moved to Kentucky about 1789 or 1790. In 1820 Rachel HOWE was age 58, son David HOWE was 19, daughter Rachel was 20, daughter Eleanor was 16, and daughter Isabella was 14. After John's death, Rachel moved to Harrison County, Indiana circa 1831 and died there on September 3, 1844. Abraham HOWE made an affidavit in 1846,

listing the children and grandchildren of John HOWE as follows:
Milcah HOWE, born October 25, 1790; Abraham HOWE, born June 1,
1792; William HOWE, born June 25, 1794; Rachel HOWE, born March 17,
1796; Isaac HOWE, born August 12, 1797; Jacob HOWE, born May 1,
1799; David HOWE, born January 27, 1801; Eleanor HOWE, born
November 15, 1802; John HOWE, born August 6, 1803; Anne HOWE, born
October 28, 1805; Isabel HOWE, born May 1, 1806; Mary HOWE, born
November 7, 1806; James HOWE, born April 15, 1807; Elizabeth HOWE,
born February 4, 1808; Elizabeth HOWE, born June 12, 1809; Nancy
SHIRLEY, born May 22, 1814; Nancy HOWE, born October 22, 1814;
Isaac HOWE, born November 26, 1816; and, Elizabeth HOWE, born March
25, 1821. The application also lists his only living children (in
1818?) as Sarah HEDDEN, David HOWE,

Abraham HOWE, Isabel THOMAS, Rachel PINDELL, Isaac HOWE, Eleanor
GOODMAN, and Jacob HOWE, and that John GOODMAN of Hardin County,
Kentucky (in 1844) may have family records. (Ref: MS:44; RSK:87;
KPR:1835)

Joseph HOWE was among the early Catholics to move from St. Mary's
County, Maryland to Nelson County, Kentucky in 1785 (Ref: KC:28).

HOWELL. George W. HOWELL was born near Covington, Kentucky on
January 7, 1832, a son of Capt. Abram P. HOWELL, a native of
Baltimore, Maryland. As part of his supply business, he manufac-
tured the "Howell Patent Rainwater Cut-Off" and the "Howell Patent
Suspension Metal Wheel." (Ref: KB 8:87).

HOWLETT. The Howlett family originally came from England and
settled in Maryland. Drusilla JOHNSON married John HOWLETT, "a
native of Baltimore, (and) accompanied a colony of people who made
the journey to Nelson County (Kentucky) in wagons, with their
teams, servants, furniture, and other equipment for life in the new
country" circa 1798 (Ref: BCK:96).

HOWSLEY. Robert HOWSLEY was born in London, England in 1710 and
married Sarah BIGGS in Maryland in 1735. He died in 1794. His son,
Robert HOWSLEY, Jr. (born 1762) married Catherine McNEAR in 1786
and they went to Bardstown, Nelson County, Kentucky in 1793. The
children of Robert HOWSLEY, Jr. were Alban Steward HOWSLEY, Stephen
Theodore HOWSLEY, Henry Townsend HOWSLEY, William McNear HOWSLEY,
Alexander HOWSLEY, Aletha Steward HOWSLEY, and Nancy Howsley HIGDON
(Ref: Data from Curtis Smith of Santa Ana, California, in KA 3:1,
July, 1967, p. 38).

HUGHES. James HUGHES was an Irishman, possibly from Maryland, who
settled on Hardin's Creek, Kentucky before 1800. (Ref: KC:54)

The following notice appeared in the Elizabethtown Advertiser on
February 15, 1804: "Lands for sale in Kentucky and Virginia (by)
Samuel HUGHES, Jr., in Hagerstown, Maryland." (Ref: WMNA 2:92).

HUKILL, HUKINS. The Hukill family was from Cecil County, Maryland.
Abiah HUKILL was born in 1759. Although his pension application
states he enlisted in Lee's Legion of Horse on Elk River, Virginia

and served under Capt. John RUDULPH, he and John Rudulph actually were from Elk River in Cecil County, Maryland and Col. Harry LEE's Legion actually was from Virginia, and recruited soldiers in Maryland. In 1818 Abiah HUKILL was in Bracken County, Kentucky and in 1821 he was in Mason County, Kentucky. He received pension S35439 (Ref: MS:65, RSK:118, KP:176; MRR:29; Mason County, Kentucky Order Book J, July, 1821, p. 204, "Declaration of Pensioners")

Daniel HUKILL was born in 1761 and enlisted under Capt. John SEARS in the 3rd Maryland Line for three years. He moved to Mason County, Kentucky in 1795. His children were Rachel, Billey, Susan, Sally and Malinda. Daniel applied for and received pension S36608 for his Revolutionary War services. Daniel HUKILL (or HUKINS) died on June 6, 1833 (Ref: MS:65; KPR:1835. Source RSK:118 erroneously lists his name as "John Hukins").

HUME. George J. HUME, of Scottish origin, migrated from Maryland to (now) Kenton County, Kentucky prior to 1786. His son, William HUME (1786-1849), was born in Kentucky and married Elizabeth ALDRIDGE (1791-1877), daughter of William and Elizabeth ALDRIDGE, both of were natives of Maryland who settled in Jefferson County, Kentucky when Louisville was just a fort. William HUME became a Baptist Minister. His children were: Lucy McKENZIE, Benjamin P. HUME, Drucilla ALLEGRE, Thomas G. HUME, Mary RECORD, Cassandra HUFFMAN, William HUME, Elizabeth STEPHENS, Martha A. BROWN, and George J. HUME (Ref: KB 8:89-90).

HUNTER. Thomas HUNTER was born April 15, 1811 in Fayette County, Kentucky. His father, George HUNTER, Jr., migrated to Kentucky from Maryland circa 1800, settled in Fayette County, married Elizabeth McKEE. Their children were James, Martha, George, Samuel, William, Archibald and Thomas. In 1824 George moved to Todd County and in 1825 he moved to Caldwell County, Kentucky, where he died in 1835 or 1836. Thomas HUNTER, at age 20, was Deputy Sheriff of Caldwell County, Kentucky. He was married first to Lucy A. ROCHESTER and second to Jane R. CRABB (Ref: KB 4:14-15).

HUSTON. Elizabeth HUSTON of Maryland married William WOOD of Pennsylvania and they were in Bracken County, Kentucky by 1818. Their son George H. WOOD was born December 20, 1818. They were in Missouri by 1853 (Ref: KM:33).

HUTCHINS. John HUTCHINS was among the early Catholics who migrated from St. Mary's County, Maryland to Nelson County, Kentucky in 1785 (Ref: KC:28).

HYNES. William HYNES of Coleraine, County Londonderry, Ireland, came to America, settled in Philadelphia, and worked with Benjamin FRANKLIN in the printing business in 1745. His son, Thomas HYNES (c1741-1796) was a Captain in the Revolutionary War and married Abigail -----, 1746-1821. Thomas HYNES moved from Maryland to Nelson County, Kentucky by way of the Ohio River in 1779. His children were Hannah, Andrew, William R., Sally, Polly, Nancy, Thomas, Rachel and Elizabeth. Andrew HYNES, Jr., brother of Thomas, migrated to Kentucky with him. He died January 21, 1849 in Nashville, Tennessee. (Ref: BCK:32-33)

Nancy Anna HYNES was born in Frederick County, Maryland in 1756 and married John COLE who was born in 1752 in King George County, Virginia. Their son, John COLE, Jr. was born in 1789 in Berkeley County, Virginia and died in 1860 in Barren County, Kentucky. John COLE, Jr. built a stone house overlooking the Barren River circa 1812. He married Sembly LAWRENCE of Culpeper County, Virginia and the 1850 Census of Barren County shows these children: John L., age 21; Nancy, age 10; and, Elizabeth C., age 8.(Ref: KA 13:2, October, 1967, p. 102)

The following appeared in the Washington Spy newspaper on August 8, 1792: "Houses for sale in Hagerstown, Maryland; also tract of 400 acres nearly adjoining Hancock Town in this county, being former mansion seat of Col. HYNES, now of Kentucky----Frederick RHORER." (Ref: WMNA 1:38).

IGLEHEART. Mary IGLEHEART married David BELL (1785-1877) some time after his arrival in Ohio County, Kentucky in 1815. Both were natives of Maryland. David BELL was in the War of 1812 also. His son, John D. BELL, was born in Ohio County, Kentucky on October 12, 1825 (Ref: KB 3:122).

IGO. Jacob IGO (possibly a son of William IGO) was born in Maryland in 1776 and married Elizabeth ANSON on December 18, 1805 in Logan County, Kentucky. They moved to Pike County, Missouri prior to 1830, with son Lewis IGO. (Ref: KA 14:2, October, 1978, p. 116; KA 15:2, October, 1979, p. 125).

INLOW. Henry INLOW, of Maryland, married Saloam -----, of Kentucky, in Bourbon County, Kentucky prior to 1820. Their son, Rev. D. V. INLOW, was born on November 24, 1820. They were in Missouri by 1829 (Ref: KM:25).

JACOBS. The following notice appeared in the Fredericktown Republican Gazette, April 14, 1802: "John JACOBS, Frederick County, about to remove to Kentucky, requests claims against him be presented." (Ref: WMNA 2:8).

JANES. John JANES and Austin JANES were among the early Catholic settlers from St. Mary's County, Maryland to move to Cartwright's Creek in (now) Washington County, Kentucky circa 1785 (Ref: KC:80).

JARBOE. There were several Catholic families named JARBOE that went to Washington County, Kentucky from St. Mary's County, Maryland in 1785. Henry JARBOE, Stephen JARBOE, Arnold JARBOE and Benjamin JARBOE were on Cartwright's Creek circa 1785. Walter JARBOE was on Hardin's Creek circa 1786. Richard JARBOE was on Cox's Creek (Fairfield) before 1800. Charles JARBOE was an Elder in Bardstown, Kentucky by 1820. (Ref: KC:56, 63, 80, 114).

JARVIS. Solomon JARVIS was born in Harford County, Maryland in 1753 and was in Kentucky by 1820. He was a Private in the Maryland

Militia in the Revolutionary War. (Ref: MRR:29) In 1825 he resided in Poplar Plains, Fleming County, Kentucky and in 1839 he was in White Sulphur, Scott County, Kentucky. His children were Lewis JARVIS, Reason JARVIS, Elizabeth RILEY, Hannah MOREN, Ann OWENS, and Betsy OLIVER. (Ref: KA 14:3, January, 1979, p. 188) Solomon JERVIS was administrator of the estate of John JERVIS on October 4, 1787 (Ref: Henry C. Peden's Heirs and Legatees of Harford County, Maryland, 1774-1802, p. 28, published by Family Line Publications, Westminster, Maryland (1989).

JEFFERSON. Thomas Lewis JEFFERSON was born in Baltimore, Maryland on February 15, 1826, the eldest son of Thomas JEFFERSON. They moved to Louisville, Kentucky in 1831 and were involved in the wholesale grocery business (Ref: KB 9:80).

JENKINS. William JENKINS was among the early Catholics from St. Mary's County, Maryland who settled on Cartwright's Creek in (now) Washington County, Kentucky in 1785. (Ref: KC:80) William N. JENKINS married Priscilla B. HOSKINS of Maryland and they were in Bullitt County, Kentucky prior to November 11, 1811 when their son Jerermiah F. JENKINS was born. They migrated to Missouri prior to 1861. (Ref: KM:34) A. L. JENKINS was born May 11, 1830 in Owen County, Kentucky, the fifth child of John G. JENKINS (1791-1883) of Maryland, and Eleanor BRANLAN of Kentucky. He married Jennie HUNT in 1852 (Ref: KB 6:120).

JOHNSON. There were several Johnson families that went to Nelson County, Kentucky from St. Mary's County, Maryland in 1785.

Leonard JOHNSON was on Pottinger's Creek with his children: John JOHNSON, Clement JOHNSON, George JOHNSON, Thomas JOHNSON, Philip JOHNSON, and Polly JOHNSON married Thomas HAYDEN and moved to Daviess County.

John JOHNSON, (1777-1833) son of Leonard, married Dorothy MILES, daughter of Philip MILES, and they had nine children: Charles, Nancy, William, John, Thomas, Elizabeth, Silvester, Ellen, and Catherine. John JOHNSON, the father, went to Nelson County, Kentucky in 1798 and settled near what is now New Hope. His son, Silvester JOHNSON (born 1813) married Mildred BOONE (1816-1875) in 1835 and served in the Kentucky Legislature in 1859. John JOHNSON married a second time to Henrietta HILL, daughter of John B. HILL, and they had four children: Priscilla, Hillery, Mary, and Sally. Clement JOHNSON, son of Leonard, was known for his remarkable fiddle playing. (Ref: KB 5:25, KB 9:88, KC:28-30)

Simeon JOHNSON had also settled on Cartwright's Creek by 1785. (Ref: KC:80)

Another Clement JOHNSON was born in Maryland in 1773 and died in 1869 in Carroll County, Kentucky. He married Rebecca DEAN who was born in 1783 in Delaware. Their children were Eleanor J. D. JOHNSON (married Henry B. THOMPSON), Henry R. JOHNSON, and Richard JOHNSON. (Ref: KA 4:2, October, 1968, p. 105)

Another John JOHNSON was born in 1763 in Maryland and was living in Stafford County, Virginia when he enlisted in the Revolution in 1782 under Capt. Leonard JAMISON. He was a driver in the artillery and was subsequently discharged at Fort Washington in 1783. He lived in Virginia until 1810 when he moved to Clark County, Kentucky. He applied for a pension in 1832, but it was rejected (R5634) according to Source MS:30.

Absalom JOHNSON was born August 21, 1757 in Baltimore County and enlisted in the Revolutionary War in 1778. He was a Lieutenant in Pennsylvania service. (Ref: MRR:30) He later went to Nelson County, Kentucky and applied for and received pension S15484 in 1832. His brother, Thomas JOHNSON, made an affidavit that he was nine years younger then Absalom and he remembers his being in the war. Ephraim JOHNSON, an uncle of Absalom JOHNSON, stated in 1833 (at age 80) he remembered Absalom being in the war while residing in Baltimore County, Maryland. (Ref: MS:59)

Charles JOHNSON was a Private in the Maryland Line and received a pension in 1818 in Ohio County, Kentucky. He was born in 1757 and died on January 14, 1833. (Ref: KPR:1835)

Elisha JOHNSON was born in Maryland and married Rhoda MARTIN. They were in Kentucky by 1810 and in Hancock County by 1830. (Ref: KA 12:2, October, 1976, p. 101)

This notice appeared in the Hagerstown Advertiser newspaper on April 17, 1807: "James CARROLL, Baltimore, offers reward for negro man who ran away from his farm on Rhode River, Anne Arundel County, named Gilbert, 35-40; he had a wife belonging to William JOHNSON, who is now moving out to Kentucky with his family; will endeavor to pass for free man named Peter MOORE." (Ref: WMNA 3:56)

Daniel JOHNSON was born in 1763 in Maryland (possibly a son of Jonathan JOHNSON) and served in the Revolutionary War from Charles County in the company of Capt. William WINTER. He was in the 1790 Maryland census and the 1820 Kentucky census. He died in Scott County, Indiana on May 31, 1847 (Ref: MGS, 14:3, August, 1973, p. 30. However, not listed in Source MRR:30).

JOHNSTON. Peter JOHNSTON, very sick, wrote his will on July 31, 1793 in Jefferson County, Kentucky (probated August 5, 1793) and gave 75 acres in Frederick County, Maryland near Fort Frederick to his brother James JOHNSTON. He mentioned his brother Jacob JOHNSTON may be deceased. Witnesses were Abraham DECKER and John MARTIN (Ref: "Abstracts from the First Wills of Jefferson County, Kentucky," by W. J. Gammon and published in NGS 6:3, October, 1917, p. 55).

JONES. Joshua JONES was born in 1759 or 1760 in (now) Harford County, Maryland and served in the Revolutionary War in the 4th Maryland Line in 1778, enlisting at Bush Town. Joshua, becoming quite ill after seven months service, stayed at the house of Araminta SHAW at Lower Susquehanna Ferry, with his Captain's permission. Not recovering enough to return, he purchased a convict servant of Joseph STEVENSON named George SOMERVILLE who substituted for him in the military. Joshua JONES afterwards married Araminta SHAW. He applied for a military pension under the Act of 1818, but never received one. In Clark County, Kentucky, in 1832, he again applied for and received pension S31175, based on the testimony of Jesse COOK (who had since moved to Ohio), James CLARK and George BUCKNER, both of Clark County, Kentucky. (Ref: MS:27; RSK:59; KPR:1835)

Thomas JONES, whose mother (unnamed) was born in Ireland in 1715 and died in Bourbon County, Kentucky about 1823, aged 108 years, was born in Virginia, married Nancy HAWKINS, and served in the Revolutionary War under General Marquis CALMES. Their son, Strother JONES, was born in Spottsylvania County, Virginia and married Elizabeth Ann JONES of Baltimore County, Maryland. She was a daughter of Abraham JONES and Polly GIDDINGS. In 1780, Thomas JONES and family moved to Bourbon County, Kentucky. William G. JONES, son of Strother and Elizabeth JONES, was born there on July 4, 1813. (Ref: MS:54; KB 3:98)

George JONES, a native of Maryland, was a Captain in the Revolutionary War and was at the surrender of Cornwallis in 1781. After the war he moved to Orange County, Virginia and then to North Carolina. Descendants of George JONES migrated to Spartanburg, South Carolina and Campbell County, Kentucky (Ref: KB 8:92).

KEECH. John J. S. KEECH was born in 1752 in Charles County, Maryland, where he enlisted in the 6th Maryland Line in 1777 under Capt. William BELL. After the war he moved to Nelson County, Kentucky and applied for a pension in 1810 and again in 1820. He received pension S36671, stating he had no wife or children. He died on May 15, 1825 (Ref: MS:59; RSK:132).

KEENE. Richard T. KEENE, of Maryland, married Priscilla WILMOT, of Virginia, and they were in Scott County, Kentucky before 1821. A son, Robert W. KEENE, was born there November 21, 1821. They subsequently moved to Missouri (Ref: KM:144).

KEFAUVER. Peter KEFAUVER was born in Maryland and served in the Revolutionary War throughout the entire struggle. After the war he moved to Roanoke, Virginia where he was a farmer and millwright. A son, David KEFAUVER, was born in Roanoke County in 1797. He married Mary DAY, daughter of Evan DAY, and moved to Grayson County, Kentucky in 1834 (Ref: KB 1:180).

KELLAM, KILLAM. Peter KELLAM was born in Hagerstown, Maryland in 1778 and married Leah SELBY in 1799 in Bourbon County, Kentucky (Ref: KA 5:4, April, 1970, p. 222; KA 2:3, January, 1967, p. 118).

KELLY. John KELLY was among the early Catholic settlers from St. Mary's County, Maryland to settle on Cartwright's Creek in (now) Washington County, Kentucky in 1785. (Ref: KC:80)

Samuel KELLY was born in Cecil County, Maryland in 1756 and enlisted in the Revolutionary War in September, 1777. After the war he lived in Prince Edward County, Virginia, and also in Pennsylvania and Tennessee. He applied for and received a pension S38112 in Morgan County, Kentucky in 1834. A fellow soldier, Thomas HAMILTON, stated that he knew him in 1777. Source RSK:130 erroneously states he served in the North Carolina militia (Ref: MS:61; MRR:31).

KELSO. Thomas KELSO was born in 1762 or 1764 and was a Private in the Maryland Militia. He received a pension while in Shelby County, Kentucky. (Ref: RSK:154; KPR:1835; MRR:31) Thomas KELSO married Penelope RUTLEDGE on January 25, 1789 (Ref: MRR:117).

KENDALL. Aaron KENDALL was born in 1757 in Philadelphia County, Pennsylvania and enlisted in the Maryland Militia in Frederick County, Maryland on April 1, 1781 for nine months under Capt. Ralph HILLERY. He married (name not given) in Frederick County on November 6, 1798 and thereafter moved to Bracken County, Kentucky. Aaron KENDALL applied for and received a pension in 1833 in Kentucky. He died April 2, 1841 and his widow died in 1849. Joseph MADDIN, of Fleming County, Kentucky, stated he knew Aaron KENDALL in Maryland when they joined in the Revolutionary War. (Ref: MS:15; MRR:31. Source RSK:44 erroneously states he served in North Carolina)

Jane KENDALL was born in Maryland and went to Kentucky at an early date. She married Haden NELSON, of Orange County, Virginia, in Fayette County, Kentucky and moved to Campbell County in 1807. Their son, Thomas H. NELSON, was born November 7, 1808 and married Sarah HAWKINS in 1833 (Ref: KB 8:122-123).

KENNEDY. John KENNEDY, of Ireland, was kidnapped and sold in Maryland circa 1740. His son, Thomas KENNEDY, was born in Maryland in 1744, went to Virginia in 1775, to Bourbon County, Kentucky in 1776, to Strades Station in 1779, was a carpenter and mason, and died in 1827. A son of Thomas was Jesse KENNEDY (1787-1863) who served in the War of 1812 and served in the Kentucky Legislature four times. He married Mary WAUGH who died in 1828. Their children were: Thomas; Franklin; Jesse G.; Joseph, 1820-1885; Washington; George; William W.; and, Mary M. KENNEDY (Ref: KB 6:152).

KENNETT. Charles KENNETT was among the early Catholics who migrated from St. Mary's County, Maryland to Cartwright's Creek in (now) Washington County, Kentucky in 1785 (Ref: KC:80).

KERRICK, KARRICK, CARRICK. Benjamin Harrison KERRICK was a Musician in the 6th Maryland Line during the Revolutionary War. He was in Washington County, Maryland from 1783 to 1791 and moved to Shelby County, Kentucky in 1791, then Spencer County in 1826 and Jefferson County in 1840. He applied for and received a pension in November, 1828, while in Spencer County. (Ref: RSK:158; MRR:31)

Othaniel KERRICK married Henrietta SMITH on November 7, 1815 in Nelson County, Kentucky, and lived in Spencer County in 1830. Moses CARRICK and John Montgomery CARRICK appear on the 1800 Tax List for Barren County. John CARRICK died in Caldwell County on December 31, 1817. James CARRICK died on September 10, 1812. Stephenson CARRICK lived in Caldwell County in 1830 and in Crittenden County in 1850 (Ref: KPG 1:3, July, 1979, p. 51).

KIBLEY. Joseph KIBLEY was born in 1763 in St. Mary's County, Maryland. He moved to Kentucky in 1805 and in 1835 he applied for a pension for his Revolutionary War service, stating he enlisted in 1781 in the militia. His application (R5905) was rejected due to lack of proof (Ref: MS:55, but Source MRR:31 states he was a Revolutionary War pensioner).

KIDWELL. Jonathan KIDWELL was born in 1752 in Charles County, Maryland and married Rebecca -----, born 1754, in 1770 in Charles County. They moved to Rowan County, North Carolina in 1777, where Jonathan served in the Revolution. In 1784 they moved to Madison County, Kentucky in 1784 and to Henry County, Kentucky in 1828. He received a pension for his services. (Ref: MS:49, RSK:95)

Matthew KIDWELL was born in April, 1752 in Frederick County, Maryland and married Martha -----, born 1752, in Charles County on May 21, 1778. Matthew entered the Revolutionary War in Charles County. (Ref: MRR:31) After the war they moved to Virginia where their son William KIDWELL was born circa 1795. In 1807 they moved to Cumberland County (now Monroe County), Kentucky. Isham D. KIDWELL, son of William, was born on January 30, 1829. Matthew applied for and received pension S30523 in 1831. His widow applied after his death in 1833 (Ref: MS:62; RSK:126; KB 2:60).

KILGOUR. William KILGOUR was a Private in the 1st Maryland Regiment in the Revolutionary War and married Eda -----, born 1760. After his death in Mason County, Kentucky, Eda married Leonard BEAN. She died prior to April, 1833. (Ref: KP:184, Mason County Court Order Book N, p. 53, April, 1833).

KING. Jeremiah KING was born in 1759 in either New Jersey or Maryland, and enlisted in the Maryland Line on May 22, 1778, serving as a Corporal. He applied for and received pension S36032 in 1823 in Jessamine County, Kentucky. He transferred to Clark County, Missouri in 1832 and applied for transfer to Fayette County in 1843. He moved back to Jessamine County "as the Missouri climate did not suit him." (Ref: MS:53; RSK:102; KPR:1835; MRR:31).

KIRK. Thomas KIRK was born in 1759 in Frederick County, Maryland and enlisted in the Revolutionary War in June, 1776. He applied for and received pension S31188 in Mason County, Kentucky in 1832. His brothers, William KIRK (born 1762 and a soldier in the Revolutionary War) and Benjamin KIRK, gave testimony that Thomas served in the Revolution. (Ref: MS:65; MRR:32; KP:181-182; Mason County, Kentucky Court Order Book M, October, 1832, p. 7)

Daniel KIRK was a native of Maryland and among the early settlers in Nelson County, Kentucky. He had a son, Henry KIRK, and a daughter, Lydia KIRK (1802-1854) who married John S. PURDY (1798-1872) in 1818 in Kentucky. (Ref: KB 5:240)

Garrett KIRK was born before 1765 and was in Cecil County, Maryland in 1790. His son, Samuel KIRK, was born in 1780. The families of Garrett KIRK and William SMITH went to Knox County, Kentucky prior to 1810 (Ref: KA 10:2, October, 1974, p. 102).

KIRKWOOD. David KIRKWOOD married Margaret LEECH on May 18, 1795 in Campbell County, Kentucky. Their marriage was proven through a Maryland Revolutionary War pension application; soldier's name not given, although it appears to have been that of David KIRKWOOD, born 1740, a Private in the Maryland Line (Ref: MRR:32, 117).

KIRTZ. Rachael KIRTZ (1794-1866) was born in Maryland and married John SAMUELS (1796-1852) of Kentucky prior to 1821. Their son, Wakefield M. SAMUELS, was born in Nelson County, Kentucky on February 17, 1821. He married Sarah L. STONER on November 12, 1844 and was County Sheriff from 1863 to 1867. He was a Police Judge and a strawberry farmer (Ref: KB:161).

KNOTT. Joseph KNOTT was among the early Catholic settlers from St. Mary's County, Maryland who migrated to Cartwright's Creek in (now) Washington County, Kentucky in 1785. James KNOTT was on Cox's Creek by 1800, and married Mary MUDD circa 1810. (KC:80; KC:114; MRR:117)

Thomas Percy KNOTT was an Episcopal Minister in Derbyshire, England. His only son, Thomas Percy KNOTT, met Jane HART and followed her to American where she was sent to school in Baltimore, Maryland and married her. One of their nine children, Thomas Percy KNOTT (3rd) was a teacher in Maryland and moved to what is now Marion County, Kentucky some time after 1794. A son of this Thomas Percy KNOTT was Joseph Percy KNOTT, who was born on March 31, 1794 near Ellicott Mills, Maryland. He was a teacher and legislator, married Maria Irvine McELROY, and died in West Point, Kentucky in 1851 (Ref: BCK:413-415).

KRIGBAUM. Jacob KRIGBAUM was born in Maryland in 1770 and married Mary ---. Their children were: John, born 1793 in Maryland, married Sarah -----; Mary, born 1794 in Maryland, married Archibald ORGAN; Sarah, born 1796 in Maryland, married Lewis TRACY; Katherine, born 1798 in Kentucky, married David RICE; Jacob R., born 1800 in Kentucky, married Maria BRANDON; Frances, born 1806 in Kentucky, married Jacob ASHURST; David K., born 1812 in Kentucky; and, William B., born 1821 in Kentucky, married Sarah Jane BAIRD. Jacob KRIGBAUM moved to Kentucky, possibly Jessamine County, and then to Ralls County, Missouri circa 1825-1830 (Ref: KA 11:1, July, 1975, p. 45).

KUGEL. John KUGEL was born in Lancaster, Pennsylvania on November 20, 1757 and enlisted in the Revolutionary War on Washington County, Maryland in July, 1776. His father had moved to Maryland when John was very young. In 1801, John KUGEL moved to Fayette County, Kentucky and then to Owen County, Kentucky in 1817. He applied for and received pension S15190 in 1833 (Ref: MS:60; MRR:32. Source RSK:138 erroneously states he served in Connecticut during the war).

LAMBERT. Mathias LAMBERT was born in Frederick County, Maryland on

March 15, 1755 and enlisted in the Revolutionary War in 1779 in Augusta County, Virginia. In 1783 he moved to Clark County, Kentucky and then Madison County, Kentucky. He married Elizabeth WILLIAMS in Madison on January 27, 1796 and they had a son, John LAMBERT. Mathias LAMBERT received a pension in 1834 and after his death his widow applied and received pension W1784 in 1850 (Ref: MS:57; RSK: 115).

LANCASTER. John LANCASTER and Raphael LANCASTER were sons of John LANCASTER and Fannie JARNIGAN who came to America from Lancashire, England and settled at "Cob Neck" on the lower Potomac River in Charles County, Maryland. Fannie JARNIGAN was from County Cork, Ireland. Raphael LANCASTER, son of Raphael, married Eleanor BRADFORD, and their oldest son, John LANCASTER, was born in 1766 and went to Kentucky in 1784 and settled in the Hardin Creek Catholic Settlement. His parents went to Kentucky in 1785. His brother, Raphael, settled near Bardstown, Kentucky in 1788. John LANCASTER married Catherine MILES in 1789 or 1790, a daughter of Philip MILES of St. Mary's County, Maryland and of the Pottinger Creek Settlement in Kentucky. John and Catherine LANCASTER had these children: Joseph B. married Anna BLAIR; Raphael married Caroline CARTER; Philip H. married Catherine HAGAN; John married Mary HAYDEN; Benjamin, 1799-1839, married Ann POTTINGER; Ellen married Judge A. H. CHURCHILL; Ann married E. B. SMITH; James Madison became a Priest; William married Malvina CHURCHILL; and, Catherine married Leonard A. SPALDING. John LANCASTER served in the Kentucky Legislature, 1799 to 1802, and in 1820. He died in 1838. (Ref: KC:48-50; BCK:376; KB 5:264)

William LANCASTER married widow Sarah BLADES on September 11, 1813 in Kentucky and their marriage was proven through a Maryland Revolutionary War pension application; soldier's name not given (Ref: MRR:117).

LANHAM. Zachariah LANHAM was among the early Catholics who migrated from St. Mary's County, Maryland to Cartwright's Creek in (now) Washington County, Kentucky in 1785. (Ref: KC:80)

Stephen LANHAM married Eleanor SELBY, both of Maryland, and their daughter Elizabeth LANHAM married William POWELL, Jr. (born in Virginia in 1811) in Kentucky, possibly Madison County. Their children were Stephen C., Joel H., Allie C., and Martha Elizabeth (Ref: KPG, 2:2, April, 1980, p. 100).

LANSDALE. Mary LANSDALE was born in 1788 in Harford County, Maryland and married Richard MENEFEE, who died in August, 1815, in Owingsville, Kentucky. Their son, Richard Hickman MENEFEE, was born December 4, 1809 in Bath County, Kentucky and married Sarah Bell JOUETT, daughter of Matthew JOUETT, on August 14, 1832. Richard died February 20, 1841 and Sarah died December 13, 1898. Their other sons were Alfred, John, Alvin, and Allen (Ref: KA 12:3, January, 1977, p. 156. Note: The Menefees were from Virginia and some are buried in the Whitley Cemetery near Stanford, Kentucky (Ref: KCR:257).

87

LAWRENCE. On January 7, 1802, Levin LAWRENCE and wife Mary of Nelson County, Kentucky, conveyed land to Edward DORSEY of Jefferson County, Kentucky, part of "John's Industry." Mary LAWRENCE was a daughter of Elias DORSEY, deceased. (Ref: BCLR Liber WG #70, p. 163)

Samuel LAWRENCE was born October 29, 1764 in Maryland and died in Kentucky on September 17, 1822. He married Sarah HOBBS in Frederick County, Maryland on June 22, 1790. She was born in 1769 and died on September 19, 1828. Their daughter, Urath O. LAWRENCE (1791--1854), married James BROWN (1780-1853), and their son, Elias Dorsey LAWRENCE (1799-1828), are buried with their parents in the Brown and Lawrence Cemetery in Jefferson County, Kentucky (Ref: KCR:228-229; MM-2:133).

LAYTON. William H. LAYTON was born in Maryland in 1755 and enlisted in the Revolutionary War in Kent County, Delaware on January 1, 1776 for one year under Capt. ADAMS. He returned home and in March, 1780 he reenlisted for three years in the 4th Maryland Line under Col. Josias Carvil HALL. He resided in Maryland until 1802 and moved to Kentucky. He lived in Harrison County and Fleming County, and in 1832 he applied for and received pension S16443 for his services. He was still alive in 1840. Source RSK:71 erroneously states he served in the Pennsylvania Line. (Ref: MS:35; MS:47; MS:60; MRR:32)

"In the year 1720, the great-grandfather of Col. John Jay LAYTON, Ohio County, Kentucky, came to America from England and settled in Baltimore with a large family, of which Col. Layton's grandfather was the youngest. He was an officer in the French and Indian War, and was an officer at Braddock's defeat. He died at Spartanburg, and his widow removed with her family of five boys and six girls to what is now Garrard County, Kentucky in the year 1800. William, the father of Col. Layton, was the youngest son and was born in North Carolina in 1790 and died in 1866. He became a Colonel in the militia and in the War of 1812. He married Mary Ann YATER in 1815 and had thirteen children." Col. John Jay LAYTON was born in 1821, served in the Mexican War in 1846, and married Miriam SHREWSBURY in 1851 (Ref: KB 3:148).

LEACH. Leonard LEACH migrated from Maryland to Kentucky in 1799, settled in Ohio County, and died there in 1840. His son, John Nelson LEACH (1807-1863) married first to Martha TAYLOR and second Joanna ARNOLD. (Ref: KB 3:159) John LEACH (1802-1859) was probably a son of Leonard also, and married Nancy -----. Their son, Alfred K. LEACH, was in the Civil War and was a Postmaster in Ohio County, Kentucky (Ref: KB 3:158).

LEAKE. "Rebel" James LEAKE was possibly born in Scotland and came to Maryland and served in the Revolutionary War in the St. Mary's County Militia. He migrated to Woodford and Scott Counties, Kentucky and died circa 1807 (Ref: S. Eugene Clements and F. Edward Wright's Maryland Militia in the Revolutionary War. Silver Spring, Maryland: Family Line Publications, 1987, p. 212; KA 9:1, July, 1973, p. 42).

87

LEATHERMAN. Michael LEATHERMAN was born in Maryland in 1753 and enlisted in the Revolutionary War in 1776, serving with Frederick GERGER and John GERGER. In 1830, in Jefferson County, Kentucky, Michael applied for and received pension S36684 for his services in Maryland and Pennsylvania. It is noted in his application that four sons and two daughters were deceased, and he stated that as his children came of age they married and left him, but his youngest son Jacob was a minor in 1815. Michael's wife Margaret LEATHERMAN died in 1824 and he then lived with his son-in-law Jacob BLANKENDECKER. He died July 6, 1831 (Ref: MS:51; RSK:99).

LEE. Philip LEE was among the early Catholic settlers who migrated from St. Mary's County, Maryland to Washington and Nelson County, Kentucky in 1785, and lived on Pottinger's Creek in 1786. While still in Maryland he was in the habit of keeping a record of passing events. From the entries in that record extending back to the year 1735, and continued after his removal to Kentucky, it appears that his neighbors in both states bore identical names. Among the names most frequently mentioned in Lee's diary are Lancaster, Coomes, Brown, Thompson, Smith, Rapier, Cash, Bullock, Hayden and Howard. (Ref: KC:28)

Samuel LEE has settled on Rolling Fork by 1791, and one Samuel LEE died in 1863 at age 85. (Ref: KC:110)

Samuel LEE married Nancy RAPIER and their children were James, Samuel, Raymond, Richard, George, Charles and William. James R. LEE was born in Marion County, Kentucky in 1811 and his wife, Susan, was born 1813. He died in 1844 and she married Francis FORD. (Ref: KB 5:177)

Matilda Ann LEE of Maryland married William SIMMONS of Bullitt County, Kentucky and their daughter Laura SIMMONS, 1838-1878, married Henry J. LYONS, 1829-1867. (Ref: BCK:226-267)

John LEE married Neomy CORD in Cecil County, Maryland on February 12, 1784. Neomy was born circa 1762, a daughter of Jacob CORD and Elizabeth COOK. John LEE moved to Fleming or Mason County, Kentucky circa 1794. Parker LEE, son of John, was born in Maryland on December 6, 1787 and died in Marion County, Ohio on April 14, 1866. He married Elizabeth SHOOTS (1797-1870) on April 22, 1813 in Pickaway County, Ohio. The other children of John LEE were Jacob Cord LEE, Samuel LEE, and Achsah LEE (Ref: KA 7:4, April, 1972, pp. 192-194; and "Wilford Lee, 1774-1849, Gentleman: Son of John LEE, Kentucky Pioneer" by Evelyn C. Adams in the Filson Club Quarterly, Vol. XXXIV, 1960, pp. 115-135, and published in Genealogies of Kentucky Families, pp. 654-674, Baltimore: Genealogical Publishing Co., 1981).

LEMASTERS. The earliest known LeMaster in America was one Abraham LEMAISTRE, a Huguenot who was born about 1637 and came to Maryland in 1668, possibly by way of Barbados, and settled in Charles County. Richard LEMAISTRE owned land in 1720-1724 in Charles and St. Mary's Counties. The will of Abraham De LeMAISTRE in 1772 names a wife and sons Richard, John and Isaac. The LeMasters also settled in Amherst and Botetourt Counties in Virginia, as well as Kentucky, where Richard LEMASTERS name appears in Bourbon County in 1788 and in Montgomery County in 1797, along with Isaac LEMASTERS and Conrad LEMASTERS and Benjamin LEMASTERS. In 1799, Isaac and Conrad were in Hamilton County, Ohio. Benjamin LEMASTERS married Polly LANGSTON on September 21, 1797 in Clark County, Kentucky and Richard LEMASTERS married Catherine LANGSTON on May 11, 1793 in Bourbon County, Kentucky. They moved to Clermont County, Ohio after 1797 and the family later moved to Bush County, Indiana (Additional information can be found in Maurine C. Schmitz and Glendola A. Peck's The Amos Family, pp. 28-31, available at the Maryland Historical Society Library, Baltimore, Maryland, 1964).

LESTER. Richard LESTER of Pulaski County, Tennessee married A. C. WRIGHT in 1839 in Hickman County, Kentucky. She was born on January 23, 1820 in Simpson County, Kentucky, a daughter of Henry WRIGHT of Maryland. He moved to Hickman County in 1839 and in 1853 he went to Texas and soon after died of yellow fever at the age of 62 (Ref: KB 6:153).

LEWIS. William LEWIS was born circa 1760 in Frederick or Montgomery County, Maryland and married Nancy ELLIS, who was born in 1764 in Maryland and died in July, 1849, in West Feliciana Parish, Louisiana. They moved to Cynthiana, Kentucky in the 1780's. Their children were: Aaron LEWIS, Hiram LEWIS, John LEWIS, Elizabeth JOHNSON, Mary Ann PERKINS, Sanford LEWIS, and Sarah LEWIS. William LEWIS died in 1809 in Harrison County, Kentucky, and Nancy married Alexander LEWIS, who had moved with them from Maryland. He died in February, 1841, in Harrison County, Kentucky. (Ref: KA 16:2, October, 1980, p. 124; MGS 26:4, Fall, 1985, p. 440)

John LEWIS and wife Sarah lived in Maryland and Virginia. Their son Samuel LEWIS was born 1784 in Virginia and married Sarah LEMASTERS in Henry County, Kentucky in 1804. They moved to Orange County, Indiana, founded the town of Orleans in 1815, and went to Texas in 1832 (Ref: KA 3:2, Oct., 1967, p.83).

LILLY. Thomas LILLY and John LILLY, brothers, of Nelson County, Kentucky, were among the early Catholic settlers from St. Mary's County, Maryland to settle on Cox's Creek circa 1785. John LILLY represented the county in the Kentucky Legislature in 1807, and Thomas LILLY married Elizabeth JENKINS in Maryland. Their children were: John LILLY; Thomas LILLY, became a physician; Richard LILLY; Harriet LILLY, married Noble WRIGHT; Matilda LILLY, married James PARSONS; Eliza LILLY, married John JOHNSON; Mary LILLY, married Sylvester BOWMAN; and, Ann LILLY, married M. J. O'CALLAGHAN (Ref: KC:114, 129).

LINDSAY. Anthony LINDSAY (1736-1808) married Rachel DORSEY (1737-1805) of Maryland and they were in Kentucky by 1784. Their son, Vachel LINDSAY (1768-1855) married in 1791 in Paris, Kentucky, to Ann CUSENBERRY (1774-1842), daughter of Moses and Ann CUSENBERRY. (Ref: KA 1:4, April, 1966, p. 135) John LINDSAY was born in Baltimore County, Maryland in 1759 and enlisted in 1777 in the

Frederick County Militia under Capt. Simon MERIDITH. In 1779 he moved to Pennsylvania to Buffalo Creek, a tract of country claimed both by Virginia and Pennsylvania. He resided in Ohio County, Virginia and in 1780 enlisted again in Westmoreland County, Pennsylvania. He went to Kentucky in 1784 and he subsequently applied for and received pension S30545 in Henry County. In 1837 he was in Hancock County (Ref: MS:50-51; RSK:95; MRR:33).

LINGENFELTER. Michael LINGENFELTER was born on November 17, 1762 in Frederick, Maryland. He enlisted in 1779 and was a Private in the Maryland Line during the Revolutionary War. After the war he lived in Maryland and Virginia, and was in Kentucky by 1832. He lived in Port William, Gallatin County, Kentucky in December, 1832 when he applied for and received pension S32379 in Oldham County, Kentucky. (The 1835 Kentucky Pension Rolls indiacte he was in Ohio County, but it was actually Oldham County, Kentucky) In 1835 he transferred to Marion County, Indiana, having two sons in Indianapolis with whom he was going to live (Ref: MS:61; MRR:33; KPR:1835).

LINK. Jacob LINK (born 1762) married Elizabeth CREAGOR (born 1769), both of Frederick County, Maryland, and moved to Bourbon County, Kentucky in 1797. Their daughter, Catherine LINK, married James BRAND, son of Dr. Richard BRAND, of Maryland, who went to Paris in Bourbon County, Kentucky from Maryland in 1797 (Ref: KB 5:110).

LINN. Ashael LINN married Miss HUNTER of Maryland circa 1795 in Jefferson County, Kentucky. Their son, Dr. Lewis F. LINN was born November 5, 1796. They were in Missouri by 1856 (Ref: KM:87).

LITSEY. Randolph LITSEY was born in 1770 in Maryland and migrated to Springfield, Kentucky prior to 1800. He was a farmer and distiller. His wife was Mary GREGORY, daughter of Richard GREGORY. Mary died about 1859 and Randolph died in September, 1849. One of their sons, Uriah LITSEY, was born in Washington County, Kentucky on October 15, 1813, and married Eleanor J. LEWIS in 1841 (Ref: KB 5:182).

LITTIG. Elizabeth LITTIG, daughter of a Sea Captain from Fell's Point in Baltimore, Maryland, married William PINKERTON (1780--1857), son of John PINKERTON of Northern Ireland. William was born in Chester County, Pennsylvania, became a Captain in the War of 1812, and died in Midway, Kentucky. His son, Rev. Lewis L. PINKERTON, M.D., was born in Baltimore, Maryland on January 28, 1812. William moved to Kentucky after the War of 1812 (Ref: KB 5:234).

LIVERS. Samuel LIVERS was an early settler from Maryland on Hardin's Creek in (now) Washington County, Kentucky circa 1786. Henry LIVERS and Robert LIVERS were in Bardstown prior to 1820 (Ref: KC:56, KC:63).

LLOYD. James LLOYD was born in Ireland and came to the United States with his parents about 1795 and settled in Maryland. He then migrated to Green County, Tennessee where he married Mary SHIELDS. Their daughter, Mary LLOYD, married Abel LLOYD and moved to Monroe County, Kentucky. They lived on Indian Creek, near Flippin, Kentucky (Ref: KB 2:62).

LOCKWOOD. Samuel LOCKWOOD was born on July 22, 1755 in Worcester
County, Maryland and his family moved to Sussex County, Delaware
circa 1760. Early in 1776 he enlisted in the militia at Lewistown,
Delaware under Capt. David HALL. In 1777 he transferred to a company under Capt. William PERRY. He also served on board a ship for
a short time, but mostly guarded the Delaware coast and the light-
house on Cape Henlopen. In 1778 he moved back to Worcester County
where he married (wife not named) and in 1791 they moved to Bourbon
County, Kentucky. He became a Minister of the Methodist Episcopal
Church. In 1833 he applied for and received pension S13789 and died
on July 28, 1834 in (now) Pendleton County, Kentucky (Ref: MS:10;
RSK:43).

LOSGDON. William LOGSDON settled in Baltimore County, Maryland in
the early 1700's. Thomas LOGSDON I, son of William, may have
married Mary JONES, daughter of Richard JONES, circa 1735. Their
son, Thomas LOGSDON II, served in the Revolutionary War, as did
their son Joseph LOGSDON, who was a guide for General George
WASHINGTON. By 1784 Thomas is in Garrett County, Maryland and
George WASHINGTON reportedly spent the night with the family. By
1787 Thomas was in Hardy County, (now) Virginia, at which time he
sold his land and went to Madison County, Kentucky in 1788. The
1791 Tax List names three Thomas Logsdons: Thomas "Old," Thomas
"Sr." and Thomas "Jr." The Logsdons later migrated to Barren County, Kentucky where Thomas (II) died in 1818. (Ref: BCF:407-408; and
article by Gloria Lucas of Sonora, California, published in the
South Central Kentucky Historical and Genealogical Society Quarterly "Traces," 16:1, Spring, 1988, pp. 8-10).

LOVE. David LOVE was a Sergeant in the 1st Maryland Line and
received a pension in Oldham County, Kentucky in 1828. He died
December 6, 1830; executor: David LOVE (Ref: MRR:34; KPR:1835;
RSK:137).

LOVELACE. Elias LOVELACE, was born January 27, 1755 in Frederick
County, Maryland and moved to Rown County, North Carolina around
1775. In May, 1776, he volunteered as a Spy for 3 months under
Capt. Samuel REESE, and served 5 months under Capt. Jacob NICHOLAS.
Elias LOVELACE married Anne ROBY, born January 3, 1757, daughter
of Thomas ROBY, on January 2 or 12, 1775. Andrew LOVELACE was born
February 3, 1776. Elias moved to Butler County, Kentucky in 1798
and to McCrackern County in 1826. He applied for and received a
pension for his Revolutionary War service in 1833. He died December
23, 1834. In 1840 his widow, age 83, applied for his pension.
Nancy HILL stated she knew them since 1778, and also Elias'
brother, Vachel. (Ref: RSK:113, MS:62) Vachel LOVELACE, brother of
Elias, was born June 12, 1758 in Frederick County, Maryland and
enlisted in Rowan County, North Carolina on April 1, 1777. He
married Margaret -----, and in 1780 moved to Graves County, Kentucky. Their children were: George, born March 13, 1780; William, born
March 10, 1783; Elizabeth, born June 21, 1785; Elias, born April
26, 1788; John, born February 9, 1790; Shelby, born January 6,
1794; and, Walter, born July 6, 1797. Vachel applied for and

received a pension in 1833. His widow filed in 1840 and received pension W9144. It appears that Vachel LOVELACE and Elias LOVELACE were sons of John Baptist LOVELACE and wife Eleanor (Ref: MS:41; MS:62; RSK:81).

LOVELL. William LOVELL, a native of Maryland, married Rachel EADES, a native of Madison County, Kentucky, and their son, William M. LOVELL, was born on September 18, 1835 in Muhlenburgh COunty, Kentucky. Michael LOVELL, a native of Maryland, married a Miss INGRAM, of Virginia, and their daughter, Mary E. LOVELL, married William K. MORGAN in Muhlenburgh County, Kentucky prior to 1840. (Ref: KB 3:100-103)

William LOVELL married Priscilla PROUT (both from Maryland) in Virginia and then moved to Allen County, Kentucky in 1812. Their daughter, Nella LOVELL, married Stephen T. BARNES (1801-1884) prior to 1825 when their son James N. BARNES was born in Allen County (Ref: KB 4:174).

LOWRY. Thomas LOWRY was born in August, 1760 in St. Mary's County, Maryland and moved with his family to Stafford County, Virginia in 1763. He served in the Revolutionary War under Capt. MOUNTJOY in 1781. His brother, Moses LOWRY, was in Bath County, Kentucky in 1832 when he stated that Thomas did serve in the war. Thomas LOWRY married Nancy DEADMAN in Orange County, Virginia on October 16 or November 21, 1805. Other marriages (relationships not stated) in the pension papers were: Reuben TERRELL to Susan MORTON, September 11, 1805; James FISHER to Fanny MASON, December 26, 1805; and, George REARDON to Sarah TEALE, April 1, 1806. Thomas LOWRY received a pension in Clark County, Kentucky in 1832, where he had been living since 1816. His widow made application in 1853 and received pension W2139 (Ref: MS:27; RSK:59).

LUCAS. Henry LUCAS was among the early Catholic settlers to migrate from St. Mary's County, Maryland to Nelson County, Kentucky in 1785. (Ref: KC:28)

Benedict LUCAS, whose father was born in Maryland and his mother in Tennessee, was born in Breckinridge County, Kentucky in 1832 and married Susan Ellen TURLEY in 1866 in Edmonson County, Kentucky (Ref: Information compiled by Dorothy Holton in the South Central Kentucky Historical and Genealogical Quarterly "Traces," 13:2, Summer, 1985, p. 60).

LUCKETT. Hezekiah LUCKETT was among the early Catholic settlers from St. Mary's County, Maryland to migrate to Nelson County, Kentucky in 1785. He died at the home of his son George LUCKETT at the age of 86, date not given. Henry LUCKETT was a settler on Rolling Fork, Kentucky circa 1791. (Ref: KC:110, 114, 131. Note: Additional data can be found in The Lucketts of Portobacco, by Harry Wright Newman in 1938, which is available at the Maryland Historical Society Library in Baltimore)

The following appeared in the Elizabeth-Town Advertiser on January 25, 1805 (and had been previously printed in a Kentucky newspaper):

"Dr. John M. LUCKETT, young physician, of eminence and respectabilty, who has been residing in Louisville about 3 years, returned from Frederick Town, Maryland on December 13th, with an aged mother and two sisters whom he had brought to share his fortunes, and who have heretofore resided in this state, on the day after his arrival he was challenged by George F. STROTHER, Esq., attorney at law, and on the day succeeding, Mrs. Luckett beheld her darling son a corpse. On the third fire he received a wound in the breast, which instantly terminated his existence, in the 23rd year of his age; verdict by coroner's inquest was murder. (Ref: WMNA 2:104)

Samuel LUCKETT was born in 1756 or 1757 in Maryland and served as a Sergeant in the Maryland Line from 1776 to 1780. His wife, Elizabeth -----, was born May 9, 1769 and their children were: Samuel LUCKETT, born March 2, 1801; John LUCKETT, born May 19, 1803; David LUCKETT, born September 26, 1805; Nancy LUCKETT, born January 13, 1808; and, Anna LUCKETT, born June 17, 1811. Samuel applied for and received pension S36051 in 1818. (Ref: MS:7; RSK:34; MRP:26; MRR:34; KPR:1835) Samuel's will was written in April, 1828, and probated in October, 1828, in Barren County, Kentucky, naming his wife ELizabeth and these children: Ann Ware LUCKETT, David LUCKETT, William LUCKETT, Frances H. LUCKETT, Samuel LUCKETT, Susanna PARNELL, Polly ELMS, John L. LUCKETT, and Nancy CREEK (Ref: KR:14).

LUCKIE. William LUCKIE of Harford County, Maryland died intestate, leaving these children: Grace LUCKIE, married John BELL; Rebecca LUCKIE, married Patterson BAIN; Polly LUCKIE, married Archibald DORSEY; Hugh Finley LUCKIE; John Bell LUCKIE; and, William A. LUCKIE. John BELL, Patterson BAIN and Hugh LUCKIE had moved to Jefferson County, Kentucky and on July 23, 1804 appointed Jane LUCKIE, widow, as their attorney in Harford County, Maryland (HCLR Liber HD #T, April, 1807, pp. 42-45).

LUSH. William LUSH was born in 1744 and applied for a pension for Revolutionary War services as a Privateer on the brig "Hawk" under Capt. James CLIFTON of Fell's Point in Baltimore, Maryland. He lived in Baltimore at the time and in 1834 he was in Hardin County, Kentucky. His claim was rejected (R6526) according to Source MS:46 (but Source MRR:34 indicates he was a Revolutionary War pensioner).

LYNCH. The following appeared in the Hagerstown Advertiser newspaper on September 5, 1810: "John LYNCH, who lives near Williamsport, intends removing to Kentucky, to sell house in Williamsport on Salisbury Street." (Ref: WMNA 3:87).

MADDEN. Walter MADDEN was an early Catholic settler from Maryland to settle on Hardin's Creek in Washington County, Kentucky circa 1786. (Ref: KC:56)

Joseph MADDEN was born in 1757 or 1758 in Frederick County, Maryland and enlisted in 1777 under Capt. William DUVALL and subsequently became a Lieutenant. In 1803 he moved to Fleming County, Kentucky where he applied for and received pension S31237 in January, 1834 (Ref: MS:35; KBG 7:1, Spring, 1980, p. 10; MRR:36.

94

Source RSK:71 erroneously states he served in Virginia).

MADDOX. Notley MADDOX was a native of Maryland, but died in Virginia. His son, John M. MADDOX was born in Virginia and married Mary SUTHERLAND. They moved to Kentucky in 1810 or 1814 and lived in Henry and Shelby Counties (Ref: KB 7:214).

MAGRUDER. Alpheus MAGRUDER was born in southern Maryland in 1803 and married Sarah MARTINIE (born 1812), probably in Henry County, Kentucky. Their sons were: David M. MAGRUDER, born 1831; and, Elias MAGRUDER, born 1833. They were in Missouri by 1852 (Ref: KM:83).

MAHONY. William MAHONY was among the early Catholics who migrated from St. Mary's County, Maryland to Nelson County, Kentucky in 1785 (Ref: KC:28).

MAKEMSON. Thomas MAKEMSON ws born in County Cork, Ireland in 1753 and came to America with his family when only two years old, settling first in Philadelphia. They moved to Maryland during the Revolutionary War and then to Kentucky after the war, possibly to a place called Ruddles Station. Thomas MAKEMSON married in 1793 to Jane LINDSEY in Harrison COunty, Kentucky, and they moved to Danville, Illinois in 1829. Andrew MAKEMSON settled on Mill Creek near Cynthiana, Kentucky in 1795. He married Ann LINDSEY in 1800 and after she died in 1813 he married Elizabeth HAND. They lost most of their family due to cholera in 1833. Elizabeth MAKEMSON of Pendleton County, Kentucky stated in an affidavit in 1829 that she was born in 1754 in York County, Pennsylvania about a mile and a half from the Maryland line. Her maiden name was Elizabeth BROWN and she married John MAKEMSON, brother of Thomas MAKEMSON, during the war and lived in Maryland about nine miles from the Pennsylvania line. Both John and Thomas served in the war. She stated that she knew their brothers Robert, Joseph, James, Andrew, and William, and their sister, Becca. After the war they moved to Kentucky, except James and William who were killed near Philadelphia during the Revolution. Katharine PATTERSON of Harrison County, Kentucky made an affidavit in 1829 (age 73) that she was raised in Harford County, Maryland about 30 miles from Baltimore and a mile from Andrew MAKEMSON, father of Thomas. She stated her maiden name was Katharine PATTERSON and she married Samuel PATTERSON who had a brother James PATTERSON who lived near York, Pennsylvania and was a Colonel in the Revolutionary War. The pension of Thomas MAKEMSON was subsequently granted (Ref: Article on the Makemson Family by Walter E. Makemson of Leesburg, Indiana in 1967, published in KA 3:1, pp. 27-28).

MAJOR. Alexander MAJOR was born on September 30, 1756 in Philadelphia, Pennsylvania, the son of James MAJOR. In 1768 he moved with his father to Baltimore County, Maryland. He substituted for his father for three months in the Maryland Militia and then moved to Frederick County, Maryland. In his pension application (S31239) in 1831, Alexander stated he moved to Virginia and then to Woodford County, Kentucky and Hopkins County, Kentucky (Ref: MS:48; RSK:98; MRP:26; KPR:1835).

MALOTT. Amos Elias MALOTT was born circa 1770 in Washington County, Maryland, a son of Benjamin MALOTT who was born in 1815 in Washington County, Amos married Christiana AMOS who was born in 1773 in Harford County, Maryland. They moved to Jefferson County, Kentucky where Amos died in 1837 (Ref: MGS 24:2, Spring, 1983, p. 173).

MARAMAN, MERRIMAN. In the Beech Fork area of Nelson County, Kentucky, the families of John LEE, Atkinson HILL, and Zachariah MARAMAN associated together. Zachariah MARAMAN went to Kentucky frolm St. Mary's County, Maryland in the mid 1780's. He was a son of John MARAMAN, wealthy slave owner and planter, whose family was affiliated with historic St. Andrew's Episcopal Church near Leonardtown, Maryland. In his will probated September 17, 1810, Zachariah MARAMAN left his wifow Ann Howard MARAMAN his plantation and slaves. He had six children, of whom Francis MARAMAN married Mary LEE and Margaret MARAMAN married Charles LEE (Ref: "Wilford Lee 1774-1849, Gentleman: Son of John Lee, Kentucky Pioneer," by Evelyn C. Adams in the Filson Club Quarterly, Vol. XXXIV, 1960, and published in Genealogies of Kentucky Families, pp. 654-674, Baltimore: Genealogical Publishing Co., 1981).

MARKWELL. William MARKWELL was born in Maryland and served in Rawling's Regiment and in the 7th Maryland Regiment in the Revolutionary War. He married Amelia -----, and moved to Fleming County, Kentucky where he died in 1816. He is buried on the Markwell farm between Poplar Plains and Hillsboro. It appears that his tombstone bears an incorrect birth year of 1769 because William was born in 1750 according to the DAR. (Ref: DAR:438; KCR:167; Archives of Maryland, Vol. 18, pp. 145, 618).

MARRIOTT. James MARRIOTT and wife Sophia moved to Hardin County, Kentucky in 1818 from Maryland. She was born in Prince George's County, Maryland on June 26, 1784 (parents not stated) and died in Hardin County, Kentucky on September 18, 1854. Their son Ephraim MARRIOTT was born in Maryland in 1809 and moved with his parents to Elizabethtown, Kentucky, where he married Artemeci HARDIN. He died in 1873. Several Marriotts are buried in the Old Harcourt Cemetery between White Hills and Glendale in Hardin County, Kentucky (Ref: KCR:186; KB 1:45).

MARSH. On April 30, 1801, Thomas MARSH and wife Sarah, and Beal MARSH and wife Eleanor, of Bourbon County, Kentucky, conveyed to Joshua MARSH of Baltimore County, Maryland, lots in "Valley of Jehosphat." (Ref: BCLR Liber WG #67, p. 231) Joshua MARSH married Temperance MARSH on December 11, 1785 in Baltimore County, Maryland. (Ref: MRR:118) Dryden MARSH, daughter of Beal MARSH, married Nimrod WOOD and their son Thomas C. WOOD was born in 1821 in Nicholas County, Kentucky (Ref: KB 7:127).

MARSHALL. Robert MARSHALL was born circa 1725, possibly a son of Richard MARSHALL of Charles County, Maryland. He died in Mason County, Kentucky circa 1801. A son Robert MARSHALL, Jr., died in Fayette County, Kentucky circa 1814, and a daughter Elizabeth MARSHALL married Jacob EDWARDS and died in Mason County, Kentucky in 1798. (Ref: MGS 26:1, WInter, 1985, p. 90)

Another Robert MARSHALL was born March 11, 1760 in Maryland and served in the Revolutionary War in the 6th Maryland Line from 1777 to 1780. In his pension claim he said he enlisted in Carlisle, Pennsylvania, but no date was given, and an inference was made to being in the Indian Wars under General WAYNE. He apparently received a pension and after his death on July 1, 1837 in Campbell County, Kentucky, his widow Nancy applied for and received pension W2141. She stated that she and Robert MARSHALL were married on October 24, 1797 by Rev. Bethenel RIGGS. Her maiden name was Nancy MARDIS. She was living in Kenton County, Kentucky in 1850, age 69. (Ref: RSK:53; MRP:27; MS:18-19; KPR:1835; MRR:118)

Thomas MARSHALL came to America from Wales prior to 1790 and settled in Maryland where his son Alexander MARSHALL was born on March 24, 1790. They soon moved to Virginia and in 1818 migrated to Hardinsburg, Kentucky. Alexander married Elizabeth HICKS (1793-1864), daughter of Jesse HICKS, and died January 6, 1867 (Ref: KB 1:141).

MATTINGLY. William, Leonard, Lucas (Luke), Basil, Zachariah, Richard, Barton, Joseph, and Philip MATTINGLY were among the early Catholic settlers from St. Mary's County, Maryland to move to Kentucky between 1785 and 1791. William MATTINGLY (followed by brothers Leonard and Lucas) arrived first with his wife, Miss SPALDING, and three son, James, Edward, and Richard. His first wife died and he married Elizabeth CLARK and had ten children: William, Mary, Benjamin, Felix, Ignatius, Julia, George, Susan, Catherine, and John. Leonard MATTINGLY, brother of William, married in Maryland and all of his children were born there: Leonard, Basil, John, William, Joseph, Ignatius, Jane, Margaret, Susan, and another daughter, name not stated. Lucas MATTINGLY, the third brother, settled on Hardin's Creek, Kentucky in 1786. Basil MATTINGLY, second son of Leonard, married Polly HAGAN, daughter of Henry HAGAN, and had these children: Mahala, married Washington MATTINGLY; Edward H., married Alethair SPALDING; Nancy, married A. J. MUDD; Mary Jane, married Joseph SPALDING; Henry, married Susan Jane SPALDING; and, Burrilla M., married J. W. MONTGOMERY. Luke, Leonard and William MATTINGLY were sons of Ignatius MATTINGLY (who died in 1789) of St. Mary's County, Maryland. Richard MATTINGLY was born in Maryland in 1756 and moved to Long Lick in (now) Breckinridge County, Kentucky in 1791. Joseph MATTINGLY was on Cartwright's Creek in (now) Washington County, Kentucky circa 1785 (Ref: KC:46-51; KC:80, 141; KB 1:152; KB 5:199; MMG 2:2, Fall, 1979, p. 89).

McADAMS. Jacob McADAMS was among the early Catholics who settled on Cartwright's Creek in (now) Washington County, Kentucky in 1785 (Ref: KC:80).

McADOW. John McADOW was born in 1745 in Harford County, Maryland and enlisted in 1777 for 4 years at Pittsburgh for the Maryland Line under Capt. Richard BROWN. He became a Sergeant during the Revolutionary War and subsequently moved to Kentucky. His pension seems to have been rejected (R6581) initially, but in Mason County,

Kentucky court in 1836, John appeared (age 91) and produced signed statements by William TURNER and Benjamin BEAN to verify his service. The court upheld the declaration that John McADOW was a veteran. In August, 1838, John McADOW's administrators were John McADOW, Larkin A. SANDIDGE, and David LINDSAY (Ref: KP:188-189; MS:65; HCP:143; MRR:34; Mason County, Kentucky Court Order Book M, October, 1836, p. 410, and Mason County, Kentucky Order Book Book N, August, 1838, p. 31).

McARDLE. John McARDLE and James McARDLE were among the early Catholic settlers to Kentucky from St. Mary's County, Maryland. They were Bardstown elders by 1820 (Ref: KC:63).

McATEE. Henry McATEE was among the early Catholic settlers from St. Mary's County, Maryland to settle in Kentucky in 1785. (Ref: KC:28)

Miss McATEE married Roswell BOARMAN in Maryland and migrated to Kentucky in 1812 with their son, Felix BOARMAN, to Lincoln County. (Ref: KB 5:55)

George McATEE married Miss HAMILTON in Maryland and migrated with the early Catholic settlers to Nelson County, Kentucky, and their daughter Ann McATEE married Henry STILES in Kentucky. (Ref: KB 5:266)

William McATEE was born June 20, 1793 in Maryland and married Clotilda ELDER, daughter of Aloysius ELDER and Elizabeth MILLS, in Frederick County, Maryland. He was a Bardstown elder in 1820 and died January 24, 1845 in Nelson County, Kentucky. (Ref: KC:63; MGS 16:2, May, 1975, p. 94)

Walter McATEE was born in Charles County, Maryland in 1756 and served in 1777 in the Maryland Militia. He later lived in Prince George's and Montgomery Counties, Maryland before moving to Nelson County, Kentucky in 1781. He applied for and received pension S31845 in 1832. Source RSK:133 erroenously states he served in the Pennsylvania Militia. (Ref: MRP:27; MS:60)

Benjamin L. McATEE, whose father came to America from Scotland in the mid-1770's and served in the Revolution, was born February 14, 1799 in Montgomery County, Maryland. The family moved to Bardstown in Nelson County, Kentucky in 1812 and Benjamin died in 1862 (Ref: BCK:595).

McBEE. Philip McBEE was born in Maryland on August 31, 1785 and died on March 25, 1864 and his wife Susannah was born in Maryland on March 7, 1788 and died on March 3, 1865. Their son, Walter McBEE was born in Maryland on February 24, 1816 and married Sarah CANNON, born October 8, 1817, on January 17, 1839. Walter and Sarah lived in Grant County, Kentucky. (McBee Family Bible record can be found in Source KB 8:106).

McCAWLEY. Thomas McCAWLEY was born in 1757 in Anne Arundel County, Maryland and served in the Revolutionary War there. He moved to

Harrison County, Kentucky in 1818 and in 1833 he applied for and received pension S31248 for war services in Virginia (Ref: MS:46; RSK:90. Note: Thomas McCAWLEY's name is spelled Thomas McCAULEY in John W. Gwathmey's Historical Register of Virginians in the Revolution, p. 515, Baltimore: Genealogical Publishing Co., 1973 reprint; originally published in Richmond, Virginia in 1938).

McCLURE. "The McClure family (of Woodford County, Kentucky) is of Irish origin, the original ancestor having immigrated from Ireland at an early day and settled in Baltimore, Maryland, where he became the father of eleven children. His son, James McCLURE, at the age of 12, left home with his parents consent and went to New Orleans where he tarried for a time and then walked to Kentucky through the Indian Territory and located in Woodford County. He served an apprenticeship to the tanner's trade, and when he had attained his majority, removed to Anderson County where he married the widow Nancy SMITH and entered upon the life of a farmer. He had three sons: William McCLURE, John McCLURE, and Virgil McCLURE. The first named immigrated to Missouri, taking with him a Kentucky wife, and died there. Virgil became a physician and located in Gallatin County, Kentucky and died in 1873. John passed his entire life in Anderson County and died in November, 1854." (Ref: KB 7:21)

Frank McCLURE married Matilda BEAN in Kentucky prior to 1820 (Ref: MRR:118).

McCOLLUM. John McCOLLUM was born in Kenton County, Kentucky in 1793 and died of cholera in 1849. His parents had moved to Kentucky from Maryland in the 1780's. His wife, Mary STEPHENS, was from Fairfax County, Virginia and their son, John J. McCOLLUM was born in 1842 in Kenton County, Kentucky (Ref: KB 8:108).

McCONNELL. Robert McCONNELL was born in Woodford County, Kentucky on November 17, 1818, the son of James McCONNELL of Fayette County, Kentucky, and Elizabeth VILEY of Scott County, Kentucky, both of Maryland born parents. (Ref: KB 7:75) James McCONNELL married Amanda SMITH after 1815 in Kentucky (Ref: MRR:118).

McCLOUD. John McCLOUD was born in Piscataway, Prince George's County, Maryland, on March 16, 1741 and lived in Fairfax County, Virginia at the time of the Revolutionary War. He stated in his pension application that he served under Capt. Charles LITTLE and guarded the home of General George WASHINGTON. He moved to Loudon County, Virginia and served again under Capt. Richard SPURR for ten months. He moved to Bourbon County, Kentucky in 1814. He applied for and received pension S13883 in 1833 (Ref: MS:11, RSK:43).

McCREADY. George W. McCREADY married in Maryland (wife's name not given) and was in Bracken County, Kentucky by 1820 where his son George J. McCREADY was born on February 20, 1820. By 1839 they were in Missouri (Ref: KM:32).

McCULLOUGH. William McCULLOUGH was a Revolutionary soldier from Harford County, Maryland who enlisted for 3 years in August, 1776 in Rawlings' Regiment in the Maryland Line. In Fleming County,

Kentucky on September 11, 1818, he applied for and received pension S36085, stating his age was 65. A letter from L. P. COOPER of Clark County, Illinois, dated Septeber 21, 1847, stated that William McCULLOUGH had died November 22, 1832 and his children all now lived in Indiana. (Ref: MS:35; KBG 7:1, Spring, 1980, p. 11; HCP:148; MRR:35).

McDANIEL. Joseph McDANIEL was among the early Catholic settlers from St. Mary's County, Maryland to settle in Washington County, Kentucky circa 1785 (Ref: KC:80).

McDOLL. The following notice appeared in the Elizabeth Town Advertiser (Maryland) on April 20, 1803: "Esther McDOLL, of Pine Creek, Lycoming County, Pennsylvania, young lady about 18, daughter and only child of Dr. John McDOLL of Kentucky, offers reward for Benjamin CONNET, about 22, middle size, swarthy complexion, long black hair tied with a ribbon, large mole over left eye, who stole gold watch and clothing" (Ref: WMNA #2, 1799-1805, p. 83).

McDOWELL. William McDOWELL was born in Maryland in 1761 and entered the Revolutionary War in Loudon County, Virginia in April, 1780 for three months and again in July, 1782. After the war he moved to Fairfax County, Virginia and then back to Loudon County. In 1809 he moved to Fayette County, Kentucky and in 1826 to Gallatin County, Kentucky. In 1833 he applied for and received pension S30580 (Ref: MS:40, RSK:77).

McGARY. William McGARY was born in 1769 in Ireland and came to America in 1790, settling in Hagerstown, Maryland where he married Ann DALY. He moved with his family to Bardstown, Kentucky in 1809. Their children born in Maryland were William, Ellen and John, and their children born in Kentucky were Mary, Margaret, Joseph, Martin, Elizabeth, Anselm and James. William moved to Breckinridge County in 1818 (Ref: KC:143).

McGILL. Thomas McGILL and Joseph McGILL were Catholics from Maryland and by 1810 were in Breckinridge County, Kentucky. Thomas McGILL and David McGILL were elders in Bardstown by 1820. Joseph McGILL lived in Anne Arundel County, Maryland circa 1800 and moved to Breckinridge County, Kentucky with children Thomas, Richard, John, Joseph, Mary W., Cody, and Susan Elder. Some of the children later moved to Meade County, Kentucky. Mary W. McGILL married Michael CODY (who was born circa 1795 in Ireland) in Kentucky circa 1825 (Ref: KC:63, 142; Information from Agnes Asscherick of Pasadena, Texas in the Anne Arundel County Genealogical Society Quarterly "Anne Arundel Speaks," 17:2, December, 1990, p. 32).

McGRAW. Christopher McGRAW enlisted as a Drummer in the 2nd Maryland Line in Winchester, Maryland in 1777 for 3 years and was discharged at Frederick, Maryland in 1780. He was born in 1751 and after the war he went to Pittsburgh circa 1780 and then to Fayette County, Kentucky circa 1790. He applied for and received pension S36096 in Jessamine County, Kentucky in 1821 (Ref: MS:34; RSK:65; KPR:1835).

McINTIRE. Thomas McINTIRE migrated from Maryland to Kentucky circa 1785 and his son John McINTIRE was born in Washington County, Kentucky (Ref: KB 5:130).

McKENZIE. The father of William McKENZIE came to American from Scotland and settled in Maryland, remaining there to the end of the Revolutionary War in which he served (name not given) and then removed to Kentucky. William McKENZIE (age 16) went by flatboat with his parents to Limestone, Kentucky and then on to Lexington where they stayed two years in Bryan's Station. They settled near Step's Cross Roads in Bourbon County, Kentucky. William McKENZIE served in the War of 1812. His son, John McKENZIE, was born March 19, 1798, married Sallie NIEL, and moved to Clark County and then Shelby County in 1830, where he died in 1870 (Ref: KB 7:211).

McMILLEN. Daniel McMILLEN married Jane SCONCE on January 17, 1811 in Cumberland County, Kentucky (Ref: MRR:119).

McPHERSON. Mark McPHERSON was a Sergeant and Lieutenant in the Maryland Line during the Revolutionary War. He married Mary MIDDLETON circa 1785 in Charles County, Maryland. In 1818 he received a pension (age 80) in Lincoln County, Kentucky. (Ref: RSK:108; KPR:1835; MRR:36, 119).

McREYNOLDS. Robert McREYNOLDS and wife Sally McDANIEL were natives of Maryland who moved to Virginia and then Kentucky in an early day. He founded one of the first Methodist Episcopal camp grounds in the state on his own farm. His father (name not given) came to America from Ireland, but was born in Scotland. M. M. McREYNOLDS, daughter of Robert, married Dr. A. S. WALKER who was born in Jessamine County, Kentucky on January 4, 1811 (Ref: KB 4:248).

MEDLEY. Ignatius MEDLEY, Thomas MEDLEY and John MEDLEY were early Catholic settlers from St. Mary's County, Maryland who settled on Hardin's Creek in Washington County, Kentucky in 1786. (Ref: KC:54, 56) Ignatius MEDLEY married Sarah BOONE, daughter of Harry BOONE, upon his arrival in Kentucky. They were related to the Cecil family of Maryland and Kentucky. (Ref: KB 5:80)

John L. MEDLEY married Ann ATWOOD; both were from Baltimore, and they were early settlers in Nelson County, Kentucky, having brought 50 slaves with them from Maryland. These Medleys were related to the Hill family of Bardstown (Ref: KC 5:152).

MEEK. Basil MEEK was born in 1740 in Maryland and enlisted in the Revolutionary War in 1777 under Capt. Hugh STINSON in the Frederick County, Virginia Militia. He also fought the Indians and served as a Spy at Fort Pitt, around Redstone, Pennsylvania. When Basil applied for his pension in Henry County, Kentucky in 1833, he stated he had been in Kentucky for 25 years. His service was substantiated by statements from Jesse MEEK and Edmund P. THOMAS (Ref: MS:49, RSK:95).

MEFFORD. The family of Jacob MEFFORD came to America from France. Jacob was born in 1764 and enlisted in Frederick County, Maryland on February 3, 1781 in Capt. CLAGGETT's Company, and was discharged in August, 1783. In 1786 he moved to Kentucky and then down to "Orleans." In 1792 he returned to his father's home in Maryland, and in 1793 he returned to Kentucky. He married Eleanor -----, on August 20, 1793 in Scott County, Kentucky. He applied for a pension in 1819 and it was granted in 1824 while he resided in Campbell County, Kentucky. In 1829 the children of Jacob MEFFORD were named and aged as follows: Polly, 26; Ellen, 27; Thompson, 12; Nancy, 10; William, 7; Jackson, 4; and, Malissa, 2. It appears he had two others not named. Jacob stated his father had raised eight sons and two of them were William and John MEFFORD of Baltimore. He stated that John also served in the Revolution and William was a Seaman. Jacob MEFFORD died on December 14, 1844 in Campbell County, Kentucky. His widow, Eleanor, applied for and was granted pension W9562 in 1848 (at age 72) while living in Lawrence County, Indiana (Ref: MS:19; RSK:52; MRR:37; KPR:1835).

MELONE, MELOAN. Andrew MELONE was born February 18, 1754 in Cecil County, Maryland, and enlisted in 1775 in the 2nd Maryland Regiment under Capt. VEAZEY. He reenlisted in 1777 for three years and fought in the Battles of Long Island, Trenton, Staten Island, Brandywine, Germantown, Princeton, White Plains, Stoney Point, and Monmouth. He married Rachel OZIER (born May 23, 1753) in 1781 or 1782 in Maryland. She had been married to Mr. YELEFRAU and had three children by him: Sarah, born March 3, 1775; Mary, born January 7, 1777; and, John, born December 20, 1778. Rachel YELEFRAU married Andrew MELONE and had these children: Thomas, born November 24, 1784; Elizabeth, born October 1, 1786; Andrew, Jr., born October 22, 1788; Isabel, born July 13, 1790; Obadiah, born October 2, 1792 and married E. W. SCRUGGS on May 8, 1828; and, Alex, born in December, 1794. Andrew MELONE and family moved to Kentucky circa 1808 and settled in Calloway County, Kentucky. Andrew applied for a pension and received it in 1828. He died in August, 1834 and his widow applied and received pension W27972. She died on July 29, 1839. Their heirs applied for a pension in 1853, namely Thomas MELONE, age 70; Elizabeth LOCKRIDGE, age 68; and, Obadiah A. MELONE, age 60 (Ref: MS:24-25; MRP:28; RSK:51; KPR:1835; MRR:119).

MELTON. Stanislaus MELTON was among the early Catholics who migrated from St. Mary's County, Maryland and settled in Nelson County, Kentucky in 1785 (Ref: KC:28).

MERRIMAN. John MERRIMAN of Maryland was an elder in Bardstown, Kentucky circa 1820 (Ref: KC:63).

MERRIOTT. William H. MERRIOTT was born in Baltimore, Maryland on February 11, 1816 and moved to Jessamine County, Kentucky in 1828, where he was a wagon maker (Ref: KB 7:80).

METCALF. Thomas METCALF was born and raised in Maryland and lost his father when only four years old and his mother (no names or dates given) a few years later. He had 4 brothers: Charles, of Bardstown, Kentucky; Elisha, of Louisville, Kentucky; William, of Lexington, Kentucky; and, John, of Covington, Kentucky; and a sister, Patsy BARR, of Lexington, Kentucky. Thomas METCALF married

Margaret HUTCHINSON and their children were: Western M. METCALF;
Tilford METCALF; James H. METCALF, born September 1, 1815 in
Fayette County, Kentucky; Archibald METCALF; John METCALF; William
METCALF; Thomas METCALF; Cordelia Metcalf MOORHEAD; Letetia Metcalf
MOORHEAD; Parthenia VALLANDINGHAM; Marth FISK; and Catherine
SHEWMAKER. Thomas METCALF died in 1874 in Grant County, Kentucky
(Ref: KB 8:113-114).

MILES. Philip MILES and son Harry or Henry MILES was among the
early Catholics who migrated from St. Mary's County, Maryland to
Kentucky, along with Barton MILES and John S. MILES who were on
Hardin's Creek in Washington County, Kentucky between 1785 and
1788. They migrated with the Hill family, with whom they were
related. (Ref: KB 5:150; KC:30; KC:68-69; KC:56; KB 5:205)

Nicholas MILES was on Cox's Creek in Nelson County prior to 1800.
(Ref: KC:117)

Dorothy MILES married John JOHNSON in St. Mary's County, Maryland
and migrated to Nelson County, Kentucky in 1798. (Ref: KB 5:25; KB
9:88)

Jesse MILES was born in Prince George's County, Maryland on July
1, 1763 and was drafted into the Revolutionary War in 1781 in
Berkeley County, Virginia and also served as a substitute for his
father under Capt. John VANMETER. He moved to Nelson County,
Kentucky and in 1833 Jesse MILES applied for and received a pension
in Bullitt County, Kentucky. (Ref: MS:17; RSK:47)

John MILES was born in 1733 in Maryland and enlisted in 1777 in
Frederick County under Capt. Jarrett BRISCOE in the 6th Maryland
Regiment for 3 years. He moved to Green County, Kentucky and
applied for and received pension S36138 in 1818. He died on March
17, 1827 (Ref: MS:53; MRP:28; RSK:83; KPR:1835 Kentucky Pension
Rolls state his name was "John Miles 2nd." Also, Source MS:53
states his pension number was S36139).

MILLER. David MILLER, son of Joseph MILLER of Ireland, was born in
Calvert County, Maryland and migrated to Kentucky in 1798. He
married Dorcas HOLLIDAY and their son, David A. MILLER, was born
August 19, 1801 in Ohio County, Kentucky. (Ref: KB 3:169)

Michael MILLER also went to Kentucky at an early date and married
Sarah DAUGHERTY. Their son, Joseph MILLER, was born November 16,
1809 in Trimble County, Kentucky. They moved to Orange County,
Indiana in 1815, then in 1836 to Missouri, to Indiana in 1838, and
back to Kentucky after the Mexican War of 1846, in which Joseph
participated. (Ref: 7:218)

James MILLER (name originally "MILLES") was a soldier in the
Revolutionary War in Harford County, Maryland. (Ref: HCP:159) In
1781 he married Mary MARTIN and between 1783 and 1828 they lived
in Pennsylvania, Maryland, Virginia, Kentucky, Ohio and Indiana.
James MILLER died in 1828 in Indiana. His children were: Martin
MILLER, Martha HOLMES, Margaret BULL, Mary CROMWELL, William

MILLER, James W. MILLER, Nancy KNOTT, Samuel MILLER, and possibly George MILLER. (Ref: MGS 14:2, May, 1973, p. 13; MM-2, p. 157)

John MILLER was born July 16, 1763 in Pennsylvania, lived in Montgomery County, Maryland, and enlisted at Fredericktown in 1781 under Capt. Joseph WARD. In 1790 he moved to Surry County, North Carolina and married Eleanor GARNER, daughter of John, on September 7, 1796, by Rev. Lazarus WHITEHEAD. Their children were: Jacob MILLER, 1798-1803; Martin MILLER, born November 4, 1800; Nancy Miller PEASEY, born September 5, 1803; and one child died in infancy. John MILLER moved to Cumberland County, Kentucky in 1810 or 1812 and received a pension in 1831. He died September 14, 1845 in Clinton County, Kentucky and his widow received pension W2647 (Ref: MS:32; RSK:62; KPR:1835; MRR:119).

MILLNER. Nicholas MILLNER was born in Harford County, Maryland on June 22, 1762 and enlisted in Washington County, Pennsylvania in 1776. After the war he married Hannah -----, near the Monongahela River in Pennsylvania, and they moved to Harrison County, Kentucky. He applied for and received a pension in 1833; children not named. His widow filed in 1836 and received pension W3028 (Ref: MS:46; RSK:90).

MILLS. Joseph MILLS was an early Catholic settler from St. Mary's County, Maryland to Washington County, Kentucky in 1785, as were John MILLS on Hardin's Creek circa 1786, and Ignatius MILLS and Bernard MILLS on Rolling Creek (Ref: KC:28, 56, 111)

Timothy B. MILLS was born in Maryland on May 13, 1797, married Mary PAYNE on March 28, 1826, and died on March 28, 1873 in Spencer County, Kentucky. Mary Payne MILLS was born on March 2, 1804 and died on August 8, 1871. (Ref: KB 7:162)

Elizabeth MILLS of Maryland married Gerard BANKS of Virginia and their son H. P. BROOKS was born in Garrard County, Kentucky on July 7, 1818. They were in Missouri by 1831. (Ref: KM:67)

William MILLS was born in 1751 or 1756 in Worcester County, Maryland and enlisted on July 15, 1780 in the Snow Hill Battalion under Capt. James PATTERSON and Col. John DANIELS. He married Miss PORTER and their son William P. MILLS served in the Maryland Militia in the War of 1812. They moved to Jefferson County, Kentucky in 1815, where William P. MILLS married Mary E. MOORE, daughter of Thomas MOORE of Delaware. Dr. Samuel B. MILLER, son of William and Mary MILLS, was born March 9, 1828 in Jefferson County, Kentucky. William MILLS filed for a pension for his Revolutionary War service but it was rejected (R7251) according to Sources MRP:29 and MS:53, although Source MRR:38 states he was a pensioner (Ref: MRP:29; MS:53; BCK:181-182; MRR:38).

MITCHELL. Ignatius MITCHELL was born in Baltimore County, Maryland and died in Mason County, Kentucky in March, 1826. He was a Sergeant in the Revolutionary War from 1777 to 1780 and received a land patent in Mason (then Bourbon) County, Kentucky on February 8, 1780. His wife was Mildred SMITH and their children were:

Charles Smith MITCHELL, Mildred E. ROBINSON, Richard B. MITCHELL, Martha ALLEN, and Ignatius MITCHELL, Jr., 1799-1882. (Ref: KP:7-9; Archives of Maryland, Vol. 18, p. 137; Mitchell Genealogical Chart compiled by William V. Norris III of New York in 1979 and on file at the Maryland Historical Society in Baltimore)

Rev. Thomas MITCHELL married Rebecca KETCHAM of Maryland and their son Thomas MITCHELL was born on October 11, 1818 in Shelby County, Kentucky. They were in Missouri by 1855. (Ref KM:149)

Dr. James A. MITCHELL was born in 1792 in Maryland and went to Kentucky in 1817. He graduated from St. Mary's College at Georgetown, Kentucky and practiced medicine and preached religion until his death on September 7, 1875. (Ref: KB 3:169)

Richard MITCHELL was also a native of Maryland and he settled in Fayette County, Kentucky in the 1790's. His son, Boswell MITCHELL, was born in Kentucky and his grandson, George S. MITCHELL, was born May 23, 1813 in Fayette County near the Clark County line (Ref: KB 7:82).

MOBBERLY. William MOBBERLY was born in western Maryland in 1808 and moved to Nelson County, Kentucky in his boyhood. He married Sarah CURTSINGER in 1830 in Washington County, and their children were Mary E., Lewis T., John W., N. B., William M., Sarah E., Susan E., and Matthew M. He died in Taylor County after 1885. His wife died in 1876 (Ref: KB 1:46).

MOLEN. Philip MOLEN was born circa 1735 in Maryland and married Mary -----, in Henry County, Virginia. Their children were: Hezekiah, born 1777; Aquilla, born 1779; Joseph; Nellie; Prissie; and, Nancie. Philip died in Wayne County, Kentucky (Ref: MGS 15:1, February, 1974, p. 18).

MOLLAHORNE. James MOLLAHORNE (MOLLIHORNE) was among the early Catholic settlers from St. Mary's County, Maryland to move to Washington County, Kentucky and settle on Hardin's Creek and Pottinger's Creek in 1785. He was the first adult of the original settlers to be buried in the Holy Cross Cemetery in 1801 (Ref: KC:28, 30, 56).

MONTGOMERY. James, John, Bernard, and Jeremiah MONTGOMERY were early settlers on Cartwright's Creek in Washington County, Kentucky, having moved there from St. Mary's County, Maryland prior to 1800. Austin MONTGOMERY was on Cox's Creek at that same time. Jeremiah MONTGOMERY was born November 17, 1781 in Maryland and married Anne ALVEY in Kentucky on April 5, 1806. He died in Washington County on April 8, 1871 and is buried at St. Rose. (Ref: KC:79-80; KC:114; KA 5:1, July, 1969, p. 50)

The father of William W. MONTGOMERY was born in Ireland (no name given) and came to America in 1792 and settled in Baltimore, Maryland where he worked as a clerk. He migrated to Hardin County, Kentucky where his only child, William W. MONTGOMERY, was born in 1809 and died in 1868. His wife was Catherine A. BROOKS (1811-1882) of Virginia. (Ref: KB 1:46)

MONTGOMERY moved from Maryland to Ohio County, Kentucky in an early day. His daughter, Nancy MONTGOMERY, married Samuel T. HOWARD and their son, Nathaniel HOWARD, was born January 12, 1830 in Ohio County (Ref: KB 3:66).

MOORE. Alexander MOORE was a Catholic and a house builder by trade. He served in the War of 1812, notably in the defense of Baltimore. He moved to Bardstown, Kentucky after that war. (Ref: KC:63)

John MOORE was born in Delaware on February 27, 1752 and served as a Lieutenant in the Virginia Militia during the Revolutionary War. He married Margaret BLACK (born January 27, 1753 in Maryland) and their children were: James, born February 28, 1808 in Bourbon County, Kentucky; John, Jr.; William; Sarah; Mary; Abraham; and, Margaret. John MOORE married secondly to Mrs. Elizabeth KIMBROUGH of Bourbon County. He died April 16, 1830 at Ruddles Mills, Kentucky. (Ref: DAR:477; Information from Margaret Henley of Oklahoma City, as published in KBG, 7:1, Spring, 1980, p. 22) Edward MOORE, son of William and Mary MOORE, was born in Queen Anne's County, Maryland on January 23, 1737 and married Amy ASHLEY on April 11, 1757 at Church Hill, Maryland. They lived in Kent County, Delaware, and Surry County, North Carolina, and Lincoln County, Kentucky. (Ref: MGS 24:2, Spring, 1983, p. 168)

Thomas MOORE was born in St. Paul's Parish, Kent County, Maryland, on March 7, 1745, the youngest son of William MOORE and wife Rachel MEDFORD. He moved to Tyrone Township, Fayette County, Pennsylvania in 1769, where he married Mary HARRISON, a daughter of Lawrence HARRISON, of the Virginia Harrisons. Thomas MOORE was a Lieutenant in the 13th Virginia Regiment in the Revolutionary War and a Captain in the 9th Virginia Regiment. After the war he served with Gen. George Rogers CLARK in Illinois. In 1802 he retired from the Kentucky Militia with the rank of Major. He was an early settler in Harrison County, Kentucky, where he died testate in January, 1824. (Ref: Article by Dr. Emmett Waits published in KA 10:2, October, 1974, pp. 73-76)

Col. James Francis MOORE, son of James MOORE and Hannah WILLMOTT, was born in Baltimore County, Maryland on August 12, 1751 and married there on February 18, 1773 to Ann STANDIFORD, daughter of William and Elizabeth STANDIFORD. They moved that same year to Bedford County, Pennsylvania. James Francis MOORE was commissioned a Lieutenant in the 12th Pennsylvania Line on March 19, 1776 and became a Captain in the 13th Pennsylvania Line, before being transferred to the 8th Pennsylvania Line in 1778 and discharged on August 2, 1779. He went to Kentucky thereafter and subsequently became Deputy Commissary General for Gen. George Rogers CLARK. He later became Trustee for Harrodsburg and Louisville in 1789. He died while attending the Kentucky Legislature on December 9, 1809. His daughter, Elizabeth, had been taken to her uncle, Nicholas Ruxton MOORE, in Baltimore County, Maryland in the Fall of 1786. She later returned to Kentucky and married Jesse PRENDERGAST in 1797. Col. James Francis MOORE's second wife was Elizabeth HIGGINS and among their children was Zerruih MOORE who married John JONES in Jefferson County, Kentucky in 1803. Additionally, Sarah MOORE, wife of John HARROD, was possibly a daughter of James MOORE and Frances GAY of Baltimore County, Maryland (Ref: "Harrod Family Genealogy and the Moore Family," by Bernice L. Swainson in the Filson Club Quarterly, Vol. XXXII (1958), pp. 107-133, and published in Genealogies of Kentucky Families, 1981, pp. 609-637).

MORGAN. Benjamin MORGAN was among the early Catholics from St. Mary's County, Maryland who settled on Rolling Fork, Kentucky prior to 1800. (Ref: KC:111)

John MORGAN and Thomas MORGAN were twin brothers born in St. Mary's County, Maryland on September 22, 1761. They both served in the Dorchester County, Maryland militia during the Revolutionary War. Thomas joined in 1776 or 1777 and John joined in 1780. In 1794 John MORGAN moved to Kentucky and in 1832 he applied for and received pension S1238 in Oldham County. His brother Thomas MORGAN moved to Kentucky in 1806 and he applied in 1828 for and received pension S2859 in Oldham County, later moving to Trimble County (Ref: MS:55; MS:61; KPR:1835; MRR:39)

On February 10, 1791, Nathaniel MORGAN advertised in the Washington Spy in Maryland that he had land for sale in Kentucky (Ref: WMNA #1, 1786-1798, p. 29).

MORTON. Isaac MORTON moved from Maryland to Hartford, Kentucky with his parents circa 1800. He married Sarah H. SHANKS and their son James S. MORTON (third of ten children) was born May 24, 1828 in Hartford, Kentucky (Ref: KB 3:172).

MOURNIN. Sarah MOURNIN, of Maryland, married Edwin CARLTON, of Maryland, and their daughter Eliza CARLTON, a native of Virginia, married Thomas FOSTER (born 1804) and moved to Kentucky. Their son, Robert E. FOSTER, was born in Gallatin County, Kentucky on May 3, 1830 and became a Druggist and Postmaster at Glencoe, Kentucky (Ref: KB 8:61).

MOXLEY. Nehemiah MOXLEY (1737-1836) of Elkridge, Maryland, married Elizabeth NORWOOD, and three of their sons, William, Ezekiel, and Jacob, settled in Montgomery County, Maryland. In the early 1800's their descendants moved to Kentucky, Ohio and other points west. Nehemiah MOXLEY participated in the burning of the brig "Peggy Stewart" in Annapolis during the Revolutionary War in protest over tea taxes. (For additional information see the book entitled Nehemiah Moxley, His Clagettsville Sons and Their Descendants compiled by Mrs. Allie May Moxley Burton of Damascus, Maryland in 1990. Also, lineage information in Sons of the American Revolution, Maryland Society No. 1749, approved application papers of Ira Dorsey Watkins in 1949).

MUDD. The Mudd family migrated from St. Mary's County, Maryland to Washington County, Kentucky with the Catholic league in 1785. William MUDD, Andrew MUDD, Luke MUDD, Ignatius MUDD, and Joseph MUDD settled on Hardin's Creek. Thomas MUDD and Raphael R. MUDD settled on Cartwright's Creek. (Ref: KC:28, 54, 56, 80)

James MUDD was probably born in Maryland circa 1790 and married Sarah SWEARINGEN in Jefferson County, Kentucky on January 27, 1816. He died in Alabama on February 13, 1847. Nicholas MUDD was born near Bryantown, Maryland in 1772 and married (1) Eleanor BURCH in Washington County, Kentucky in 1800; (2) Eleanor FERGUSON in Washington County, Kentucky in 1803; (3) Ann SEMMES in Bardstown, Kentucky in 1811. He died in 1823. John Thomas MUDD was born in Maryland circa 1795 and married in 1818 to Ann Ellen QUEEN in Nelson County, Kentucky. (Ref: Maryland Historical and Genealogical Bulletin, Vol. 21. No. 1, p. 15) Nicholas MUDD of Maryland married Martha JANES of Virginia and their son Robert MUDD was born October 9, 1817 in Washington County, Kentucky. They were in Missouri by 1843, and Dr. James R. MUDD was there by 1849 (Ref: KM:161).

MUIR. Dr. William MUIR was born in Scotland in 1754 and came to America prior to 1795 and settled in Maryland. His daughter, Mary S. MUIR, was born in Virginia in February, 1796, and Dr. Muir moved to Nelson County, Kentucky in 1802. He died there in 1836 or 1838. Mary S. MUIR married William McGILL in 1819. Jasper MUIR, son of Dr. William Muir, was born in Maryland and married Isabella BROWN, daughter of Peter BROWN of Maryland, in Nelson County, Kentucky. Their son, Peter B. MUIR, was born October 19, 1822 in Kentucky and married Sophronia RIZER. Jasper died in 1830 and Isabella in 1833. (Ref: KB 1:140, BCK:10-11)

Margaret C. MUIR, of Maryland, married James M. ROGERS, of Kentucky, on November 11, 1824 in Bardstown, Kentucky, and their son, William M. ROGERS, was born in Owensboro, Kentucky on October 31, 1825 (Ref: KB 7:232).

MULLICAN. John H. MULLICAN was born near Emmittsburg, Maryland circa 1795 and moved to Washington County, Kentucky when very young. His father was a native of Ireland. John H. MULLICAN married Susan HAYDEN, daughter of Stanley HAYDEN, who was born in 1795 and died in 1878 in Nelson County, Kentucky. Their son, John Simeon MULLICAN, was born on March 22, 1838 and became Sheriff of Daviess County, Kentucky (Ref: BCK:484-485).

MURPHY. Abner MURPHY (Orthodox Quaker) was born circa 1775 in Maryland. His father (Irish Quaker) had migrated from Northern Ireland to Maryland in 1773. Abner MURPHY married Sarah GATTAN (born 1775, Dundee, Scotland; died 1853, Knox County, Ohio) and their children were: Hiram, Robert, William, Jane, Mary, Basil, Rachel, Eleanor, Sallie, and Elias. William MURPHY was born April 17, 1804 in Maryland and married Sarah Ann McKINNEY in 1830. Their son, Abner Goff MURPHY, was born October 18, 1831 and became President of Logan Female Academy in Russellville, Kentucky. (Ref: BCK:64)

Hezekiah MURPHY married Sarah COTTON on April 17, 1794 in Nelson County, Kentucky (Ref: MRR:120).

MURRAY. Col. John MURRAY served in the War of 1812 and was a native

of Maryland. He moved to Washington County, Kentucky after the war.
His daughter, Minerva J. MURRAY, was born in Kentucky and married
John M. BROWN (Ref: KB 9:11).

NALLY, NALLEY. Bernard NALLY was among the early Catholics who
migrated from St. Mary's County, Maryland to Washington County,
Kentucky in 1785. (Ref: KC:28)

John NALLEY was born in Maryland in May, 1786 and went to Nelson
County, Kentucky in 1787 with his uncle (no name given) and died
in 1863 in McLean County, Kentucky. He married Ruth TAYLOR (1793-
1875), daughter of Philip TAYLOR, in 1808 and left descendants in
Daviess, Ohio, and McLean Counties. A son, Allison NALLEY, was born
in 1825 (Ref: KB 3:73; KA 8:1, July, 1972, p. 54).

NASH. Noble NASH was born in Maryland. He moved to Bagdad, Kentucky
prior to 1800. His son, Harmon NASH, was born in 1803 in Shelby
County and married Sarah GATES, daughter of Elijah GATES of
Georgia. Their son, Dr. Noble F. NASH, was born in 1831 (Ref: KB
7:223).

NAYLOR. Nicholas NAYLOR enlisted in Prince George's County,
Maryland on January 22, 1776 in the Revolutionary War and served
under Capt. George STRICKER in the 9th Company of Light Infantry.
He became a Sergeant and also served in the 1st Maryland Line. He
married Mary SELBY, a daughter of William Magruder SELBY and Martha
WILSON, on February 15, 1783. Nicholas NALER (NAYLOR) appears on
the Fayette County, Kentucky Tax List on July 2, 1789. The Fayette
County deposition of Isaac NAYLOR, age 56 on November 13, 1805
stated his brother was Nicholas NAYLOR. Prior to 1797 Nicholas
NAYLOR was guardian of the children of Thomas LEVENS of Washington
County, Pennsylvania. Ann LEVENS was a niece of Thomas SELBY, and
Mary SELBY, wife of Nicholas NAYLOR, has a brother Thomas SELBY.
In Green County in 1797, Thomas and Rebecca SELBY granted power of
attorney to Richard LEVENS of Bullitt County, Kentucky to represent
their interests in the estate of Thomas LEVENS of Washington
County, Pennsylvania. Nicholas NAYLOR, Benjamin NAYLOR and James
NAYLOR appear in Adair County (originally part of Green County,
Kentucky) in 1801. Nicholas sold his land in 1806 and moved to
Barren County, Kentucky. Benjamin NAYLOR married Deborah SELBY, a
daughter of William Wilson SELBY, in Prince George's County,
Maryland on August 31, 1785 and was in the Green County, Kentucky
militia in 1799. His will in 1834 in Adair County, named children
Elizabeth, Samuel, William, James, Deborah, Reason, Benjamin,
Alexander and Otha. James NAYLOR was born in March, 1771, in Prince
George's County, Maryland and married Sarah SELBY (1779-1861),
daughter of James Wilson SELBY, on February 5, 1798 in Green
County, Kentucky. James NAYLOR died July 11, 1835 in Williamson
County, Tennessee. His children were Mary, Joshua, Rachel,
Elizabeth, James, Phebe, Sarah and Lydia (twins), Susanna,
Alexander and Lavinia. George NAYLOR married Eleanor BERRY on June
2, 1785 in Prince George's County, Maryland. George Truman NAYLOR
was born in Maryland on June 10, 1786 and his father, George
NAYLOR, moved to Albemarle County, Virginia, married secondly to
Jane NEWCOMB on November 22, 1793. They moved to Garrard County,

Kentucky and appear in the 1810 and 1820 census records. George NAYLOR was a son of Batson NAYLOR (died 1769) and Margaret FIELDS, who was a daughter of Elisha FIELDS. George Truman NAYLOR moved to Missouri in 1827. (Ref: KA 20:1, p. 40; MM-2:165; Archives of Maryland, Vol. 18, pp. 19, 146; and research by Henry A. Naylor, Jr. of Baltimore, Maryland, Mary S. Naylor of White Pigeon, Michigan and Mary K. McCaffree of Jefferson City, Missouri, 1985-1987).

NEALE. Thomas and Letty NEALE, of Maryland, settled about 1787 in Bourbon County, Kentucky. His will was written on February 2, 1820 and probated in March, 1823. His children were: Anna NEALE, married Edward ORTON; Rebecca NEALE, married Elijah AMOS; Martha NEALE, married Ditto AMOS; Fanny NEALE, married Thomas ELLIS; Joseph NEALE; James NEALE, married Elizabeth HORNBACK; Sally NEALE, married Henry ASHCRAFT; Thomas NEALE, Jr., married Juliann BEVANS; Lettie NEALE, married James ELLIS; Rosemary NEALE, married James BARNETT; and, Nancy NEALE, married William ELLIS (Ref: The Amos Family, by Maurine Schmitz and Glendola Peck, p. 21, copy available at the Maryland Historical Society, 1964).

NEELEY. James NEELEY and David NEELEY were among the early Catholic settlers from St. Mary's County, Maryland to settle on Cartwright's Creek in Washington County, Kentucky prior to 1800 (Ref: KC:80).

NEIKIRK. John NEIKIRK was born in Hagerstown, Maryland and went to Kentucky with the Aker family prior to 1815. He was a blacksmith by trade in Maryland and in Pulaski County, Kentucky. He died in 1859. His son, William NEIKIRK (second of fifteen children) was born on October 19, 1819 in Pulaski County, and became a Methodist Episopal Minister (Ref: KB 5:220).

NEWBOLT. John NEWBOLT was born in Maryland and migrated to Kentucky before 1800 with the Roberts and Spalding families, and settled near Lebanon. His son, William NEWBOLT, was born in 1800 in Nelson County, Kentucky, married Cecilia PENICK (1810-1875) in 1828, and died in 1860 (Ref: KB 5:221).

NEWTON. John NEWTON was born in 1756 and enlisted into the 2nd Maryland Regiment in Anne Arundel County in October, 1776, under Capt. John SMITH, and served for six years and nine months. He moved to Kentucky and applied for and received pension S35536 in Hardin County in 1819. He died February 9, 1830 (Ref: MS:45; MRP:30; RSK:87; MRR:40).

NICHOLLS. Henry NICHOLLS was born in Maryland in 1772 and went to Kentucky as a young man, settling in Nelson County. In 1814 he married Catherine HARRIS and they had two sons and two daughters, one of whom was Henry M. NICHOLLS, born in November, 1829 (Ref: KB 5:221).

NOE. Samuel NOE was the son of James NOE who located in Bourbon County, Kentucky in an early day, and was the son of Aquilla NOE, of Scotland, who came to American and settled in Maryland. His sons, James, John and Aquilla, migrated to the South. Samuel NOE married Mary HUGHES (Ref: KB 3:73).

NOLAND, NOLAN. James NOLAND was born in Charles County, Maryland in 1740 and moved to Loudon County, Virginia where he married Barbara -----, on December 26, 1774. She was only 14 or 15 when they married. She was born May 28, 1759 or 1760. In 1775 James enlisted for 12 months. He was a Captain and in his pension application he states the Tories had a $500 price tag on his head. They later moved on to Rowan County, North Carolina and then to Estill County, Kentucky in 1812. He applied for and received a pension for his services. After his death on December 26, 1833, his widow applied and received pension W9202. The pension record shows these children: Stephen NOLAND, born June 6, 1776; Silas NOLAND, born October 11, 1778; Rasha NOLAND, born July 29, 1781; Francis NOLAND, born in 1784; two other children not named; and, John NOLAND, born June 9, 1792. Barbara NOLAND was living in LaPorte County, Indiana in September, 1844, with her children. (Ref: MS:33-34; RSK:64; MRP:30) Jesse NOLAND was a brother of James NOLAND. He was born in Charles County, Maryland in 1761 and enlisted in 1780 for 3 years in Rowan County, North Carolina, but with the Tories being so bad, he moved with his widowed mother to Virginia and then came back in 1781 and volunteered again. He went to Kentucky in 1784 to Estill County, where he applied for and received pension S14039 in 1832 (Ref: MS:33; RSK:64).

NORRIS. Henry NORRIS and Rudolphus NORRIS were among the early Catholic settlers who went from St. Mary's County, Maryland to Washington County, Kentucky in 1785, settling on Pottinger's Creek. (Ref: KC:28, 30)

William NORRIS was a native of Maryland and an early settler of Pendleton County, Kentucky. His daughter, Frances A. NORRIS, was born in that county (died 1889) and married John H. FRYER (1833- -c1900) of Butler, Kentucky, and a son of Walter FRYER of Scotland who migrated to Kentucky in an early day (Ref: BCK:243).

OARD. William OARD was born in Maryland in 1754 and was a soldier in the Revolutionary War. He went to Washington County, Kentucky circa 1800-1810 and then to Clark County, Indiana circa 1815. He died in 1833 in Parke County, Indiana. His children were Lucinda HOGAN, John OARD, Sarah BULLOCK, and Augustus OARD (Ref: KA 12:1, July, 1976, p. 44).

O'BRYAN. Henry O'BRYAN was born in Charles County, Maryland in 1783 and moved with his parents to Nelson County, Kentucky in 1792. He married Mary McATEE in Kentucky on November 27, 1809. A hatter by trade, he died December 24, 1858. (Ref: KA 11:3, January, 1976, p. 163)

Peter O'BRYAN married Jane GARDNER and moved to Nelson County, Kentucky from St. Mary's or Charles County, Maryland, with his two sons, Lewis and William (Ref: KPG 1:4, Oct., 1979, p. 55).

O'CONNOR. Thomas O'CONNOR was born in Maryland in 1736 or 1746 and enlisted in the 1st Maryland Regiment in 1776 under Capt. Patrick

SIMMS. He moved to Nelson County, Kentucky and applied for and received pension S35541 in 1818 (Ref: MS:59; MRP:30; RSK:132; KPR:1835; MRR:40).

O'DANIEL. John O' DANIEL was born in 1757 and was a Private in the militia in Virginia service. He married Sarah RUDE on April 10, 1794 in Nelson County, Kentucky. Their marriage was proven through his Maryland Revolutionary War pension application, according to Source MRR:120 (Ref: MRR:40).

OFFUTT. Augustine OFFUTT and Z. B. OFFUTT were among the early Catholic settlers who migrated from St. Mary's County, Maryland to Cartwright's Creek in Washington County, Kentucky prior to 1800. (Ref: KC:80)

Andrew OFFUTT was born in Maryland in 1773 and married Elizabeth WARFIELD in 1802. They later went to Kentucky and settled in Spencer County. (Ref: A 1946 letter from Mrs. William E. Bach of Lexington, Kentucky, contained in the Layton Genealogical Collection, G5077, Box 8, at the Maryland Historical Society)

Ruth C. OFFUTT was born in Maryland in 1801, married John SHOEMAKER (born 1787 in Pittsburgh and died 1852 in Spencer County, Kentucky) and their son, Dr. Thomas Jefferson SHOEMAKER, was born in Spencer County on June 5, 1837 (Ref: KB 4:257).

OGDEN. Benjamin OGDEN was born in Baskinridge, New Jersey in April, 1764 and enlisted in 1778 or 1779 under Capt. MITCHELL. His guardian demanded and secured his release because of his youth. In 1780, at age 16, he enlisted under Capt. FREEMAN and served to the surrender of Cornwallis in 1781. He moved to Baltimore, Maryland in 1783 and lived with his brother, Col. Amos OGDEN, until 1784. In 1785 he became "a Methodist itinerant preacher." In 1832 he applied for and received pension S31281 ($80 a year) while residing in Caldwell County, Kentucky (Ref: MS:23; RSK:50).

O'HARA. James O'HARA, a native of Ireland, came to America in 1798 and settled in Maryland. In 1820 he went to Kentucky and settled in Woodford County, where he studied law. He removed to Owen County and practiced his profession. His wife was Lucy HARDY, of Scott County (Ref: KB 8:124).

OLIVER. Nathan OLIVER was born in Maryland circa 1785 and was possibly a son of Leven OLIVER. He lived in Price George's County, Maryland in 1810 and went to Kentucky thereafter (Ref: MGS 24:4, Fall, 1983, p. 369).

O'NEIL. Jonas O'NEIL and Thomas O'NEIL were among the early Catholic settlers from St. Mary's County, Maryland who went to Cartwright's Creek in Washington County, Kentucky before 1800 (Ref: KC:80).

ORENDORF. "Driven from Germany by Louis XIV on account of their religious beliefs, the Orendorfs fled to England and eventually made their way to the United States some time prior to the

Revolutionary War. Some of the members settled in Virginia, some in Pennsylvania, and others in Maryland, and a number of the men became good soldiers in the cause of liberty....Mary Madaline ORENDORF (age 17) was present at an entertainment given a number of patriot officers in Baltimore during the Revolutionary War. General Horatio GATES proposed....but she refused because he was old enough to be her father. She afterwards married a son of Jonathan HAGER, founder of historical old Hagerstown. Her husband died in a few years, leaving her with one child and a large estate....She rejected a proposal of marriage from famous Maryland lawyer Luther MARTIN and subsequently married a Col. LAWRENCE of Virginia." (Ref: BCK:132-134).

ORNDORFF, ORENDORF. Mrs. Mary ORNDORFF, relict of the later Christian ORNDORFF (formerly of Washington County, Maryland) died in the 68th year of her age in Logan County, Kentucky on October 4, 1823. Christian died September 14, 1823 in Logan County, Kentucky, at about age 72. Elizabeth Ann ORNDORFF died in the 97th year of her age on July 16, 1829, widow of Major Christian ORNDORFF, formerly of Washington County, Maryland. "It is supposed that not less than 500 of her children's children are now living. Up to the 6th generation witnessed her interment." (Ref: NAW:49, 111; KB 4:141; MRR:41).

OSBORNE. Walter OSBORNE and William OSBORNE were Bardstown elders in 1820, and were descended from the Osbornes who had migrated to Kentucky from Maryland circa 1785 (Ref: KC:63).

OWEN. Thomas OWEN married Sally FARMER, and their son Robert OWEN married Nancy FOSTER, and their granddaughter Lydia OWEN married in 1818 to William N. ELSBERRY, who was born in 1792 in Maryland. They settled Clark and Bourbon Cunties in Kentucky (Ref: Information from Mrs. John E. Palmer of Santa Ana, California, published in KPG 1:3, July, 1979, p. 46).

OWENS. George OWENS (OWINGS) was born March 14, 1749 in Baltimore County, Maryland and enlisted in the Revolutionary War in 1776 under Capt. James WINCHESTER. He moved to Calloway County, Kentucky and applied for and received pension S14073 in 1832. (Ref: MS:25; RSK:51; KPR:1835; MRR:41)

Cidia OWENS was born in 1773 in Washington County, Maryland and her brother Richard OWENS was born in 1783. They moved to Pendleton County, Kentucky where Richard OWENS married Sydney ROBINSON, widow of William ROBINSON, in 1810. Their son, Sidney OWENS, born in 1812, later moved to Henderson County, Illinois (Ref: KA 11:4, April, 1976, p. 214).

OWINGS. Joshua OWINGS married Rachel SPEARS, both natives of Maryland, and they migrated early to Kentucky. Their daughter, Mary W. OWINGS, married Lucas STANFORD, a soldier of the War of 1812, and their son, John L. STANFORD, was born on December 3, 1823 in Simpson County, Kentucky and later became a Judge (Ref: KB 4:241).

OWSLEY. William OWSLEY came to America from London, England and settled first in Maryland and then went to Virginia. He soon migrated to Garrard County and is buried in Lancaster, Kentucky. His son, Joel OWSLEY, was born in Lincoln County, Kentucky on June 28, 1790, and became a Doctor. He married Mary Ann LEWIS in April, 1812. Their son, William F. OWSLEY, was born July 9, 1813, and became a Judge (Ref: KB 5:223).

PACA. By her attorney, William ALLEN of Harford County, Maryland, Hellen PACA, "now of Logan County, Kentucky," conveyed part of "Paca's Park" to Josias William DALLAM of Harford County, Maryland, on November 6, 1810 (Ref: HCLR Liber HD, No. V, 1810, pp. 488-489).

PADEN, PEDEN. Frances (Frankey) PADEN, daughter of John PEDEN (PADEN) and Elizabeth MILLS, was born on the Eastern Shore of Maryland and married Stephen Holland TILGHMAN on July 12, 1761 in Somerset County. Stephen was born in 1738 and died in 1810. Frances TILGHMAN died in 1811 in Kentucky (county not stated) and a son, Joshua B. TILLMAN (TILGHMAN) was born in 1762 and married Chloe TAYLOR. (Ref: MM-1:179; Information from Gay Scarborough of Jackson, Tennessee in 1990; Peden-Paden-Peyton of Maryland by Lorenzo Q. Powell, Jr., 1985; The Boston Family of Maryland by Matthew M. Wise, 1987. The latter two publications are available in the Maryland Historical Society Library in Baltimore).

PADGET. Robert PADGET was born circa 1780 in Maryland was in Clark County, Kentucky by 1806. In 1811 he married Harriet TRAYLOR, daughter of Cary TRAYLOR (Ref: MGS 27:2, Spring, 1986, p. 255).

PAIN. In support of the Revolutionary War pension claim of Raphael WINSETT in 1840, Francis PAIN (age 83) stated he was born and raised in St. Mary's County, Maryland and he was a neighbor of Susannah CISELL when she married Raphael WINSETT in 1783. About a year later he moved to Nelson County, Kentucky with them and has been their neighbor (Ref: MS:59).

PARKER. Richard PARKER was among the early Catholic settlers from St. Mary's County, Maryland who migrated to Washington County, Kentucky and settled on Cartwright's Creek in 1785. (Ref: KC:68)

Henry PARKER and Robert PARKER, twin brothers, married Susan HOBBS and Kitty HOBBS, sisters, and about 1795 they left Frederick County, Maryland and went to Fayette County, Kentucky. (Ref: KA 9:3, January, 1974, p. 161)

Thomas PARKER moved from Maryland to Kentucky (no date given) and settled on Cane Ridge, four miles from Paris, Kentucky. His daughter Priscilla PARKER married Jesse HUGHES (died in 1854) of Bourbon County, Kentucky (Ref: BCK:102).

PARSONS. Clement PARSONS was among the early Catholics who settled in Kentucky from St. Mary's County, Maryland. He was on Rolling Fork near Lebanon, Kentucky prior to 1800 (Ref: KC:111).

PATTERSON. "Katherine PATTERSON, of Harrison County, Kentucky, age 73 in January, 1829, testified that she was raised in Harford

County, Maryland about 30 miles from Baltimore and one mile from Andrew MAKEMSON, father of Thomas, and knew Thomas served in the army during the Revolution as she often saw him during that time. She states her maiden name was Katherine PATTERSON and she married Samuel PATTERSON, who had a brother, James PATTERSON (who lived about 14 miles from Little York, Pennsylvania) who went out in the Revolution as an Ensign and was promoted to Lieutenant, and at last to Colonel. Her own brother (name not stated) was in the Flying Camp with her brother-in-law and both returned home." (Ref: KA 3:1, July, 1967, p. 27).

PATTON. Matthew PATTON, Sr. was born in May, 1750 in Augusta (now Pendleton) County, Virginia, and moved to Baltimore, Maryland when a young man. In 1775 he was one of 60 men who organized the Baltimore Independent Company under Capt. Mordecai GIST, and they served Maryland during the resistance to British oppression. By war's end he was a Major. (Source MRR:41 states he was a Sergeant) In 1834 he applied for and received pension S31294 in Christian County, Kentucky. (Ref: MS:31; RSK:56; KPR:1835)

Samuel PATTON was born in 1753 in Maryland and enlisted as a Sergeant in 1776 under Capt. KELLY at Sharpsburg, Maryland. In 1830 he applied for and received pension S31901 while living with his son (unnamed) in Hardin County, Kentucky (Ref: MS:45; RSK:88; KPR: 1835; MRR:41).

PAUL. George S. PAUL was born in 1766 in Washington County, Maryland and enlisted in the Revolutionary War in Berkeley County, Virginia on April 1, 1781. After the war he moved to Fayette County, Pennsylvania and then to Breckinridge County, Kentucky about 1796. He married Elizabeth PURCEL in Hardin County, Kentucky on July 20, 1817. In 1832 George S. PAUL applied for and received a pension for his services. Fellow soldier Barney MILLER testified for him. On April 8, 1853 Elizabeth PAUL, widow, age 64, applied for and received pension W5471 in Hardin County (Ref: MS:16, RSK:46).

PAYNE. Charles PAYNE and Patrick PAYNE were among the early Catholic settlers from St. Mary's County, Maryland to move to Washington County, Kentucky in 1785. Also, John PAYNE was on Cox's Creek by 1800. (Ref: KC:28, 80, 114)

Mary PAYNE was born March 2, 1804 and died August 8, 1871. She married Timothy B. MILLS on March 28, 1826. He was born May 13, 1797 in Maryland and died March 28, 1873 in Kentucky. Bettie C. MILLS, their daughter, was born in Spencer County, Kentucky and married Stephen CAMPBELL (Ref: KB 7:162).

PEAK. Francis PEAK was among the early Catholic settlers to move from St. Mary's County, Maryland to Washington County, Kentucky with the "Maryland League" in 1785 (Ref: KC:28).

PEARCE. George PEARCE was born in Maryland in 1749 and was a Private in the Maryland Line during the Revolutionary War. He applied for and received a pension in either Simpson or Warren

County, Kentucky in 1823. (Ref: MGS 6:16, Pension Resolution 37; KPR:1835; MRR:41 states he was born in 1760) "Wesley PEARCE was born and raised near Evansville, Virginia and emigrated to Brown County, Ohio, near Maysville, Kentucky, about 1825 and died in 1877, age 74. He was a son of Samuel PEARCE of Preston County, West Virginia. The Pearce families of Virginia, Maryland and Delaware are of Scotch and Scotch Irish descent, the father, Samuel PEARCE, immigrating to America about 1752 from Lurgan, Ireland.... having suffered religious persecution in Scotland." (Ref: KB 5:227).

PEDIGO, PEDIFORD. Edward PEDIGO (PEDIFORD) was born in Maryland on December 24, 1732 and served as a Private in Virginia during the Revolutionary War. He married Mary ELKIN and moved to Kentucky. He died in 1834 or 1835 and is buried in the Old Mulkey Meetinghouse Graveyard in Monroe County, Kentucky (Ref: KCR:320; DAR:524).

PENDER. Thomas PENDER was in 1757 in Maryland and enlisted in the Maryland Line in Montgomery County, Maryland in 1778. He married and had these children born in Maryland: Hester; Elizabeth; and, Thomas, Jr., born 1789. He was in Ohio County, Kentucky by 1802. He filed for a pension in 1818. Source MS:61 states it was rejected (R8085) but the 1835 Kentucky Pension Rolls and Sources RSK:136 and MRR:42 indicate he did receive a pension. Thomas died January 14, 1833. His widow, Anna PENDER, age 43, filed her claim in 1853 while residing in Daviess County, Kentucky (Ref: MS:61, MGS 24:2, Spring, 1983, p. 168; KPR:1835).

PENISTON. Robert P. PENISTON of Virginia married Nancy NUTTALL of Maryland prior to 1812 in Jessamine County, Kentucky. Their son Theodore PENISTON was born in Kentucky on May 6, 1812 and their son Robert P. PENISTON was born on December 27, 1813. They were in Missouri by 1831 (Ref: KM:91).

PENN. Benjamin PENN was born in 1753 and enlisted in the Revolutionary War in May, 1776 at Elkridge in Anne Arundel County, Maryland. He served in the 1st and 2nd Maryland Regiments (his name might appear as Benjamin PAYNE in the records) under Capt. Joseph BURGESS for about 15 months. Benjamin married Rebecca RYAN in 1774 in Montgomery County, Maryland. She was only 14 years old, and their first child was born about two years later. Their children were: Axey MARSHALL, Ann McCANN, Zacheus PENN, Ephraim PENN, Polly WARFIELD, Charles PENN, Benjamin PENN, Betsey ONANN, Noah PENN, Joseph PENN, and Rebecca SHADWICK. Benjamin moved to Kentucky where in 1820 he applied for and received a pension in Franklin County. He was in Harrison County, Indiana prior to 1825 and transferred back to Jefferson County, Kentucky in 1826. He died there on May 10, 1827. His widow, Rebecca, filed for and received pension W8510 in Franklin County, Kentucky on December 16, 1836. She died January 10, 1840 (Ref: MS:52; MS:37-38; RSK:100; KPR:1835; MRR:42).

PENNY. Asa (Asalom) PENNY and wife, Comfort, resided in Caroline County, Maryland in 1800 and were in Bourbon County, Kentucky in 1810. Their children born between 1787 and 1807 were Isaac, Peter, Lewis, Nathaniel, William, Allen, and Nancy. Asa PENNY died in April, 1816, in Lewis Township, Clermont County, Ohio. Comfort

PENNY is listed in the 1820 census there (Ref: MGS 27:4, Fall, 1986, p. 496).

PERRYMAN. William PERRYMAN came to America from England in the early 1700's and settled in Maryland. His son, William PERRYMAN, served in the Revolutionary War as a teamster. He suffered a hearing loss from frost bite while in service. He was an early pioneer of Kentucky in what is now Russell County. He received a pension in 1833 (age 75); died at the age of 100. His son, William PERRYMAN, Jr., was born in 1781 and went to Kentucky with his parents in 1806. He married Sabrina JOHNSON (1784-1863) and died in 1865. They had 12 children (Ref: KB 5:229-230. Source RSK:147 states he served in the Virginia militia during the Revolution).

PETERS. Frazier PETERS, born 1805 in Maryland, married Elizabeth COURTNEY in Mason County, Kentucky on July 17, 1826. Their children were Robert PETERS, Josephine PARKER, Isabelle CUNNINGHAM, Matilda MARTIN, and Elizabeth VAUGHAN (Ref: KA 6:4, April, 1971, p. 211).

PETTIT. Thomas PETTIT was born in 1764 in Maryland and enlisted in 1779 in Frederick, Maryland in the 3rd Maryland Regiment under Capt. LYNN. He married Sarah CLOOT, daughter of Simon CLOOT, on November 1, 1788 in Harrison County, Virginia. In his pension claim in 1820 in Henry County, Kentucky, Thomas stated he had a child who is married and a son who is in the U. S. Army but did not know if he was living or not. Thomas PETTIT died February 24, 1846. His widow applied for and received pension W10874 (Ref: MS:50, RSK:152, KPR:1835).

PHEBUS. George PHEBUS was born in 1762 and was a Private in the Maryland Militia in the Revolutionary War. He married Mary MUIR in 1782 in Somerset County, Maryland and moved to Kentucky with their Alkire and Walston kinfolk (Ref: MRR:42; MGS 24:4, Fall, 1983, p. 368).

PHILLIPS. John PHILLIPS was born May 7, 1734 in Cecil County, Maryland and when young moved to Frederick County, Maryland. He then to Rowan County, North Carolina where he was drafted into the military under Capt. John LOPP. In 1832 he applied for and received pension S31905 while residing in Christian County, Kentucky. (Ref: MS:31; Source RSK:56 gives his age as 100 in 1832 and states he was in the Maryland Militia, as does Source MRR:42)

Another John PHILLIPS died in Baltimore County, Maryland in 1827 and in his will he mentioned his land in Franklin and Washington Counties, Kentucky. His executors were John PHILLIPS and Lemuel PHILLIPS. (Ref: Abstracts of Wills of Baltimore County, Maryland, Book 13, 1827-1831, p. 2, by Annie W. Burns, 1938)

William PHILLIPS and wife Margaret, along with William's three oldest brothers, went to Kentucky in 1779 from Maryland by way of Pennsylvania. They stayed in Allegheny County, Pennsylvania about a year and then went to Kentucky down the Ohio River to Louisville. They later went on to Washington County and settled and built Hardin's Creek Fort. In 1800 William moved to Lebanon, Kentucky and died there on March 22, 1834. His son, Felix Grundy PHILLIPS, was born in 1807, married Frances Moss PENICK, and died in 1875 in Marion County, Kentucky (Ref: KB 5:233).

PIERCEALL. Richard PIERCEALL was born March 25, 1744 in St. Mary's County, Maryland and enlisted on December 27, 1776 in Leonardtown under Capt. John Allen THOMAS in the Maryland Line. He was discharged five months later and subsequently joined again under Capt. Charles JORDAN. Richard PIERCEALL moved to Washington County, Kentucky in 1795 with his wife and six children (unnamed) but sons Clement PIERCEALL and Joseph PIERCEALL had migrated earlier to Cartwright's Creek, Kentucky circa 1785. Richard moved to Green County, Kentucky circa 1830 where he applied for and received pension S1245 in 1833. In 1840 he was living with his son-in-law James NEWCOMB (Ref:MS:43; KA 11:3, January, 1976, p. 164; KC:111; MRR:42; and Source RSK:84 erroneously states he served in the Virginia militia).

PIGMAN. Rhoda PIGMAN, a native of Maryland, married Stephen B. STATELER, a native of Pennsylvania, and moved to Kentucky prior to 1800 when Hartford was a small fort. Their son, Ignatius P. STATELER was born in Ohio County (Ref: KB 3:79).

PILCHER. Robert PILCHER moved from Maryland to Stafford County, Virginia where his son, James PILCHER, married Phoebe FIELDING circa 1745 and their son Joshua PILCHER was born circa 1749. Joshua PILCHER's sons were in Kentucky by 1800: Fielding PILCHER in Woodford County; Joshua PILCHER in Fayette County; and, Shadrach PILCHER in Jessamine County. Shadrach PILCHER married Sarah PROCTOR (1771-1866) and was in Morgan County, Illinois by 1830 (Ref: Information from Richard Slatten of Ashland, Virginia, as published in KPG 2:1, January, 1980, p. 49).

PINDELL. Dr. Richard PINDELL was born in Maryland in 1751 and married Eliza HART. He was a Surgeon in the 1st Maryland Line during the Revolutionary War. His son, Thomas Hart PINDELL, was born in 1790 in Maryland and served in the War of 1812. The Pindells moved to Fayette County, Kentucky and Richard received a pension (Resolution 58) in 1826 for his services. He died March 16, 1833 and is buried in Lexington Cemetery. Thomas Hart PINDELL married Mary EDMISTON of Mifflin County, Pennsylvania (1791-1826) and died in 1858. Their son Richard PINDELL (1812-1870) was born in Lexington, Kentucky and died in Cleveland, Ohio. They had two other children who died in infancy: Thomas Hart PINDELL and Jane Edmiston PINDELL (Ref: MGS 6:16; KCR:153; KPR:1835; MRR:42; DAR:536).

PITT. Archibald PITT was among the early Catholic settlers from St. Mary's County, Maryland who settled in Washington County, Kentucky on Cox's Creek prior to 1800 (Ref: KC:114).

PLUMMER. Benjamin PLUMMER, whose family is of English origin, was born June 15, 1793 in Maryland, a son of James PLUMMER and Dorcas CASH. They migrated to what is now Mason County, Kentucky in 1795 when Benjamin was only 18 months old. In 1805 they moved to Fleming

County. Benjamin PLUMMER served in the War of 1812 under General Wilkinson and Captain Matthew, and he was wounded at Dayton, Ohio. On August 15, 1816 he married Mary M. SEEVER, daughter of Henry SEEVER and Elizabeth MYERS of Pennsylvania (Ref: KB 5:235).

POINTS. Luke POINTS, of Virginia, married Mary HUTCHESON, of Maryland, and their son, Squire William POINTS, was born in 1813. Both families were early settlers in what is now Grant County, Kentucky (Ref: KB 8:128).

PORTER. Ephraim PORTER was born in 1760 or 1761 in Maryland and enlisted in 1777 under Capt. Charles HERMAN. He lived for 9 years in Washington County, Maryland and then moved west to Fayette County, Kentucky. He lived there 15 years and then moved to Woodford County for 11 years and then on to Todd County. He applied for and received pension S15562 in 1834. (Ref: MS:55; MRP:32; RSK:159; KPR:1835; MRR:42)

Richard PORTER was a native of Maryland and one of the early settlers of Nelson County, Kentucky. He later moved to Jefferson County where he died. His daughter, Elizabeth PORTER, married Horatio DEBO (Ref: KB 5:100).

POWELL. Peter POWELL was among the early Catholic settlers who migrated from St. Mary's County, Maryland to Nelson County, Kentucky circa 1785, settling on Cartwright's Creek in (now) Washington County, Kentucky (Ref: KC:80).

PRATHER. Baruch William PRATHER (1742-1822) was born in Frederick County, Maryland, a twin of William Basil PRATHER. Baruch married Sarah HIGGINS on November 15, 1775 and they were in Fayette County, Kentucky by 1810. They are buried in the Prather Cemetery near Spears, Kentucky. (Ref: KA 8:4, April, 1973, p. 211; MM-1:142)

John Hunt PRATHER was born in Prince George's County, Maryland, married there, and moved to Rowan County, North Carolina. He died in Madison County, Kentucky in 1813 (Ref: KA 10:2, October, 1974, p. 99).

PRIBBLE. James PRIBBLE, son of Stephen PRIBBLE, was born in 1762 in Baltimore County, Maryland and in 1783 he married Margaret PRIBBLE in 1783 in Washington County, Pennsylvania. He served in the Revolutionary War as a Spy. Job PRIBBLE, Rueben PRIBBLE, and Thomas PRIBBLE, Jr. also served in the Revolutionary War and in wars against the Indians. James moved to Bourbon County, Kentucky in 1789 and in 1817 he was in Bracken County where he had a trading post at Augusta Hill. He died in Pendleton County in 1851. (The Pribbles, or Prebles, were from Baltimore and Harford Counties, Maryland. Additional information on Pribbles is contained in an article written by Mrs. Robert J. Burton of Albuquerque, New Mexico, and published in KA 12:1, July, 1976, pp. 19-23).

PRICE. Ignatius PRICE, whose father was from Maryland, was born in Nelson County, Kentucky in 1795. He was a blacksmith and wagonmaker in Bardstown. His daughter, Ann E. PRICE, was born in 1822 and married James DALMAZZO (1792-1845) who had come to America from Turin, Italy in 1808. They died in Switzerland County, Indiana. Ignatius PRICE died in 1840 in Nelson County, Kentucky (Ref: BCK:437).

PROTZMAN. On February 10, 1791, Laurence PROTZMAN advertised in the Washington Spy that he had land for sale in Kentucky (Ref: WMNA 1:29).

PROUT. Priscilla PROUT married William LOVELL, both natives of Maryland, and lived in Virginia. Their daughter Nella LOVELL was born in 1800 in Virginia. They moved to Allen County, Kentucky circa 1812. Nella LOVELL married James N. BARNES and lived in Simpson County, Kentucky. (Ref: KB 4:174) However, Simpson County, Kentucky Records published by the Simpson County Historical Society in Franklin, Kentucky in 1975 indicates that Nellie BARNES (November 14, 1799 - February 5, 1887) was wife of S. T. BARNES (p. 187).

PURDY. Henry PURDY was born in Maryland and went to what is now Marion County, Kentucky in an early day. He married to a Miss SMITH, then a Miss STATEN, and then a Miss HANLEY. He died in 1833. Altogether he had 21 children. One son, John S. PURDY (1798-1872) was born in Nelson County, Kentucky and married Lydia KIRK (1802-1854) in 1818 (Ref: KB 5:240).

PUSEY. Joel PUSEY married Anna ROOP in Baltimore, Maryland and moved to Meade County, Kentucky circa 1818. He died in 1876 and she died in 1849. Their children were: Evan PUSEY, W. H. PUSEY, Dr. H. R. PUSEY, J. R. PUSEY, Dr. D. C. PUSEY, Sarah PUSEY, and Dr. Robert B. PUSEY (Ref: KB 1:48-49).

QUEEN. James QUEEN was among the early Catholic settlers from St. Mary's County, Maryland to move to Nelson County, Kentucky in 1785 (Ref: KC:28).

RAGLAND. John RAGLAND was born in 1749 and enlisted in the Revolutionary War in Virginia in 1775 under Col. Patrick HENRY and also served in the Maryland Line. When he filed for his pension (S35602) in Warren County, Kentucky in 1824, he said his wife was deceased and he had three sons (names not given) living with him, ages 12, 15 and 18 (Ref: MS:54; RSK:162; KPR:1835).

RALEIGH. Basil RALEIGH, Henry RALEIGH, and John RALEIGH were settlers from Maryland who were resided at Rolling Fork, Nelson County, Kentucky prior to 1800 (Ref: KC:111).

RALEY. Thomas RALEY was possibly born in 1814 in Maryland and married Isabella CLEMENTS in Nelson County, Kentucky in 1852. Their sons were James Hiram RALEY, born 1853, and Thomas Abner RALEY, born 1854. Thomas RALEY died in 1857 (Ref: KA 12:2, October, 1976, p. 105).

RAMSEY. Mary RAMSEY married Arch COOPER in Maryland and went to Kentucky circa 1800 with their son Joseph COOPER, age 11. They settled in Clark County where Joseph was a blacksmith and farmer. He married Priscilla BAXTER and their son A. R. COOPER was born on March 1, 1821 (Ref: KB 7:168).

RANEY. Thomas RANEY left Maryland and settled on Hardin's Creek circa 1786 in what is now Washington County, Kentucky. Irish born Robert RANEY and Patrick RANEY were also in this area prior to 1800 (Ref: KC:54, 56).

RAPIER. Capt. James RAPIER and his son Charles and William left Maryland and settled near Bardstown, Kentucky between 1776 and 1786 in the Poplar Neck community. (Ref: KC:57)

Samuel LEE migrated to Nelson County, Kentucky from Maryland and settled near Rolling Fork. He married Nancy RAPIER and had 13 children, including James, Samuel, Raymond, Richard, George, Charles and William, and several daughters. James R. LEE was born in Marion County in 1811. (Ref: KB 5:177)

Charles RAPIER left Maryland circa 1800 and married Elizabeth GWYNN of Nelson County, Kentucky. Their son Nicholas A. RAPIER was born on April 2, 1821, moved to LaRue County, and married Charlotte Mary BOONE (Ref: KB 5:242).

RAY. John RAY was born in Maryland in 1754 or 1756 and enlisted in the Revolutionary War while residing in Anne Arundel County, Maryland in 1776. He moved to Kentucky in 1779 and in 1780 resided in (now) Bullitt County. His wife was Margaret -----. John RAY applied for a pension in 1832 in Union County and although sources MS:54 and MRP:32 indicate it was rejected (R8612), the 1835 Kentucky Pension Rolls and Sources RSK:161 and MRR:43 all indicate he was pensioned for his war service in Maryland. Mary Ann RAY, daughter of a different John RAY, was born in Queen Anne's County, Maryland on November 29, 1738 and died at a daughter's home in Warren County, Kentucky on July 13, 1813. She married James STRINGFIELD, Sr. who was born in Surry County, Virginia on December 19, 1735 and died after 1815 in Barren County, Kentucky. Their known children were: John, born 1762; James, born 1765; William; and, Delilah, who married James BRITTAIN, possibly in Burke County, N.C. The three sons moved to Illinois. (Ref: Mrs. Shirley B. Cawyer of Stephenville, Texas, in the South Central Kentucky Historical and Genealogical Society Quarterly "Traces," 14:3, Fall 1986, p. 94)

Nicholas RAY, a native of Maryland and whose father served in the Revolutionary War, was the first Ray to go to Kentucky. He was a contemporary of Daniel BOONE and was one of the "inmates" of the fort at Boonesborough. He later went to Washington County. His son Samuel T. RAY (1804-1884) married Margaret McELROY in Marion County. (Ref: KB 5:244)

Another Nicholas RAY was born near Point of Rocks, Maryland on November 4, 1782, a son of Nicholas RAY, Sr. who migrated to Washington County, Kentucky in 1796. Nicholas RAY, Jr. married Mary SMITH, daughter of Presly SMITH and Nancy KINCHELOE, in 1810. Their children: Susan S. SHACKLEFORD; Nicholas S. RAY; Presly S. RAY; and

Joseph F. RAY. (Ref: KB 2:93)

Mr. R. COFFIELD was born in what is now Crittenden County, Kentucky in 1832, a son of Isaac S. COFFIELD (born 1789 in Edgecombe County, N.C.) and Lucinda RAY, probably born in Kentucky, and her parents were early settlers from Maryland. Isaac died in 1843 and Lucinda died in 1832. (Ref: KB 4:36)

F. M. DULEY was born in 1818 in Livingston County, Kentucky, a son of Enoch DULEY and Polly A. RAY of Maryland. Enoch died in 1864 and Polly died in 1847 (Ref: KB 4:114).

REDDEN. Shadrach REDDEN, son of Nehemiah REDDEN (died 1795) and Leah MELVIN (died 1800) of Worcester County, Maryland, was born circa 1770 and went to Kentucky circa 1805. Nehemiah's children were: James REDDEN, John REDDEN, Stephen REDDEN, Shadrach REDDEN, Mary REDDEN, and Esther BLADES. Shadrach died in Kentucky in 1828. His son, Purnell Burch REDDEN, was born in 1802 (Ref: KA 6:1, October, 1970, p. 49; KA 14:3, January, 1979, p. 185; Worcester County Wills Liber JWB, p. 213, and Worcester County Wills Liber JBR, p. 133).

REECE. John REECE was born in 1764 in Bucks County, New Jersey and his parents soon after moved to York County, Pennsylvania. He enlisted in April, 1781 in York County under Capt. Thomas McCURDY. After his discharge, he moved to Maryland for a few years and then went to Berkeley County, Virginia in 1790. He then went back to Cumberland for a year and then to Madison County, Kentucky. He was in Barren County, Kentucky in 1800. In 1834 he applied for a pension in Hart County, Kentucky but it was rejected (R8647), probably due to lack of proof of service (Ref: MS:46).

REED. George REED was born in February, 1748 and enlisted in the Revolutionary War in Montgomery County, Maryland in 1775 at Bladensburg. A fellow soldier, Thomas SULLIVAN, stated he served with George during the war and lived with his family. George REED later migrated to Breckinridge County, Kentucky where he applied for and received pension S30609 or S30669 in 1831. (Ref: MS:16; MRP:32; RSK:46; KPR:1835)

Isaac REED (1775-1847) moved from Maryland to Lexington, Kentucky circa 1795 and owned a boot and shoe factory. He married Rebecca PRALL. Their children were: Henry W. REED; John P. REED; Emeline TIMBERLAKE; Mary J. BRIDGES; Andrew J. REED; and, William Logan REED, born 1819 (Ref: KB 5:244).

REEDING. When John HOWARD, a Revolutionary soldier from Frederick County, Maryland, applied for his pension while living in Mason County, Kentucky in 1818, Solomon REEDING stated he was born in the neighborhood of John HOWARD and he had been acquainted with him since 1792 (Ref: MS:64).

REESE. On October 1, 1801, Daniel REESE and wife Elizabeth of Mason County, Kentucky, conveyed a deed to Solomon DISNEY in Baltimore County, Maryland. It was part of "Bond's Care" and part of "Buck

Range." Elizabeth REESE was a daughter of Thomas BOND (Ref: BCLR Liber WG #72, p. 259).

RENICK. William RENICK (born 1762) and wife Betsey, both of Maryland, migrated to Barren County, Kentucky prior to 1804. Their son Strother RENICK was born January 19, 1804 in Barren County. They moved to Missouri by 1820 (Ref: KM:16).

REVEL. William REVEL was born January 18, 1801 in Maryland and married America REED (October 8, 1813 - September 26, 1877). He died in Campbell County, Kentucky on November 1, 1869 (Ref: KA 10:3, January, 1976, p. 152).

REYNOLDS. The father of William M. REYNOLDS (name not stated) was a wealthy Maryland farmer who was one of the first purchasers of Kentucky lands, and on his descending the Ohio River with his family, was attacked by Indians and killed in his boat. His family was taken prisoner and carried to Canada, where they suffered a long and rigorous imprisonment, and subsequently the loss of a large landed estate in Kentucky. The family was eventually released and returned home to Maryland (Ref: NAW:49).

RHINEHART. William and Sallie RHINEHART went from Maryland to Kentucky in the early 1800's, settling in Marion County. Their son, Thomas C. RHINEHART, was born there in 1819 and married Sarah FUNK, daughter of John FUNK (Ref: KB 5:246).

RHODES. Abram RHODES was among the early Catholics who migrated from St. Mary's County, Maryland to Nelson County, Kentucky circa 1785. (Ref: KC:80)

Elias RHODES migrated to Kentucky from Maryland in 1795 and settled on Long Lick. On June 1, 1807 his marriage to Margaret MATTINGLY, daughter of Richard MATTINGLY, was peformed by Father BADIN. Their children were: Ellen, Richard, Nancy, John, Thomas, Francis, Ely, Winifred (Sister Macaria of the Loretto Society) and Agnes. (Ref: KC:141)

Bennet RHODES was another early settler in Kentucky on Hardin's Creek, and he married Nelly MEDLEY. Two of the sisters of Bennet RHODES, Mary and Nancy, were of the Sisterhood of Mary at the Foot of the Cross, when the community so called was first established by Father NERINCKX (Ref: KC:53).

RHORER. Jacob RHORER was born in Maryland on August 8, 1794 and went to Kentucky with his parents in 1795, settling in Jessamine County. A farmer and cooper by trade, he became a Preacher in the United Christian Church in 1816. Jacob's wife was Mary HOOVER. She died on July 2, 1851 and he died on September 19, 1871. His father was Jacob RHORER, of Germany, who settled in Maryland, and his wife's father was Moses HOOVER, a preacher, born in Maryland (Ref: KB 7:95).

RICHARDSON. Daniel RICHARDSON was born circa 1750 on Kent Island in Queen Anne's County, Maryland, married Nancy -----, and had eighteen children; names not given. They moved to Virginia circa 1788 and then to Kentucky and Missouri. (Ref: MGS 25:3, Summer, 1984, p. 342)

David RICHARDSON was born in Maryland in 1753 and served as a Private in the Maryland Line during the Revolutionary War. He applied for and received a pension in Mercer County, Kentucky in 1831. (Ref: KPR:1835)

Jonathan RICHARDSON stated in his pension claim in Harrison County, Kentucky (which was rejected) that he was married in Bohemia, Maryland and served in the Revolutionary War. His daughter was Rebecca Richardson MASON. (Ref: MS:47. Source MRR:44 states his widow applied for a pension)

William RICHARDSON was born in Baltimore, Maryland and was a Colonel in the 5th Maryland Line on December 10, 1776. His son, Joseph Crowley RICHARDSON, was an Ensign in a Baltimore Regiment during the Revolutionary War and later migrated to Fayette County, Kentucky where his son Samuel Q. RICHARDSON was born. Samuel married Mary H. HARRISON of Virginia and their son, Robert Carter RICHARDSON, was born in Louisville, Kentucky on May 18, 1826. Samuel and Robert were attorneys. (Ref: BCK:430-431; Archives of Maryland, Vol. 18, p. 240)

Nancy REDMAN was born in Maryland in 1808 and married Moses RICHARDSON in Jessamine County, Kentucky around 1821. Her mother Margaret RICHARDSON and brother George RICHARDSON were also in Kentucky by 1821. (Ref: MGS 24:3, Summer, 1983, p. 260)

Noble RICHARDSON was a son of John RICHARDSON of Maryland, and a Revolutionary War soldier. He went to Kenton County, Kentucky circa 1793. He married Malinda OSBORN, daughter of Sinclair OSBORN of Orange County, Virginia, and had two sons, Robert S. RICHARDSON and John T. RICHARDSON (Ref: KB 8:136).

RICHEY. John RICHEY was born in 1755 and was a Private in the Maryland Line during the Revolutionary War. He applied for and received a pension in Allen County, Kentucky in 1825 (Ref: RSK:31; KPR:1835; but not listed in Source MRR:44).

RICKETTS. Robert RICKETTS was born on January 15, 1765 near Hagerstown, Maryland. His pension (S17047) states he served for six months in 1780 under Capt. James JOHNSON in the Pennsylvania Militia. He was living in Cumberland County, Pennsylvania when he entered the service again in 1782 for three months under Capt. Robert SAMUELS. He migrated to Kentucky and his name appears on the 1780 Tax List of Mason County. His brother, Nathan RICKETTS, was in Kentucky with him. Robert married Susannah -----, born 1767 in Maryland, and their children were John RICKETTS, Robert RICKETTS, Jr., Phoebe SHADDAY, and Margaret KELSO. In 1804 Robert was in Dearborn County, Indiana where he died February 14, 1853 and Susanna died February 20, 1853 (Ref: The Amos Family, by Maurine Schmitz and Glendola Peck (1964), pp. 47-50, in the Maryland

Historical Society Library in Baltimore) Note: There were Ricketts in Kent and Cecil County, Maryland also, but no relationship to those in Frederick has been found. One Thomas RICKETTS also settled early in Jessamine County, Kentucky and married into the Davis family (Ref: KB 7:4).

RIDGE. William RIDGE, a Revolutionary War soldier, married Rebecca SPRINGER of Frederick County, Maryland and had these children: Charles, Benjamin, Katherine, Rebecca, Cornelius, Elizabeth, Levi, Eden, Susan, and Ephraim. William RIDGE and wife Rebecca both died in Washington County, Kentucky circa 1810 (Ref: KA 13:2, October, 1977, p. 107).

RIFFE. Christopher RIFFE was born in 1765 in Maryland and married Elizabeth CASEY of Virginia circa 1783 and migrated to Bourbon County, Kentucky in 1784. They lived at Bryan's Station, Boonesborough, and Logan's Station and in 1788 at Carpenter's Station. In 1793 they moved southeast of Middleburg and became one of the first settlers in Lincoln County (now Casey County) where Christopher was elected to the Kentucky House of Representatives in 1808. His son, Peter B. RIFFE, was born in 1807 and was in Missouri by 1880 (Ref: BCK:284; KM:39).

RIGDON. James RIGDON was born in March, 1762 in Baltimore, (now Harford County) Maryland and enlisted in October, 1776 under Capt. Robert HARRIS. He married Rebecca JARVIS and moved to Kentucky in 1807, and married second to Elizabeth PEACHY on August 3, 1812. They settled in Fleming County in 1820. He filed for and received a pension in 1832 and died on August 15, 1835. His widow filed and received pension W8551. (Ref: MS:35; RSK:71; MGS 27:2, Spring, 1986, p. 255; KBG 7:1, Spring, 1980, p. 11; KPR:1835; MRR:44, 121).

RIGGS. Charles RIGGS was born June 8, 1756 and resided on the Potomac River near Hoe's Ferry in Charles County, Maryland. He enlisted on March 29, 1777 at Portobacco for three years in Col. John STONE's Maryland Troops and became a Corporal in the Maryland Line. (Ref: MRR:44) He applied for and received pension S32484 in Greenup County, Kentucky in 1832 and soon thereafter moved to Wabash County, Illinois and requested his pension to be transferred. (Ref: MS:42, MRP:33, RSP:86)

Edmund RIGGS married Jane WILSON in 1799 in Montgomery County, Maryland and moved to Jessamine County, Kentucky. They had five sons: Robert, Barzel, James, Edmund and Douglas (Ref: MGS 14:2, May, 1973, pp. 14-15).

RILEY. Amos RILEY of Maryland married Susan PHILIPS of Virginia and they were in Jefferson County, Kentucky by 1810. Their son, Judge Amos RILEY, was born June 10, 1810 and was in Missouri by 1837 (Ref: KM:87).

RINEY. By 1800 the following men of the Riney family of Maryland had settled on Cartwright's Creek in Washington County, Kentucky: Jonathan, Zachariah, Jesse, James, John, Basil, and Clement (Ref: KC:80).

RIPPERDAM. Frederick RIPPERDAM married Sarah CHITICKS in Germany and came to America, settling first in Maryland or Pennsylvania, and then migrated to Kentucky. They were one of the earliest settlers to Fort Boonesborough. Frederick's brother (unnamed) was killed by Indians. In 1782 Frederick moved to what is now Boyle County where he died circa 1825 at age 85. His daughter, Susan RIPPERDAM, married Henry FIELDS and their son William M. FIELDS was born November 10, 1815 near Danville, Kentucky (Ref: KB 5:116).

RITTER. Richard RITTER was born in Cecil County, Maryland and died July 28, 1840 in his 74th year in Mason County, Kentucky. He is buried in the Washington Baptist Church Cemetery. (Ref: KCR:301) Note: Source KCR may contain a copying error because a Richard RUTTER was born in Cecil County, Maryland on November 1, 1765, according to records of St. Mary Anne's Church in Cecil County, Maryland. The age of this Richard RITTER and this Richard RUTTER matches. The parish records have been copied in Henry C. Peden's Early Anglican Church Records of Cecil County, published by Family Line Publications, Westminster, Maryland (1990).

ROBARDS. Joanna ROBARDS married Squire HALL, a merchant of Baltimore, Maryland. Their son, William M. HALL, was born in Baltimore on May 31, 1816. The Halls moved to Kentucky and settled first in Henry County, where son Squire HALL was born on December 25, 1823, and later moved to Shelby County. William M. HALL married Mary CORLEY in 1839 (Ref: KB 7:186).

ROBB. Frederick ROBB was born in Maryland in 1789 and went to Jessamine County, Kentucky when a young boy with his father. He married Mary NEAT, a native of Maryland, and their son, G. W. ROBB, was born March 13, 1825. Frederick ROBB died in 1861 in Franklin County, Kentucky and Mary ROBB died in 1855. (Ref: KB 7:97) Another son, J. C. ROBB, was born in Jessamine County on October 23, 1826 and served in the Confederate Army under Col. Thomas HUNT (Ref: KB 1:15).

ROBERTS. Edward ROBERTS was born in 1754 and resided in Allegany County, Maryland. He enlisted in the Revolutionary War on August 20, 1776 at Fort Pleasant, Virginia. On July 5, 1784 he married Christena BRAY in Allegany County and their children were: Elizabeth, born December 22, 1785; Henry, born July 16, 1787; William, born January 27, 1788; John, born November 24, 1789; Ann, born February 22, 1791; Jane, born April 10, 1794; Polly, born July 22, 1796; Edward, born October 30, 1798; and, Chapman, born December 27, 1801. In 1792 Edward ROBERTS moved to Jessamine County, Kentucky and in 1819 applied for a pension in Montgomery County, Kentucky. He then moved to Clinton County, Ohio and died. His widow applied for and received pension W8560 in 1844 in Clinton County, Ohio and then moved to Jefferson County, Iowa. (Ref: MS:58; RSK:127)

Patrick Henry ROBERTS was born in Maryland in 1758 and served in the Revolutionary War in 1777. He married Catharine AUSTIN on June 20, 1810 in Baltimore, Maryland. Two of their children were John

ROBERTS and Edmund ROBERTS. Patrick Henry ROBERTS applied for a pension in 1830 in Franklin County, Kentucky. He died May 23, 1839 and in 1853 his widow, ag 63, applied for and received pension W1164 (Ref: MS:39; RSK:74).

ROBERTSON. Zachariah ROBERTSON served in the Maryland Line during the Revolutionary War, enlisting in Anne Arundel County in 1781. His age on his pension application in 1820, while living in Pendleton County, Kentucky, according to Source MS:46, was 57, but Source RSK:89 states he was 74 in 1819. This latter age is also indicated in the 1835 Kentucky Pension Rolls. Source MRR:44 states he was born in 1762. Zachariah received pension S35632 in Harrison County, Kentucky and later transferred to Vermilion County, Illinois. His wife was Elizabeth -----, and their children were Rachel, Margaret, Matilda, James, Delilah and Pruda. He later transferred back to Kentucky (Ref: MS:46-47; RSK:89).

ROBEY, ROBY. Hezekiah ROBEY of Maryland was among the early setlers on Cartwright's Creek in (now) Washington County, Kentucky circa 1785. He was in Bourbon County, Kentucky by 1806. His son, Hezekiah ROBEY was born March 15, 1806. They migrated to Missouri. (Ref: KM:27)

Thomas ROBY of Maryland married Elizabeth CLOUD of Kentucky and their son Hezekiah C. ROBY was born on March 6, 1807 in Jessamine County, Kentucky. They were in Monroe County, Missouri by 1849 (Ref: KM:91).

ROE. Edward ROE was born in Maryland on September 15, 1790. He migrated to Kentucky circa 1817 with Thomas STONE and James STAFFORD. His son, Islam M. ROE, was born in Kentucky in 1817 and married Ellen H. GILBERT, who was born in 1821 in Virginia. Edward ROE died October 24, 1860 in Lewis County, Kentucky (Ref: MGS 16:3, August, 1975, p. 162).

ROGERS. Daniel ROGERS of Maryland had settled on Cox's Creek in Nelson County, Kentucky by 1800. His son was Rev. Joseph ROGERS. (Ref: KC:114, 131)

Jonathan ROGERS, a native of Maryland, was a Magistrate in Ohio County, Kentucky for many years. His son, William L. ROGERS, was born there in 1822 and died in 1876. (Ref: KB 3:186)

Byrd ROGERS, of Virginia, married Mary TRUMAN, of Maryland, in Kentucky circa 1801 (Ref: MRR:122. See additional notes in this text as pertains to the Truman-Rogers family history).

ROHRER. Samuel ROHRER was born August 9, 1787 in Washington County, Maryland and died March 1, 1862. He married Magdalena ROHRER (July 20, 1791 - March 16, 1875) and their children were Martin, Jacob, and Solomon B. ROHRER. They may have later settled in Kentucky. (Ref: MGS 24:1, Winter, 1983, p. 90)

Catherine ROHRER, daughter of Major Christian ORNDORFF of the Revolutionary War, was born July 25, 1763? and died January 24,

1854. She married John ROHRER who was born April 23, 1765 and died July 18, 1855. They are buried in Smith-Rohrer Graveyard near Russellville in Logan County, Kentucky. (Ref: KCR:275)

Frederick ROHRER advertised in the Washington Spy (Maryland) on February 10, 1791 that he had land for sale in Kentucky (Ref: WMNA 1:29).

ROLL. Michael ROLL was born in Pennsylvania in 1762 and enlisted in the Revolutionary War in Frederick County, Maryland in 1776 at age 14. He again enlisted in 1778 in Cumberland County, Pennsylvania in 1778, having moved there from Frederick County, Maryland. In 1797 he moved to Hardin County, Kentucky where he lived until 1832 when he moved to Muhlenberg County. He applied for and received pension S38340. The affidavit of Elizabeth VOUGHT in 1834 (age 66) stated Michael's father was John ROLL (Ref: MS:62; RSK: 131).

RONEY. Roger RONEY of Maryland was an early settler to Kentucky who settled on Rolling Fork in Nelson County by 1800 (Ref: KC:111).

ROSS. George ROSS of Maryland was an elder in Bardstown, Kentucky by 1820. (Ref: KC:63)

W. S. ROSS was born in 1799 in Bladensburg, Maryland and was raised in Chambersburg, Pennsylvania. He migrated to Union County, Kentucky in 1821 and died there in July, 1861. His wife, Ellen DADE, was born in Montgomery County, Maryland in 1797 and died in Union County, Kentucky in February, 1865. (Ref: KB 4:94)

Lawrence ROSS married Cassandra LUTES in 1808 in Estell County, Kentucky. Their marriage was proven through a Maryland Revolutionary War pension application; soldier's name not given (Ref: MRR: 122).

ROWDEN. George ROWDEN was born on March 25, 1743 in Calvert County, Maryland and enlisted in the Revolutionary War in Camden County, South Carolina in May, 1778. Prior to the war he lived in Calvert County, Maryland and Frederick County, Virginia. He was also a Private in the Maryland Militia. After the war he moved to Madison County, Alabama and then Warren County, Tennessee and then to Graves County, Kentucky in 1830. He applied for and received pension S15623 in 1834 (Ref: MS:41; RSK:82; KPR:1835).

ROYSE. Solomon ROYSE was born in Orange County, New York on September 11, 1763 and moved to Alexandria, Virginia circa 1770. He then moved to Washington County, Maryland where he served in the Revolutionary War. He also served in the North Carolina Line. In 1792 he moved to Bourbon County, Kentucky and in 1798 he settled in Adair County, Kentucky. He applied for and received a pension in 1831 and also received bounty land warrant 26476-160-55 in 1854. He died April 14, 1858. He was married to Sarah STOTTS in Green County, Kentucky on November 3, 1796 by Rev. Benjamin LYNN. His widow received pension W3598 (Ref: MS:1; MRP:34; RSK:31; MRR:45, 122).

RUDD. James RUDD moved with his family from Prince George's County, Maryland to Springfield, Kentucky in 1796. His wife was Susanna BROOKE and their children were William, Charles, Henry B., John, Richard, James, Margaret, and Christopher. James RUDD died in 1816 and his wife in 1822 (Ref: KC:79).

RUGGLES. James RUGGLES was born in 1763 and in his pension application he claimed to have served in the company of Capt. BELL in Maryland in 1777. His claim was rejected in 1836 (R9067) in Greenup County, Kentucky. (Ref: MS:43; but Source MRR:45 indicates he was pensioned)

Another James RUGGLES was born in Maryland in 1784 and died in 1857 in Indiana. He married first to Sarah CONWAY in 1804 in Mason County, Kentucky and second to Margaret CLANCY in 1813 in Fleming County, Kentucky. His brother, Jonathan RUGGLES, married Mary GWIN, widow of Nicholas WALLINGFORD, in 1837 in Mason County, Kentucky (Ref: KA 5:1, July, 1969, p. 49).

RUSSELL. James RUSSELL was born in 1791 in Maryland and married Nancy CHURCHWELL in 1814. He died in Mercer County, Kentucky in 1873. (Ref: KA 3:3, January, 1968, p. 130)

Andrew RUSSELL, son of Joseph RUSSELL, was born in 1800 in Lincoln County, Kentucky near Fort Logan. His grandfather (unnamed) came to America from Scotland with his two brothers and first settled in Baltimore, Maryland. Andrew RUSSELL married Elizabeth ECHOLS. He died in 1852 and she died in 1873. (Ref: BCK:555-556; KB 5:252)

The will of George RUSSELL of Fayette County, Kentucky was written on May 29, 1807 as he was about to descend the Ohio and Mississippi Rivers to New Orleans. It was probated in Gallatin County, Kentucky on March 13, 1815, naming Mark PRINGLE of Baltimore, Maryland his executor, and leaving all of his estate to Sarah Stewart BOOT, wife of Capt. William R. BOOT of the U. S. Army (Ref: KA 13:2, Oct., 1977, p. 82).

RYAN. Richard RYAN was an early settler from Maryland who migrated to Cartwright's Creek in (now) Washington County, Kentucky circa 1785 (Ref: KC:80).

SALSMAN. Lot SALSMAN was born on January 6, 1809, a son of Jacob SALSMAN of Maryland who migrated to Kentucky or or before this date. Lot SALSMAN married Matilda WITTEN and died on December 11, 1876 in Grayson County, Kentucky. His son, Squire SALSMAN, was born in 1850 and was senior member of the firm of Salsman & Litsey, merchants (Ref: KB 1:189).

SAMPSON. Richard SAMPSON, born 1780 in Maryland, married Mary WATKINS, born 1789 in Virginia, and by 1815 they were in Madison County, Kentucky. Their son Thomas W. SAMPSON was born there on October 6, 1815 and their son John H. SAMPSON was born on April 6, 1818. They were in Missouri by 1839 (Ref: KM:111).

SAMUELS. Rachael KIRTZ was born in Maryland in 1794 and died in

Nelson County, Kentucky in 1866. She married John SAMUELS (1796--1852) of Kentucky and their son, Wakefield M. SAMUELS, was born in Nelson County in 1821 (Ref: KB 6:161).

SANDERS. Anthony SANDERS was a young, unmarried Catholic from Maryland who settled in Bardstown, Kentucky in 1790. (Ref: KC:57)

John SANDERS was born in Maryland on April 14, 1751 and enlisted in the Revolutionary War in Berkeley County, Virginia in 1778. He lived in Virginia for 6 years, in Scott County for 2 or 3 years after the war, and in 1801 moved to Owen County, Kentucky. He applied for and received pension S16521 in 1832 (Ref: MS:60; RSK:139).

SANDS. Eleanor SANDS, widow of William SANDS, was born in Maryland on August 14, 1778 and died in Kentucky on February 3, 1856. She is buried in Maple Grove Cemetery in Logan County, Kentucky (Ref: KCR:288).

SANSBURY. Nicholas SANSBURY was an early Catholic who moved from Maryland and settled on Cartwright's Creek in (now) Washington County, Kentucky circa 1785 (Ref: KC:80).

SAPPINGTON. Sylvester SAPPINGTON was born in Maryland circa 1762. He married Sarah -----, and their children were: Mary, Richard, Keziah, Elizabeth, Margaret, Morena, and James J. Sylvester moved to Wheeling, West Virginia, then to Fayette County, Kentucky, and then to Clark County, Kentucky. He died in Winchester, Illnois on September 24, 1844 (Ref: MGS 25:2, Spring, 1984, p. 202).

SARGEANT, SERGEANT. William SARGEANT was born in Montgomery County, Maryland in 1760 and enlisted in the Revolutionary War in Frederick County, Maryland on September 17, 1777. He lived in Maryland and Loudon County, Virginia before the war and afterwards he moved to Butler County, Kentucky. In 1834 he applied for and received pension S38356 in Bracken County (Ref: MS:15; RSK:45; KPR:1835; MRR:45).

SAUNDERS, SANDERS. George SAUNDERS was born in Maryland in 1786 and moved to Fleming County, Kentucky. The name of his wife is unknown, but their sons were: Joel, born 1831; James, born 1832; Robert, born 1834; and, Jackson, born 1836 (Ref: MGS 24:1, Winter, 1983, p. 88).

SCHMETZER. On October 24, 1787 this notice appeared in the Maryland Chronicle in Fredericktown, Maryland: "Henry FOURNIER to petition at next General Assembly for act to record deed to tract of land purchased of Peter SCHMETZER who has gone to Kentucky." (Ref: WMNA 1:12).

SCHOOLFIELD. Isaac Bosman SCHOOLFIELD was born in Maryland and migrated to Kentucky in 1814, settling in Bracken County near Augusta. He married Mary ATKINSON of Maryland and their son, George T. SCHOOLFIELD, was born December 31, 1799 in Maryland. George married Mary MAXWELL in 1840 in Kentucky and moved to Missouri in

1873, dying there in 1874 or 1877 (Ref: BCK:251; KB 5:255).

SCOTT. Baptist SCOTT was named in the will of James SCOTT in 1749 in Cecil County, Maryland. He had a brother John SCOTT, a sister Margaret SCOTT, and nephews James SCOTT and James COCHRAN. Baptist SCOTT died in 1803 in Clarke County, Kentucky (Ref: MGS 23:4, Fall, 1982, p. 355).

SCROGGIN. Thomas C. SCROGGIN was born on July 24, 1764 in Somerset County, Maryland. He enlisted in the Revolutionary War in August, 1780 and after the war he lived in Delaware. In 1792 he moved to Kentucky and applied for and received pension S16524 in 1833 in Franklin County (Ref: MS:39; RSK:75; KPR:1835; MRR:46).

SELBY. George Washington SELBY, and wife Rosy Ann -----, moved to Kentucky from Maryland in the 1820's. Their sons were Micajah, John T., George W. Jr., and Andrew Jackson. (Ref: KPG 1:3, July, 1979, p. 44)

Joshua SELBY married Mary RIGGENS of Maryland in Nicholas County, Kentucky. Their son, William M. SELBY, was born January 18, 1820. They migrated later to Missouri (Ref: KM:133).

SEWELL. Joseph SEWELL was born in Elkridge (now Howard County) Maryland in 1753 and enlisted in the Revolutionary War in Wilkes County, North Carolina. Source RSK:62 states he was in the South Carolina State Troops. Two years after the war he moved to Carter County, Tennessee where he lived for 30 years, and then moved to Kentucky. In 1832 he applied for and received pension S31354 in Cumberland County, Kentucky (Ref: MS:33).

SEXTON. George SEXTON, son of George SEXTON and grandson of Hopewell N. SEXTON, Jr., married circa 1767 in Frederick County, Maryland (wife's name not given) and his children were: James SEXTON, born 1768; Joshua SEXTON, died in Gallatin County, Illinois; George SEXTON, born 1775 and died 1852 in Missouri; Daniel SEXTON, died 1843 in Desha County, Arkansas; and a daughter who married a MARTIN. George SEXTON moved to Cumberland County, Kentucky circa 1798 and had left Kentucky by 1820, destination not stated (Ref: KA 16:4, April, 1981, p. 242).

SHANKS. John SHANKS was born in 1754 in Maryland and served in the Revolutionary War in 1780. He was first pensioned on April 14, 1789 as an invalid soldier by the Orphans Court of Anne Arundel County, Maryland. He subsequently moved to Kentucky and applied for and received pension S37393 in Meade County in 1826 or 1827. He had moved to Kentucky because his children had moved there and he requested his pension be transferred. He later lived in Nelson County, Kentucky and appointed John BOYLE of Garrard County to be his attorney for purposes of obtaining his land warrant. John SHANKS died March 23, 1829 and bounty land warrant 262-100 was issued to his widow, Ann SHANKS (Ref: MRP:35; MS:58; RSK:120; KPR:1835; MRR:46).

SHARP. William SHARP was born in Baltimore County, Maryland and married Elizabeth JAMES on September 20, 1762. He served in the Revolutionary War in Baltimore County in 1777, but he never filed for a pension. He migrated to Kentucky and died there, and his widow filed for a pension in January, 1845, in Casey County, Kentucky but her claim (R9430) was rejected according to Source MS:21. (However, Source MRR:46 indicates that William SHARP did receive a pension, and Source HCP:240 indicates that William SHARPE was a member of the Baltimore Mechanical Company of Militia in 1776).

SHELBY. Evan SHELBY came to America with his father and family from Wales and settled near Hagerstown, Maryland. His son, Isaac SHELBY, was born December 11 1750 near North Mountain, a few miles from Hagerstown. He moved into western Virginia in 1771 and fought the Indians at the Battle of Kanawha in 1774. In 1775 he was a surveyor for Henderson and Company in Kentucky, and in 1776 was a Captain in Virginia during the Revolutionary War, ultimately being promoted to Colonel under General MARION. In 1782 Isaac SHELBY was elected to the North Carolina Assembly and in 1782-1783 he surveyed land in Kentucky for North Carolina soldiers. He married Susanna HART, daughter of Nathaniel HART, in April, 1783. In 1792 Isaac SHELBY became the first Governor of Kentucky. He died July 19, 1826. (Ref: BCK:516-522, and additional data on Evan SHELBY is in Source KB 4:160)

Moses SHELBY was born near Hagerstown, Maryland on November 8, 1761. He was a Captain in the War of 1812, joining the Army of Harrison in the Summer of 1812 and at the age of 63 he fought in the Battle of the Thames. He married Elizabeth NEAL, born in 1763, and died circa 1828 at New Madrid, Kentucky; she died circa 1819. Moses' descendants settled in Georgia and Mississippi (Ref: National Society of the War of 1812 Register, published by the Society in 1972, p. 217).

SHELTON. Wilson SHELTON was born in 1747 in Charles County, Maryland and served in the Revolutionary War in Stafford County, Virginia. He received a pension in 1835 while in Henry County, Kentucky. His daughter, Nancy SHELTON, married David ADAMS in 1812 in Shelby County, Kentucky. Wilson died in Parke County, Indiana after 1838. (Ref: MGS 25:2, Spring, 1984, p. 209)

Joseph SHELTON married Priscilla RIGGS after 1800 in Kentucky. Their marriage was proven through a Maryland Revolutionary War pension application; soldier's name not given (Ref: MRR:122).

SHERMAN. Charles R. SHERMAN married Julia A. PORTER of Maryland and they were in Jefferson County, Kentucky by 1825. Their son, William SHERMAN, was born March 15, 1826 in Kentucky, and by 1840 they were in Missouri (Ref: KM:88).

SHIPLEY. Samuel SHIPLEY enlisted in the Revolutionary War on June 3, 1778 in Trenton, New Jersey. Although Source MS:62 states he was born in 1751 and served in New Jersey, Source RSK:126 states he was age 96 in 1831 and served in the Maryland Line, which is so indicated on the 1835 pension rolls. Also, Maryland Archives, Vol.

18, p. 247, states that Samuel SHIPLEY was a Private in the 6th Maryland Line from June 3, 1778 to March 22, 1779. Samuel did receive pension S37392 in Monroe County, Kentucky in 1831 for his Maryland service (Ref: MS:62; MRP:35; RSK:126; KPR:1835; MRR:47).

SHIPP. R. H. SHIPP was born in Bourbon County, Kentucky in 1797 and was a Baptist Minister. His father, Colby SHIPP, was a Revolutionary War soldier from Culpeper County, Virginia. R. H. SHIPP married Margaret CLARK, daughter of Amos CLARK of Maryland who settled in Owen County, Kentucky. T. J. SHIPP, son of R. H., was born in 1827 (Ref: KB 8:148).

SHORT. Peyton SHORT advertised land for sale in Kentucky in the Elizabeth-Town Advertiser newspaper in western Maryland, March 23, 1797 (Ref: WMNA 1:66).

SIMMONS. Jesse SIMMONS was born in Prince George's County, Marylnd and married Rachel WELLS on September 13, 1781. Their daughter, Elizabeth SIMMONS, was born circa 1782 in Berkeley County, (West) Virginia and married Minor LEEWRIGHT in 1803. Jesse SIMMONS died in Bullitt County, Kentucky in 1819 (will probated February 10, 1819) and Rachel SIMMONS died on July 5, 1815. (Ref: KA 2:3, January, 1967, p. 116)

William SIMMONS was born in Maryland in 1752 and married Nancy -----, in 1770. William served in the Revolutionary War in Prince William County, Virginia in 1777. He moved to Nelson County, Kentucky for 3 years and then moved to Henry County, Kentucky. In 1832 he applied for and received pension S30704 (Ref: MS:49; RSK:96; MRR:47).

SIMPSON. Walter SIMPSON, James SIMPSON, and Grace Newton SIMPSON were from Maryland and had settled on Cox's Creek in Nelson County, Kentucky by 1800. (Ref: KC:114, 131)

James SIMPSON, son of Benedict SIMPSON, was born, raised and married in Maryland. He moved his family to Washington County, Kentucky after 1812, having at the time 6 children. His wife was Eliza EDELIN. Another son, Martin SIMPSON, was born in Kentucky on October 15, 1822 (Ref: KB 5:258).

SIMS, SIMMS. John SIMMS of Maryland had settled in Kentucky on Cartwright's Creek circa 1785, and Samuel SIMS of Maryland had settled on Hardin's Creek circa 1786 in (now) Washington County. Francis SIMS was on Rolling Fork in Nelson County, Kentucky before 1800. (Ref: KC:56, 80, 111)

James L. SIMS married Matilda MUDD circa 1810 in Kentucky. Their marriage was proven through a Maryland Revolutionary War pension application; soldier's name not given (Ref: MRR:123).

SKAGGS. Archibald SKAGGS was born January 1, 1759 in South Carolina. His parents moved to Halifax County, Virginia and then Botetourt County, Virginia and then Montgomery County. Archibald entered the Revolutionary War in 1779 and his cousin, Henry SKAGGS, served with him. Archibald married Barbara -----, born in 1773. They moved to Adair County, Kentucky where Archibald applied for and received pension S31367 in 1832. He died April 21, 1833 (Ref: MS:12; RSK:31; and The 1835 Kentucky Pension Rolls states "dead by 1834").

SKINNER. Henry SKINNER was a native of Baltimore, Maryland and was educated there for the medical profession. He was appointed Surgeon in the Regular Army and circa 1810 he was stationed at Fort Massac, Illinois. At Eddyville, Kentucky he married Aurelia LYONS, whom he met in Washington, D.C., where her father was a member of Congress. Henry SKINNER retained his Army position until his death on June 22, 1819. His wife died in 1831. Henry's father was Frederick SKINNER who was born in England in 1750 and came to America where he married Miss STUART of Virginia and settled in Baltimore. Henry and Aurelia had two children: Beulah L. SKINNER, and Frederick H. SKINNER, who was born on June 22, 1815 in Eddyville, Kentucky. Thomas C. SKINNER, son of Frederick H., was born in 1844 and was a Confederate officer in the Civil War (Ref: KB 4:161-162).

SMALL. In 1808, John SMALL settled in the southern portion of Todd County, Kentucky near the village of Allensville, having previously lived in Shelby County, Kentucky. He was a native of Maryland. His son, James SMALL, was a young boy in 1808 and upon attaining age, he married Nancy H. BOONE, who was related to the pioneer Daniel BOONE (Ref: KB 4:142).

SMALLWOOD. Bean SMALLWOOD was born in Maryland on January 16, 1759 and entered the Revolutionary War in 1776 under Capt. Thomas BERRY in Frederick County, Virginia, and served two years in the 8th Virginia Regiment. He reenlisted and served until February 16, 1779 in the 4th Virginia Regiment under Capt. Leonard COOPER, and was wounded in the left thigh. Bean SMALLWOOD and Elizabeth RENICRID(?) were married on January 10, 1780 in Frederick County, Virginia by Rev. Isaac MARKS, a Baptist Preacher. They had a large family and their know children were James and Ann. Bean SMALLWOOD moved to Russell County, Virginia after the war and in 1794 he moved his family to Kentucky. In 1818 he applied for and received a pension in Bath County, Kentucky. He died there on October 11, 1834 and his widow filed for and received pension W8738 in 1839. Affidavits indicate she had relatives in Floyd County, Indiana. (Ref: MS:5-6; RSK:38)

Randall or Randolph SMALLWOOD was born in Maryland circa 1780 and was on the Tax List of Madison County, Kentucky from 1801 to 1805, the 1810 census of Shelby County, the 1820 and 1830 and 1840 censuses of Estill County, and the 1850 census of Owsley County, Kentucky. His wife was Rachel -----, and their children were: Margaret, 1807-1878, married William H. TINCHER; James, 1809-1852, married Caroline BULLOCK; Elizabeth, born 1814, married John McGUIRE; and, William J., 1819-1875, married first Margaret HAMILTON and second Susan ROACH. (Ref: KA 12:2, October, 1976, p. 106).

SMITH. There were several Smith families among the early Catholic settlers from St. Mary's County, Maryland who migrated to Nelson County and Washington County, Kentucky circa 1785-1800, including Samuel SMITH, Benjamin SMITH, William SMITH, Richard SMITH, Giles SMITH, and Benedict SMITH. They settled on Cartwright's Creek, Hardin's Creek, and Cox's Creek. Benjamin's wife was Christiancy BLANDFORD. Among the children of Giles were Daniel, John and Levi. By 1820 Bennet SMITH and Roger SMITH were elders in Bardstown. (Ref: KC:56, 63, 78, 114)

Aquilla SMITH (born 1760) was a Private in the 7th Maryland Line and an invalid soldier who pensioned in 1823 or 1833 in Lewis County, Kentucky. (Ref: MGS 6:62; 1965; KPR:1835; MRR:47)

Dr. Anthony W. SMITH was born in Lunenburg County, Virginia and was a Surgeon in the War of 1812. He received his medical degree from the University of Pennsylvania in 1818, relocated to Baltimore, Maryland, and married Margaret E. B. WHEELER of Easton, Maryland. She died prior to 1826 and Dr. Smith returned to Virginia and married Ann M. McROBERT of Prince Edward County, Virginia in 1826. He died in 1858. His descendants moved to Kentucky. (Ref: BCK:40)

Benjamin SMITH was born in Maryland in 1761 and served in the 6th Maryland Line during the Revolutionary War. He applied for and received pension S46547 in 1828 in Nelson County, Kentucky. His service was verified by Charles BEAVER who was a Lieutenant and now lived in Nelson County. Benjamin was still living in 1840. (Ref: RSK:133, MS:59, KPR:1835; MRR:47)

Daniel SMITH was born in Maryland and a brother of Richard B. SMITH who died in 1817 in Bourbon County, Kentucky. Daniel died in 1835 in Nicholas County, Kentucky. (Ref: KA 2:3, January, 1967, p. 118; KA 5:4, April, 1970, p. 222)

Edward Miles SMITH was born in Charles County, Maryland and served in the 3rd Maryland Line during the Revolutionary War as Sergeant in 1777 and then Lieutenant in 1781. A year after peace was declared he married Theresa DYER of Prince George's County, Maryland in a Catholic ceremony. All their children except Daniel were born in Maryland: Patrick, Edward M., Horatio, George, Francis L., John B., Levi I., and Daniel. Edward Miles SMITH died in 1802. In 1826 his widow received bounty land warrant 1180-200 or 1800-200. In 1840, Theresa SMITH, widow, age 82, applied for and received pension W8736 in Washington County. Being a "lunatic" at the time, she was living with her son Levi in Springfield. (Ref: MS:55-56; MRP:36; MRR:48)

Gerard SMITH was born in Maryland in 1755 and served in the Revolutionary War. He pensioned in 1819 in Scott County, Kentucky, but the 1835 Kentucky Pension Rolls indicate he was "dropped---not continental." (Ref: RSK:149; KPR:1835)

Henry SMITH was born February 26, 1759 in Prince George's County, Maryland and resided in Frederick County, Maryland at the time of his enlistment in the Revolutionary War in August, 1777. He was discharged at Philadelphia in March, 1778. In 1800 he moved to Jefferson County, Kentucky and in 1808 he went to Shelby County. In 1834 he applied for and received pension S31374 in Campbell County, Kentucky. (Ref: MS:20; RSK:155; MRP:36; KPR:1835; MRR:48)

James SMITH was born in September, 1755, and at the time of his enlistment circa 1776 in the Revolutionary War he resided in Frederick County, Maryland. He married Alice Margaret TRUAX, born in 1757, in Loudon County, Virginia on January 28, 1783. In 1832 they resided in Adair County, Kentucky where James applied for and received a pension. He referred to his children, but not by name, and mentioned a crippled son. In 1835 they were in Gibson County, Indiana. James SMITH died on January 29, 1836 and his widow applied for and received pension W9657 in 1842. (Ref: MS:1; MRP:36; RSK:31; KPR:1835; MRR:48)

John SMITH was born in 1759 in Hagerstown, Maryland and enlisted in the Revolutionary War in 1776. Prior to the war he lived in Pennsylvania and Maryland, and afterwards he moved to Montgomery County, Kentucky. In 1818 he received pension S37412. (Ref: MS:58; RSK:127; MRR:48)

Another John SMITH was born in Montgomery County, Maryland on February 2, 1753, served in the Revolutionary War under Capt. Benjamin SPEAKER, and also substituted for his brother Bazil SMITH in the militia under Capt. Amon RIGGS. John SMITH married Elizabeth -----, and left for Kentucky on May 12, 1796 and arrived in Clark County on June 16, 1796. In 1832 he applied for and received pension S1255 in Clark County, Kentucky. His service was verified by John OWENS and George HEATHMAN. John SMITH died on July 22, 1835 and his widow obtained his pension in 1838. (Ref: MS:28; RSK:59; MRP:36; KPR:1835; MRR:48)

Michael SMITH was born in 1752 in Washington County, Maryland and enlisted in the Revolutionary War in Hagerstown in June, 1776 under Capt. CRESAP. He served throughout the war, was in the Battle of Long Island, was taken prisoner, and was subsequently released a few months later. It appears that Michael SMITH married twice and had a son Peter SMITH by his first wife, name unknown. He married Nancy LEVITE, a widow, on September 18 or November 20, 1797 in Montgomery County, Kentucky. Peter SMITH and Michael SMITH both signed the marriage bond. In 1832 Michael SMITH applied for and received a pension in Harrison County, Kentucky. He died November 24, 1842. Nancy SMITH died December 28, 1850 in Rush County, Indiana, having earlier received pension W6088. In 1856 the heirs of Michael and Nancy SMITH applied for any arrears of their pensions, namely: George M. SMITH; Amanda McCONNELL, wife of James McCONNELL of Rush County, Indiana; Elizabeth CARPENTER, wife of Squire C. CARPENTER of Bath County, Kentucky; and, John SMITH of Pike County, Missouri. Michael's son, Peter SMITH of Bourbon County, Kentucky, is not mentioned at this time. (Ref: MS:11-12; MS:47; MRR:123; MRP:36; MRR:48. Source RSK:91 erroneously states that Michael Smith served in the Massachusetts Line)

Jacob SMITH, son of Revolutionary War soldier Adam SMITH of

Pennsylvania, moved with his mother to Maryland. He moved to Kentucky some time in the 1790's by way of the Ohio River to Maysville, and then to Mercer County where he married Mary BARKER in 1800. In 1808 they moved to Logan County and in 1811 to Butler County, where Daniel M. SMITH was born on December 14, 1811. He was the first white child born in Morgantown, Kentucky. Jacob SMITH died in 1854. (Ref: KB 3:45)

William B. SMITH was born near Nicholasville, Kentucky on September 4, 1823. His parents were Andrew SMITH of Fayette County, Kentucky, born August 15, 1797 and died December 20, 1877, and Sophia YOST of Maryland, born July 19, 1799 and died October 9, 1871 (Ref: KB 7:106).

SOPER. John SOPER of Maryland migrated to Kentucky circa 1799. His son, James SOPER (1792-1861) married Elizabeth BIBB (1808-1870), daughter of Elijah BIBB, in Jessamine County, Kentucky. Their children were: Nancy A. ALLIN; William B. SOPER; James R. SOPER; Benjamin Franklin SOPER; David M. SOPER; John E. SOPER; Oremandel T. SOPER; and, Amos B. SOPER (Ref: KB 5:263).

SPALDING. Benedict SPALDING followed his brother-in-law Robert ABELL in 1790 to Kentucky from St. Mary's County, Maryland, and settled on Rolling Fork in Nelson County. His wife was Alethia ABELL and their children were: Richard SPALDING married Henrietta HAMILTON; Thomas SPALDING married Susan ABELL; Joseph SPALDING married Elizabeth MOORE; William SPALDING married Elizabeth THOMPSON; Ignatius A. SPALDING married Ann POTTINGER; Benedict SPALDING married Mary HAMILTON; Ann SPALDING married Clement HAMILTON; Ellen SPALDING married BASIL RINEY; Elizabeth SPALDING married John WATHEN; Catherine SPALDING married Richard FORREST; Mary SPALDING married Henry H. WATHEN; and, Alethia SPALDING married Francis SIMS. They were all devout Catholics. (Ref: KC:109-110; KB 5:80, 151, 264)

Joseph SPALDING and John SPALDING were also among the early Catholics from Maryland who settled in Nelson County, Kentucky in 1785, and James SPALDING was on Cox's Creek by 1800. (Ref: KC:28, 111, 114)

Aaron SPALDING was born in Maryland in 1752 and served in the Maryland Line during the Revolutionary War. He received a pension in Washington County, Kentucky in 1819 and died on June 29, 1825. George SPALDING was also in Washington County and received a pension in 1825. He was born in 1758 and was in the Maryland Line during the Revolution. He married Susanna SHUTTLEWORTH on June 12, 1811 (Ref: RSK:164; MRR:49, 123).

SPARKS. On December 4, 1807, in Shelby County, Kentucky, Mathew SPARKS and wife Prudence, and Benjamin SPARKS and wife Elizabeth, appointed Bloys WRIGHT of Harford County, Maryland to be their attorney to sell a tract of 114 acres adjoining Isaac WHITTICAR. The conveyance was recorded in Harford County on October 25, 1811 (Ref: HCLR Liber HD #X, pp. 339-441).

SPARROW. Elias SPARROW was born in Maryland circa 1785 and went to Kentucky circa 1800. He married Nancy BARKER (born in 1795 in Logan County, Kentucky) on January 9, 1811 in Logan County, Kentucky (Ref: KPG 1:3, July, 1979, p. 51).

SPEAK, SPEAKE. George SPEAK was born in Maryland in 1758 and was a Private in the Maryland Line during the Revolutionary War. He received a pension in 1818 in Mercer County, Kentucky and died there February 26, 1828 (Ref: RSK:121; KPR:1835; MRR:49).

SPEAKS. Basil SPEAKS and Urban SPEAKS was among the early Catholics from St. Mary's County, Maryland who settled in Nelson County, Kentucky in 1785. James SPEAKS had settled on Cox's Creek by 1800. (Ref: KC:28, 80, 114)

Hezekiah SPEAKS (or SPEAKE) was born in Prince George's County, Maryland in 1755 or 1757 and was a Private in the Maryland Line under Capt. Enos CAMPBELL in 1776 and Capt. Nathaniel PIGMAN at the Battle of Germantown. Hezekiah SPEAKS married Elenor TUCKER, daughter of Edward TUCKER of Montgomery County, in Georgetown, Maryland (now Washington, D.C.) around the first of the year 1783. In 1832 Hezekiah applied for and received a pension in Bourbon County, Kentucky. Affidavits as to his service were given by John TUCKER and Ann HUGHES. Hezekiah died January 1, 1837. In 1842 his widow received pension W8748 and the names and ages of her children at that time were: John, the oldest, now deceased; Elizabeth, age 56; William, now deceased; Sarah, age 51; Elenor, age 49; Nancy, age 47; Mary, now deceased; Cassy, now deceased; Ally, age 40, and wife of Michael ASHFORD; and two more children, names not given by the deponent, Ally ASHFORD (Ref: MS:12; RSK:43; KPR:1835; MRR:49).

SPINK. Ignatius SPINK and Raphael SPINK were among the early Catholics from St. Mary's County, Maryland who migrated to Nelson County, Kentucky and settled on Cartwright's Creek by 1788 in (now) Washington County (Ref: KC:80).

SPRADLIN. Jesse SPRADLIN married Sally STONE after 1800 in Kentucky. Their marriage was proven through a Maryland Revolutionary War pension application; soldier's name not given (Ref: MRR:123).

SPRINGER. On February 27, 1808, the following notice was in the Fredericktown Herald newspaper in Maryland: "Sale at the house of William SPRINGER in Fredericktown for the creditors of William SPRINGER, an insolvent debtor, store goods; and at the house of Benjamin STALLINGS in Fredericktown, a tract of land lying in Nelson County, Kentucky----W. C. HOBBS, Trustee." On September 15, 1808 the following appeared in the Frederick Republican Advocate newspaper: "Sale of tract near Bardstown, Nelson County, Kentucky, by order of the creditors of William SPRINGER----William C. HOBBS, Trustee." (Ref: WMNA 3:18, 121).

STAFFORD. John STAFFORD was born in Dorchester County, Maryland on March 21, 1767 and enlisted in the Maryland Line in January, 1781. According to his pension application, he lived prior to the war in Dorchester County, Maryland and Dickson County, Tennessee and Smith

County, Tennessee and Caswell County, North Carolina, and since the
war he lived in Dickson County, Tennessee and in 1832 removed to
Graves County, Kentucky. He married Mary -----, in 1822 in Dickson
County, Tennessee. In 1834 John applied for and received a pension
and his widow later received pension W11554. He had also received
bounty land warrant 50888-160-55 (Ref: MS:41; RSK:42; MRP:37; KPR:
1835; MRR:49).

STANFORD. Mary E. OWINGS was born in Kentucky, a daughter of Joshua
OWINGS and Rachel SPEARS, natives of Maryland and early settlers
in Kentucky. Mary W. OWINGS married Lucas STANFORD, a soldier in
the War of 1812 in South Carolina, and their son, Judge John L.
STANFORD, was born in Simpson County, Kentucky on December 3, 1823
(Ref: KB 4:241).

STANDIFORD. Rebecca STANDIFORD was born on July 27, 1782 in
Baltimore County, Maryland and married Ebenezer BARTLETT, son of
William BARTLETT of Virginia and Kentucky, circa 1798 or 1799.
Their children (not in order of birth) were: Eliza McCABE; Franklin
J. BARTLETT; ELizabeth HILDRETH; Sarah LAPHAM; Lucinda FRISTOE;
Silas BARTLETT; Mary Jane SANFORD; Sally Ann CRAENDER; Henry J.
BARTLETT; and, Malinda DUNCAN BOWER. Ebenezer and Rebecca BARTLETT
resided in Fleming County, Kentucky and possibly Nicholas County
before moving to Hancock County, Illinois where he died in 1843 and
she died in 1845 (Ref: KP:4-6, and Agreement between Heirs of
William Bartlett in Nicholas County, Kentucky, Deed Book H, p. 368,
June 5, 1822).

STEVENS. James STEVENS was among the early Catholics from St.
Mary's County, Maryland who settled in Nelson County, Kentucky in
1785. John STEVENS was an elder in Bardstown by 1820. (Ref: KC:28,
63)

Another John STEVENS migrated to Kentucky from Maryland circa 1809
and settled in Ohio County where his son Richard STEVENS married
Sarah TAYLOR, daughter of Richard TAYLOR, native of Maryland. (Ref:
KB 3:191, 194)

Richard STEVENS died in Maryland in 1798. He had married Lydia
GARNER (born 1741 at Ellicott Mills, Maryland) and lived in
Frederick and Montgomery Counties. Their children were John Garner,
William, Thomas, Richard, Henry, Elizabeth and Charlotte. They
moved to Ohio County, Kentucy after 1800 (Ref: MGS 24:2, Spring,
1983, p. 168).

STEVENSON. Thomas STEVENSON, a native of Frederick County, Mary-
land, married Sarah EVANS, daughter of Job EVANS, also of Frederick
County. In 1786 they went by faltboat down the Ohio River to Mays-
ville, Kentucky and settled at Kenton Station in Mason County,
Kentucky. A son, Daniel STEVENSON, married Elizabeth WEST. (Ref:
BCK:25-26) On September 26, 1807, Thomas STEVENSON of Mercer
County, Kentucky sold part of tract "Edwards and Wells Valleys and
Hills" in Baltimore County, Maryland to Sater STEVENSON for $1,000
(Ref: BCLR Liber WG #95, p. 690)

Samuel STEVENSON (1765-1821) married Lucy DORSEY (1769-1822) and their son Wesley STEVENSON (born May 17, 1812 in Baltimore County, Maryland) died in Kentucky circa 1842. He married Miss DORSEY and their children were Samuel STEVENSON and Rachel STEVENSON (Ref: "Descendants of Edward Stevenson of Baltimore County," by Robert W. Barnes, 1966, p. 10, at the Baltimore County Genealogical Society).

STEWART. Charles STEWART was born in Maryland in 1753 or 1754 and was a Sergeant of Artillery in the Maryland Line during the Revolutionary War. He received a pension in 1818 in Scott County, Kentucky (Ref: MRR:50; KPR:1835. Source RSK:151 erroneously states he was in the Virginia militia).

STIBBENS. William STIBBENS was born in 1786 in Ireland and came to America and settled in Maryland. His son, Charles, was born in 1811 at Pipe Creek, Maryland. They went to Kentucky thereafter. William STIBBENS is in the 1850 census of Bullitt County, Kentucky. Charles STIBBENS went to Texas in the Mexican War of 1846 and stayed there (Ref: KA 16:4, April, 1981, p. 246).

STILES. Henry STILES, son of Philip STILES and Miss O'BRIAN, was born in Maryland in 1770. The family migrated to Nelson County, Kentucky with the early Catholics circa 1785, and Henry was wounded in a fight with Indians while coming down the Ohio River. He married Ann McATEE, daughter of George McATEE of Maryland, and died in 1839. Their son, Edward L. STILES, was born in Kentucky on August 15, 1825 (Ref: KB 5:266).

STINSON, STEVENSON. John STINSON (or STEVENSON?) was born July 6, 1755 in Bucks County, Pennsylvania and his father moved to Maryland circa 1764. John's brother Isaac STINSON (or STEVENSON?) moved to Clark County, Kentucky and his brother William STINSON (or STEVENSON?) moved to Hendricks County, Indiana. John STINSON was commissioned an Ensign in the Linganore Battalion of Frederick County Militia on June 22, 1778, was in actual service for two months under Capt. Peter LITTLE, later was a Lieutenant in Capt. GRAYBILL's Company, and also guarded prisoners in 1781. His brother William also served with him. In 1783 John STINSON moved to Virginia, leaving his father in Maryland, and in 1793 moved to Clark County, Kentucky. He applied for and received pension S30717 in 1832 (Ref: MS:28; RSK:59; MPR:38; MRR:50; KPR:1835; Archives of Maryland, Vol. 18, p. 244).

STONE. Cudbeth STONE was born in Maryland in 1756 or 1758 and enlisted in the 7th Maryland Line from St. Mary's County, Maryland on March 29, 1780 for three years. He married on March 17, 1784 to Sally -----, who was a few years older than him. They had two children and later moved to Floyd County, Kentucky where Cudbeth applied for and received a pension in 1818. The following was extracted from his pension abstract: "He made his will in Floyd County, Kentucky, the farm on which Jesse SPRADLIN my son-in-law now lives, lying on left fork of Abbott Creek, being same purchased of William STONE and deeded me by John STONE, Book D, page 515, Floyd County, Kentucky, and page 513, which land I give to the children of Jesse SPRADLIN, or children he may have by his wife Sally SPRADLIN, formerly Sally STONE, and give my son Enoch STONE, legacy." Cudbeth STONE died June 24, 1844. His widow applied and received pension W3050 (Ref: MS:39; RSK:73; KPR:1835).

STONER. John STONER married Mary JACK on April 20, 1815 in Nelson County, Kentucky. John served in the Maryland Line during the Revolutionary War (Ref: MRR:50, 124).

STUART. John STUART was an elder in Bardstown, Kentucky by 1820 and was a descendant of the early Catholics who settled Nelson County from St. Mary's County, Maryland (Ref: KC:63).

SUMMERS. George SUMMERS married Jane SMITH on May 19, 1787 in Prince George's County, Maryland and died September 10, 1811 in Washington County, Kentucky (Ref: MGS 24:3, Summer, 1983, p. 262).

SUTHERLAND. Traverse SUTHERLAND was born in Charles County, Maryland in 1745 and enlisted in the Revolutionary War in Culpeper County, Virginia in July, 1777. He moved to Shelby County, Kentucky in 1818 and then to Henry County where he applied for and received pension S31398 in 1833. His record states his daughter was Nancy WILSON. (Ref: MS:49, RSK:96)

Walter E. SUTHERLAND was born in Charles County, Maryland in 1749 and enlisted in the Revolutionary War in 1775. The Sutherland family Bible contained this information: "Walter E. married Ann, July 30, 1780; Sarah, born April 11, 1781; William M., born September 11, 1784; Verlinda B., born January 23, 1787; Elizabeth, born September 11, 1788; Walter E. married his second wife, Sarah, April 22, 1798; Thomas, born March 4, 1799; Enos, born June 22, 1800; Travis, born June 3, 1805; Luanor, born March 20, 1807; Walter, born January 25, 1809; Elizabeth, born February 15, 1811; Beldad, born February 13, 1813; Enos married Sally, August 28, 1823; Merline, born May 30, 1823; Emily Jane, born November 8, 1824; Eliza Ann, born October 18, 1828; Mary, born August 19, 1833; Travis, born April 2, 1831; David, born August 19, 1833; John M., born January 9, 1842; Thomas was put on muster list June 6, 1816; Thomas married Elizabeth, October 14, 1819; John B. married Rebecca, June 9, 1842." In 1800 Walter E. SUTHERLAND moved to Clark County, Kentucky and in 1805 he moved to Henry County. He applied for and received a pension in 1831, with affidavits submitted by his brother Traverse SUTHERLAND and his niece Mrs. Nancy WILSON. Walter also received bounty land warrant 24998-160-55. He died on March 21, 1837 and his widow later received pension W10266. (Ref: MS:49-50; RSK:96; MRP:38; KPR:1835; MRR:50)

William SUTHERLAND was born in Maryland in 1748 or 1749 and enlisted in Hagerstown, Washington County, Maryland in 1776. He was married to Catherine ENSMINGER in Rockbridge County, Virginia on August 6, 1789 by Rev. John BROWN. They moved to Casey County, Kentucky where William applied for and received a pension in 1833. Jacob COFFMAN, age 70, of Mercer County, Kentucky stated in 1833 that he knew William SUTHERLAND in Maryland. William died July 20, 1843. His record indicates he had a daughter Nancy SUTHERLAND and two children over age 50 in 1843. His widow applied for a pension in Boyle County, Kentucky on November 9, 1843, age 76, and received pension W8771 (Ref: MS:21; RSK:55; MRP:38; MRR:50; KPR:1835).

SWEARINGEN. Mary SWEARINGEN, of Maryland, married Charles DRAKE, of Virginia, and by 1823 they were in Bullitt County, Kentucky. Their son, George W. DRAKE, was born there on October 8, 1823. They were in Missouri by 1833. (Ref: KM:34)

Obediah SWEARINGEN, son of Thomas, was born circa 1760 in Montgomery County, Maryland. He married Rachel -----, and they were in Bullitt County, Kentucky by 1810. (Ref: MGS 26:4, Fall, 1985, p. 446)

Van SWEARINGEN was born in 1754 and was a Lieutenant in the Maryland Line. He also served in Kentucky (Ref: MRR:50)

Mrs. Susanna SWEARINGEN, relict of Col. Charles SWEARINGEN, died at her residence on Conococheague Manor in Allegany County, Maryland, in the 82nd year of her age, married for upwards of 59 years. She raised a large family, with branches now in Maryland, Virginia, Kentucky and Illinois (Ref: NAW:33).

SWINGLE. George SWINGLE was born in Lancaster County, Pennsylvania on December 11, 1757 and enlisted in the Revolutionary War in Washington County, Maryland in June, 1776, rising to the rank of Major. After the war he lived in Washington County, Maryland for about 15 years and then moved to Jefferson County, Tennessee for 12 years. He went to Kentucky in 1807 or 1808 and lived in Lewis County and Montgomery County for 10 or 15 years. He applied for and received pension S4914 in 1833 in Lewis County, Kentucky, stating he had a son George SWINGLE, Jr., born in 1780. He transferred to Cincinnati, Ohio in 1838, but was in Franklin County, Kentucky in 1840. (Ref: MS:39; RSK:76; MRR:51)

John SWINGLE, Jr. was born in Maryland in 1754 and served as a Private in the Maryland Militia. He applied for and received a pension in 1831 in Lewis County, Kentucky (Ref: RSK:107; KPR:1835; but not listed in Source MRR:51).

SWON, SWAN. Capt. John C. SWON was born on May 16, 1803 in Scott County, Kentucky and subsequently moved to Missouri. His father (not named) was born in Maryland (Ref: KM:146).

TABB. On September 11, 1815, a deed was recorded in Mason County, Kentucky which was a conveyance from Samuel SMOOT and Lydia his wife, Edward TABB and Letitia his wife, Ann GIll, and Erasmus GILL, all of Mason County, Kentucky, to Mary JOHNSON of Charles County, Maryland. The tract "Foxes Range" consisted of 165 acres and was bequeathed to Robert GILL, Jr. by the will of his father, Robert GILL, in 1777. Edward TABB married Letitia GILL in Mason County, Kentucky by license dated May 20, 1813. Erasmus GILL was bondsman. It appears that the Gills were from Charles County, Maryland and the Tabbs were from Amelia County, Virginia (Information from Mrs. Lula Reed Boss of Maysville, Kentucky in 1970 and published in KA

142

6:2, pp. 68-71).

TALBOT. William TALBOT (1742-1819) and son Nathaniel TALBOT migrated from Montgomery County, Maryland to Kentucky prior to 1800 (Ref: MGS 24:3, Summer, 1983, p. 259).

TANNEHILL. James TANNEHILL was born in Maryland in 1760 and enlisted in the Revolutionary War in June, 1776 in Frederick County, Maryland. He moved to Somerset County, Pennsylvania in 1796 and in 1819 he moved to Virginia. In 1824 he went to Daviess County, Kentucky and in 1832 applied and received pension S14643. An affidavit about his service was made by fellow soldier William L. BARNARD (Ref: MS:33; MRP:38; MRR:51; RSK:63; KPR:1835).

TARLTON. On May 10, 1806, the following notice appeared in the Frederick-Town Herald newspaper: "Persons indebted to Jeremiah TARLTON on account of late sales of property before his removal to Kentucky should leave claims in hands of John Hanson THOMAS." (Ref: WMNA 3:5) Jeremiah TARLTON was a Corporal in the Maryland Line (Ref: MRR:51).

TARR. Charles TARR was born on August 8, 1761 at Snow Hill in Worcester County, Maryland and married Marion RICHARDSON, who was born on March 4, 1772. They moved to Bourbon County, Kentucky in 1780 and had 12 children, names not given in this record. In 1829 they went to Adams County, Illinois and Charles TARR died there on May 18, 1835 (Ref: KA 2:2, July, 1966, p. 38).

TAYLOR. Bartholomew TAYLOR was born on February 17, 1755 in Somerset County, Maryland and enlisted in the Revolutionary War in 1778. He moved to Bracken County, Kentucky in 1796 and applied for and received pension S31411 in 1834. (Ref: MS:13; RSK:45; MRP:38; MRR:51; KPR:1835)

John TAYLOR was born in Maryland in 1754 and enlisted in Baltimore County in 1776. He married Ruth BAILEY (born circa 1760) in Montgomery County, Maryland on March 16, 1780 and their children were: Elizabeth, born January 1, 1781; Mary, born September 27, 1782; Jemima, born November 5, 1784; John, born February 8, 1787; Lesson, born May 4, 1791; Hillery, born September 22, 1793; Mahala, born November 16, 1795; Washington, born January 24, 1798; and, Walter, born August 22, 1800. John TAYLOR moved to Kentucky after 1789 (according to a fellow soldier Benjamin DALY who made an affidavit that he knew him in Maryland in 1789) and lived in Bourbon County, Nicholas County and Harrison County. He applied for and received a pension in 1818 in Harrison County, Kentucky. (Source MRP:38 states he died May 12, 1827 in Nichols County, Virginia, but since there is no such county, perhaps they meant Nicholas County, Kentucky) John's widow also received pension W8780. (Ref: MS:47, RSK:89, KPR:1835)

Another John TAYLOR was born in Maryland in 1750 and served in the 4th Maryland Line under Capt. William RILEY during the Revolutionary War. He fought and was wounded in the Battles of Monmouth and Camden, was taken prisoner for 16 months, escaped, and continued in the service until peace was declared. This he stated under oath in Harrison County, Virginia on April 22, 1818. In Hardy County, Virginia, on September 12, 1820, he made a further statement under oath that he had been farmer and shoemaker but due to wounds he received in the war he could not pursue either occupation. He also said he had a wife and they live with their children (no names given) who were all over age 21. The muster rolls of Maryland verified that he served from May 1, 1778 and was reported missing on August 16, 1780. John TAYLOR requested that his pension (which began in 1818) be transferred on August 20, 1833 to Boone County, Kentucky so he could live with his son Samuel TAYLOR. (Ref: MS:8; RSK:39; MRR:51; KPR:1835)

On April 7, 1807, Asa TAYLOR of Fayette County, Kentucky appointed Jesse TAYLOR and James TAYLOR of Harford County, Maryland, his attorneys to collect his wife's share of the estate of her decease father, Samuel KIMBLE, and to sell 50 acres of the land in Harford County. Isaiah TAYLOR attested to this matter in Harford County on March 10, 1813, stating he was present in Kentucky in 1807. (Ref: HCLR Liber HD #X, 1813, pp. 236-237)

Richard TAYLOR migrated to Ohio County, Kentucky circa 1809 from Maryland with John STEVENS. His daughter, Susan TAYLOR, married Richard STEVENS, son of John STEVENS (Ref: KB 3:191).

TEVIS. Rev. John TEVIS was born in Baltimore County, Maryland on January 6, 1792 and went to Kentucky with his parents in 1807. His father, Robert TEVIS, Jr. (1752-1846) became an Ensign in the Soldier's Delight Battalion in Baltimore County during the Revolutionary War. In 1815 John TEVIS became a Minister in the Methodist Episcopal Church. On March 9, 1824, he married Julia A. HIERONYMUS, daughter of Pendleton HIERONYMUS, in Abingdon, Virginia. They moved to Kentucky in 1825 and established Science Hill Academy. Robert TEVIS died on August 25, 1846 in Shelby County, Kentucky. Rev. John TEVIS died January 23, 1861 (Ref: KB 7:252; and, Henry C. Peden's Revolutionary Patriots of Baltimore Town and Baltimore County, Maryland, 1775-1783, pp. 269-270, Westminster, Maryland: Family Line Publications, 1988).

THAWLES. Isaac THAWLES was among the early Catholics who migrated from St. Mary's County, Maryland to Nelson County, Kentucky in 1785 (Ref: KC:28).

THEOBALD. Griffin P. THEOBALD was born in Owen County, Kentucky on December 6, 1830, a son of Henry B. THEOBALD and Lucy BACON, both native Kentuckians. Henry's father migrated to Kentucky from Maryland prior to 1792 and settled near where Georgetown now stands. Griffin served in the Mexican War in 1846 for one year (Ref: KB 9:178-179).

THOMAS. John T. THOMAS was born in 1760 in Somerset County, Maryland and enlisted in the Revolutionary War on April 15, 1778 in Elkton, Maryland and was a member of Lee's Legion. After the war he moved to Bracken County, Kentucky where he applied for and received pension S37488 in 1821. At that time he said his wife was deceased and that they had the following children: Nancy and Priscilla, twins, age 17; William, age 14, a very sickly child; and, Margaret, age 11. (Ref: MS:13, RSK:44)

Nathan THOMAS was born in Maryland in 1758 and enlisted in the Revolutionary War under Capt. Allen THOMAS in 1776. He married Margaret ----- in 1782 and they had six or seven children. Nathan THOMAS applied for a pension in 1818 in Mason County, Kentucky and it appears from Source RSK:118 and The 1835 Kentucky Pension Rolls that he received a pension. However, Source MS:65 gives his claim a rejection number (R10507) and also states that Nathan died in 1820 (Source RSK:118 gives the date as July 24, 1822) and Margaret died in April, 1841. It also appears that someone attempted in 1856 to obtain pension benefits by taking the affidavits of Hiram RUMMANS, Hiram WALLINGFORD, and William BEATTY, who were acquainted with Nathan THOMAS. (Ref: MS:65)

Nathan G. THOMAS married Clarissa EDELIN, possibly a daughter of Edward EDELIN and Susannah WATHEN of Charles County, Maryland, on May 10, 1792 in Frederick County, Maryland. They moved to Boone County, Kentucky where Nathan died in 1819. (Ref: MGS 24:2, Spring, 1983, p. 178)

Thomas THOMAS married Nancy Ann NALL and moved from Maryland to Kentucky in 1795. Their son, William H. THOMAS, was born in Hardin County on June 6, 1806 and married Nancy WILLIS. (Ref: KPG 1:3, July, 1979, p. 50)

Another Thomas THOMAS was born in Prince George's County, Maryland and died in 1798 in Washington County, Kentucky. His wife was Ann SELBY or Mary NAYLOR. (Ref: KA 15:1, July, 1979, p. 61)

William THOMAS migrated from Maryland to Kentucky before 1800 and settled in Washington County. His son, J. W. THOMAS, was born near Fredericksburg, Kentucky and died a few months before the birth of his son, J. W. THOMAS, Jr., on March 10, 1827, in Marion County, Kentucky. (Ref: KB 5:281)

Barak G. THOMAS was born in ELkton, Maryland in 1789 and was of Welsh ancestry. He moved to Charleston, South Carolina when young and became a master machinist of steam engines. He married Sarah Ann HOWE and moved to Lexington, Kentucky in 1833. He died in 1849. (Ref: BCK:212-214)

James THOMAS was born in Maryland in 1755 and married Rebecca LOGSDON on April 8, 1793 in Kentucky. Their marriage was proven through his Maryland Revolutionary War pension application (Ref: MRR:51, 124).

THOMPSON. The Thompsons were among the early Catholics who migrated from St. Mary's County, Maryland to Nelson County, Kentucky in the 1780's. Richard THOMPSON, Bennet THOMPSON, and John THOMPSON were on Hardin's Creek circa 1786. George THOMPSON, Gabriel THOMPSON, and J. B. THOMPSON settled on Cartwright's Creek circa 1788. Col. Valentine THOMPSON was on Cox's Creek prior to 1800. (Ref: KC:56,

80, 114, 130)

Barnard (Bernard) THOMPSON served in the Revolutionary War in Maryland and was a Dragoon in Armand's Corps. He migrated to Washington County, Kentucky where he received a pension effective August 19, 1828. (Ref: RSK:165 and Pension Resolution 38; MGS 6:78, 1965; MRR:51)

George THOMPSON was born in Maryland in 1763 and his son William THOMPSON was born in 1806 in Baltimore County. William married in 1827 to Hannah HOWARD (1808-1845) in North Carolina. She died in Warren County, Kentucky and William died in 1852 in Hart County, Kentucky. (Ref: KB 1:101; KPG 2:1, January, 1980, p. 43)

Another William THOMPSON was born in St. Mary's County, Maryland in 1748 or 17499 and was mustered into the Revolutionary War in Hagerstown. He resided about 16 miles from Fort Frederick. In 1798 he moved to Nelson County, Kentucky where he applied and received pension S30735 in 1833. (Ref: MS:59; MRP:39; RSK:133; MRR:51; KPR:1835)

Richard THOMPSON, son of Joseph THOMPSON, was born in St. Mary's County, Maryland circa 1766. When only 10 years old he went to sea and afterwards became captain of his own ship. He married Elizabeth KIRK of Maryland in 1801 and they migrated to Kentucky in 1803, settling near Raywick. Their son, Daniel B. THOMPSON, married Malinda MATTINGLEY (Ref: KB 5:282).

TIPTON. William TIPTON was born on January 1, 1754 in Baltimore County, Maryland and enlisted in the Revolutionary War in 1776 in Frederick County, Virginia. He married Mary -----, and after the war they migrated to Montgomery County, Kentucky. William applied for and received pension S14700 in 1832 (Ref: MS:58; RSK:129; MRR:51).

TOLEMAN. Mary HEVERN (whose father, not named, served in the Revolutionary War) married Mr.TOLEMAN, a native of Maryland who went to Kentucky as a young man and settled in Bracken County. Their daughter, Nancy TOLEMAN, married Charles A. FIELD, son of William FIELD of Virginia. Charles was born on August 8, 1815 at Germantown, Kentucky and died in November, 1880 near Augusta, Kentucky (Ref: BCK:222-223).

TOON. Henry TOON was born in Maryland in 1752 and enlisted in the militia in 1779. He migrated to Owen County, Kentucky where he applied for and received pension S14711 in 1833 (Ref: MS:61; RSK:139; MRP:39; MRR:52; KPR:1835)

Standish L. TOON was born circa 1780, possibly in Maryland, and died in Washington County, Kentucky in May, 1833. His wife was Mary HARRALL and their children were: William, Hillary, Lloyd, Sarah, and Pious. They settled in Graves County, Kentucky. Another source states Standish TOON married Jenny BRADFORD in Kentucky in 1801 (Ref: KPG 2:2, April, 1980, p. 103; KPG 2:3, July, 1980, p. 121).

TOWNSEND. Sarah TOWNSEND, of Maryland, married Edward McCRAY, of Delaware, and they were in Bourbon County, Kentucky by 1819. Their son, William McCRAY, was born on October 28, 1819 in Kentucky and they were in Missouri by 1828 (Ref: KM:25).

TOWSON. In Baltimore County, Maryland in 1809, the court case of George SHEALEY vs. Heirs of William TOWSON (Chancery Paper #2382, Maryland State Archives) contains the following information: Philemon TOWSON deposed that he was the son of Ezekiel TOWSON, and the brother of William TOWSON, and of Elizabeth, wife of Lewis HECK, and also the brother of Ruth who married William DAUGHERTY who lives in western Virginia. Nathan TOWSON, son of Ezekiel, deposed that Ezekiel TOWSON died in 1805 leaving six children then living. Nathan also deposed that Ezekiel TOWSON gave land in Kentucky to his sons Ezekiel and Nathan (Ref: Article by Peggy Kiegler and Robert Barnes in "The Notebook," published by the Baltimore County Genealogical Society, Vol. II, No. 1, February, 1986).

TRACY. Charles TRACY was born in November, 1759 on Cabin John Creek in Montgomery County, Maryland and substituted for Mordecai OXFORD in the Revolutionary War in 1777 under Capt. PIGMAN. He fought in the Battle of Germantown. He was discharged at White Marsh, Pennsylvania, and again enlisted under Capt. Thomas BEALL in Montgomery County, Maryland. He served in the western frontier this time, went to Pittsburgh and down the Ohio River, and was discharged at Ft. Lawrence. In 1781 he served again under Capt. John NICHOLS and guarded the prisoners at Fort Frederick, Maryland. Charles TRACY went to Fayette County, Kentucky circa 1789 and then on to Clark County. He married Sarah NOE, daughter of Peter NOE, and their children were: Catherine, Lobiada, Telatha, Asa, Obediah, Noland, Jerusha, Naomi, Rosana, and Winifred. In 1832 Charles applied for and received pension S31437 and died on March 19, 1834 (Ref: MS:29; MRR:52; KA 16:1, July, 1980, P. 57; KPR:1835; and pension abstracted by Edward H. West in "Tracy Families of Maryland," and available at the Maryland Historical Society Library in Baltimore 1960).

TRAIL. William T. TRAIL was born near Baltimore, Maryland on September 7, 1800 and migrated with his parents (unnamed) to Kentucky when just an infant, settling on the present site of Covington. He married Mary M. SAMPSON and their son, G. A. TRAIL, was born in Boone County, Kentucky on March 25, 1824. William T. TRAIL died in Livingston County on February 27, 1862. Mary TRAIL died January 2, 1869 (Ref: KB 4:133).

TRAPNELL. On January 13, 1806, Vincent TRAPNELL and wife Mary, both of Mercer County, Kentucky, conveyed land to Isaac AMOSS (of James) in Baltimore County, Maryland. (Ref: BCLR Liber WG #89, p. 256) During the Revolutionary War, Vincent TRAPNELL was confined in the Baltimore jail by order of the Council of Safety on January 29, 1777, and he later petitioned the General Assembly, stating he had been jailed "for a misdemeanor that he was guilty of and which he did through distraction and inadvertency." He stated he always maintained the cause and was heartily sorry for his actions. He prayed for release from confinement so that he could take care of his family (Ref: Archives of Maryland, Vol. 16, pp. 142-143).

TRAVIS. Catherine TRAVIS, of Maryland, married Alexander BEATY, of Virginia, and they were in Cumberland County, Kentucky by 1804. Their son, William T. BEATY, was born there on October 27, 1824, and they were in Saline County, Missouri by 1830 (Ref: KM:49).

TRIMBLE. The will of William TRIMBLE was written August 9, 1830 and probated December 21, 1830 in Baltimore County, Maryland. He mentions his wife Elizabeth TRIMBLE, his half sister Margaret ESDALE of Ireland, his brother James TRIMBLE, his sister-in-law Mary REESE, his sister-in-law Rachel TROXELL, and his nieces and nephews, including the "two children of my half sister Jane, who died in the State of Kentucky." (Ref: Annie W. Burns' Abstract of Wills of Baltimore County, Maryland, Book 13, 1827-1831, p. 109, and available in the Maryland Historical Society Library).

TRUMAN. Major Alexander TRUMAN (c1750-1792) was a son of Henry TRUMAN and Ann MAGRUDER of Prince George's County, Maryland, and a grandson of Thomas TRUMAN and Sarah BRISCOE. Alexander served in the Revolutionary War from June, 1776 to January 1, 1783 as a Captain in the 6th and 2nd Maryland Continental Lines. He married Margaret REYNOLDS, daughter of William REYNOLDS (owner of Reynolds Tavern in Annapolis) and Mary HOWELL (his second wife) in Anne Arundel County, by license May 29, 1781. Their children were Alexander Magruder TRUMAN, Thomas TRUMAN, and Mary Ann TRUMAN. Margaret TRUMAN died in 1786 in Maryland. Alexander TRUMAN joined the U. S. Army in 1790 and became a Major in 1792. While on a peace mission to the Indians in the Miami Valley of Ohio, he was killed in April, 1792, about five miles west of the present town of Sidney. Guardianships were appointed for his three orphan children and they eventually migrated west to Kentucky and Missouri. Mary Ann TRUMAN (1785-1822) and her brothers moved to Kentucky circa 1800 and settled on land granted them by the Federal government due to their father's death while in the service. She met and married Byrd ROGERS, Jr. (1770-1835), a son of Byrd ROGERS and Mary TRICE, of Virginia, who were in Fayette County, Kentucky in 1800. Byrd ROGERS, Sr., died there in February, 1801. Byrd and Mary Ann ROGERS moved to Barren County, Kentucky and are buried near the community of Griderville. Their children were: William Byrd ROGERS (1804--1884) who married Nancy Elizabeth BAGBY (1806-1889) in Barren County; Peter ROGERS, who died in Charleston, Illinois; Philip ROGERS; Mary B. JETT; John ROGERS; Margaret McFERRAN; and, Henry M. ROGERS. Charles Bagby ROGERS (1840-1919) was a son of William Byrd ROGERS and a great-grandson of Major Alexander TRUMAN. He was a Confederate soldier under Gen. John Hunt MORGAN in the Civil War, and married Sarah Moss FORBIS (1843-1921) in 1863. Their daughter, Janie Terry ROGERS (1867-1960) married Elmore "Mote" PEDEN (1865-1941) in 1887. He was a son of Edmund Harlin PEDEN (1838--1914) and Sallie D. WATTS (1842-1880) who married in Barren County, Kentucky in 1859. Elmore PEDEN's only son, William Henry PEDEN (1891-1944), married Pearl Eugenia CRENSHAW (1892-1976) in 1913, and one of their sons, Henry Clint PEDEN, Sr. (born 1921) married Mary Catherine FRANK (born 1926, Baltimore County, Maryland) in Cecil County, Maryland on June 14, 1942. Major Alexander

TRUMAN was an Original Member of the Society of the Cincinnati in 1783 and that membership has been held since 1986 by his 5th great grandson, Henry Clint PEDEN, Jr. (born 1946) of Bel Air, Harford County, Maryland (Ref: Truman and Related Families of Early Maryland, by Henry C. Peden, Jr., pp. 29-33, Bel Air, Maryland: Published by author, 1987; DAR Genealogical Records Committee Report, 1955-1956, pp. 54-55, in the DAR Library, Washington, D.C.; Harry Wright Newman Genealogical Collection at Charles County Community College, Learning Resource Center, LaPlata, Maryland; Genealogy of the Pedens of Kentucky, 1756-1986, by Henry C. Peden, Jr., Bel Air, Maryland: Published by author, 1986).

TUCKER. Thomas TUCKER and Zachariah TUCKER were among the early Catholic settlers who migrated from St. Mary's County, Maryland to Nelson County, County circa 1786 and settled on Hardin's Creek in (now) Washington County. (Ref: KC:56)

John TUCKER was born in Maryland in 1756 or 1757 and served in the Revolutionary War from Montgomery County, Maryland in 1777. He migrated to Kentucky and married Nancy MITCHELL in Bracken County on January 10, 1818. He applied and received a pension in 1833. He also received bounty land warrant 15446-160-55. His widow applied in 1851 while living in Mason County and she received pension W2279 (Ref: MS:14; MRP:39; RSK:45; MRR:52; KPR:1835).

TULL. Thomas TULL, son of Thomas TULL and Sarah HANDY, married Ann COX, widow of William COX. Their children were: Thomas TULL, died October 28, 1758 (sic) in Somerset County, Maryland; Handy TULL, died August 1, 1796 in Woodford County, Kentucky; John TULL, died in 1780 in Somerset County, Maryland; Rachel TULL; Mary TULL; and, Jane TULL (Ref: MGS 14:2, May, 1973, p. 32).

TURNER. Solomon TURNER was born in 1758 or 1760 in Maryland and enlisted in the 7th Maryland Line under Capt. Mountjoy BAILY in 1778. He married Cassandra HARVEY in Frederick County, Maryland on July 22, 1785 and the marriage was witnessed by his brother Evan TURNER, age about 12 years old. Evan later moved to Jackson Cuunty, Virginia. Solomon and Cassandra TURNER migrated to Hardin County, Kentucky prior to 1800. A son, James W. TURNER, was born May 14, 1799 and married Rachel BRYANT on February 17, 1825. Solomon TURNER applied for and received a pension in 1818. He died April 14, 1820 and his widow married Wright TAYLOR on December 14, 1829. Wright died May 27, 1836. By 1843 Cassandra TAYLOR was in Porter County, Indiana (age 74) and she applied and received pension W9847. (Ref: MS:45; RSK:87; MRR:52; KPR:1835)

James TURNER and wife Mary GLOVER or Mary CURRY (?) were from the Eastern Shore of Maryland, and they went to Bracken County, Kentucky in 1810. They had four daughters and a son, John G. TURNER, who lived in Lewis County, Kentucky until 1852. (Ref: KBG 8:1, Spring, 1981, p. 35)

Josiah TURNER, father of Rev. J. P. TURNER, was among the early Catholics who migrated from St. Mary's County, Maryland and settled in Nelson County, Kentucky circa 1785 (Ref: KC:80).

TYDINGS. Edward E. TYDINGS was born in 1791 in Anne Arundel County, Maryland and subsequently lived in Louisville, Kentucky. He had moved to Monroe County, Missouri by 1830. He may have been related to Rev. Richard TYDINGS, Methodist Minister who died in Louisville, Kentucky in 1865 (Ref: KBG 8:1, Spring, 1981, p. 37).

USELTON. John USELTON and George USELTON migrated from Maryland to Woodford County, Kentucky just after the Revolutionary War. They were in Fayette County in 1789 and later in Warren County, Kentucky. Their sons (unnamed) lived in Bedford and Rutherford Counties, Tennessee (Ref: KA 8:1, July, 1972, p. 49).

VALLANDINGHAM. Esther B. VALLANDINGHAM was born circa 1795 in Maryland and married Francis E. KIMBLEY (born 1791), son of Andrew KIMBLEY, in Muhlenburg County, Kentucky. Their son, Ezekiel V. KIMBLEY, was born on March 4, 1817 in Muhlenburg County (Ref: KB 3:155).

VANCE. William VANCE was born in Maryland circa 1750 and was an early settler in Green County, Kentucky, where he died in 1832. His wife was Fanny WOOLDRIDGE of Kentucky, and their daughter Margaret VANCE married Pleasant HUDSON, a son of John P. HUDSON of South Carolina and Virginia. Their son, Drury HUDSON, was born on March 5, 1823 in Green County, Kentucky (Ref: KB 5:155).

VEATCH. Jeremiah VEATCH was born in Frederick, Maryland in 1759 or 1760 and enlisted in the Revolutionary War as a Private in the Maryland Line. He moved to Washington County, Pennsylvania during the war and was married near Barrowstown to Priscilla -----, on July 18, 1782 by Rev. John CORBY. The family Bible lists these children: Ann, born August 4, 1783; Nathan, born July 29, 1785; Elizabeth, born February 2, 1788; Dorcas, born March 13, 1790; John, born July 22, 1792; and, Frances Ann, born October 19, 1794. Jeremiah migrated to Kentucky where he applied for and received a pension in Jessamine County in 1833. He died January 30, 1836 and his widow applied and received pension W8800. She died February 13, 1853 (Ref: MS:53; RSK:103; MRR:52; KPR:1835).

VILEY. Elizabeth VILEY, whose parents (unnamed) were from Maryland, was born in Scott County, Kentucky circa 1800 and married James McCONNELL, a representative of Fayette County, Kentucky, who died in 1857. Their son, Robert McCONNELL, was born in Woodford County, Kentucky on November 17, 1818 and became President of the Woodford Bank. (Ref: KB 7:75) They were probably related to Willa VILEY and Lydia SMITH whose son, Warren VILEY, was born in Scott County, Kentucky on August 3, 1817, and subsequently moved to Woodford County in 1838, settling at "Stonewall." (Ref: KB 7:117).

VINSON. Elizabeth VINSON was born in Maryland circa 1785 and married James HIGDON (born circa 1768) around 1800. In 1808 they moved to Kentucky with their children and first settled in Washington County. In 1809 they moved to Grayson County, where James HIGDON died in August, 1833. Elizabeth HIGDON died in February, 1850. Augustine HIGDON was born in Maryland on July 13,

1803 and was one of nine children born to James HIGDON and Elizabeth VINSON. He married Theresa ROBY on February 12, 1828 in Kentucky (Ref: KB 1:179-180).

WALDRON. Richard WALDRON of Harford County, Maryland, wrote his will on June 22, 1796 and it was probated on May 2, 1797 in Harford County. He mentioned his wife Phebey WALDRON and gave her all of his estate, being part of "Major's Choice." He mentioned his daughters (but not by name) and his son, David WALDRON, stating that David had "received 100 pounds due me in the State of New York and the tools he carried to Kentucky, and no more." (Ref: Harford County, Maryland Wills Liber AJ No. R, pp. 242-243).

WALKER. Joseph WALKER was born in Maryland and when about six years old went to Kentucky with his parents (names and date not given) and settled in Nelson County. Joseph WALKER married Nancy CLARK, daughter of Nathaniel CLARK who moved to Kentucky from Pennsylvania, and their son Presley WALKER was born on October 12, 1823 (Ref: KB 7:260).

WALLACE. Charles WALLACE was born in Baltimore, Maryland in 1777 and married Nancy BENTON (born January 24, 1783) on April 16, 1797. She was a daughter of Joseph and Ann BENTON of Montgomery County, Maryland. Charles and Nancy moved to Ohio County, Kentucky in 1798 where he built the first water mill in that county on Rough Creek. He also built the first courthouse and jail in Hartford, Kentucky, and he opened his house to public preaching. He and his wife were zealous members of the Methodist Episcopal Church. He died October 14, 1838. His wife died September 17, 1856. Their son, Samuel WALLACE, was born in Ohio County on April 25, 1825. (Ref: KB 3:201)

William G. WALLACE was born on November 20, 1801 in Maryland and moved with his father, Arthur WALLACE, to Kentucky in an early day. William was a tanner by trade, as was his father. William married Amanda REDDING in Ohio County, Kentucky and died there in 1881 (Ref: KB 1:192).

WARFIELD. The Warfields have been a prominent family in Maryland since colonial times. Briefly, Richard WARFIELD came to Maryland from England in 1637 and settled nine miles from Annapolis. A son, John WARFIELD, had a son Benjamin WARFIELD, who had a son Elisha WARFIELD who went to Kentucky in the Autumn of 1790. Benjamin WARFIELD, son of Elisha, was born February 8, 1790 near Annapolis, Maryland and went with his family to Bryan's Station in Fayette County, Kentucky. He married Sarah CALDWELL (1799-1836) and their son William WARFIELD was born May 30, 1827 in Lexington, Kentucky (Ref: BCK:525-526)

Roderick WARFIELD, son of Joshua WARFIELD, was born on October 16, 1786 in Maryland and married Miss Ann S. STOCKETT. They moved to Hardin County, Kentucky in 1816 by way of Wheeling and down the Ohio River. Roderick died on January 20, 1862. His son, Thomas N. WARFIELD, was born on June 27, 1823 near Elizabethtown, Kentucky. (Ref: KB 1:162) William Gerard WARFIELD was born in Maryland and married Susanna RYAN. They were in Bourbon County, Kentucky by

1805. (Ref: KA 14:3, January, 1979, p. 178; AAG I:375-474; and additional data on the Warfields is in The Founders of Anne Arundel and Howard Counties, Maryland, by J. D. Warfield, originally published in 1905 and reprinted in 1990 by Family Line Publications, Westminster, Maryland).

WARMACK. William WARMACK was born in 1762 in Maryland and enlisted in the Revolutionary War in 1780 in the Maryland Line. He married Rachel ----- (born circa 1778) and in his pension application in 1822 he stated he had "two children married and nine living at home, eight of them being girls, four of whom are nearly grown, and one of them deranged." William WARMACK received pension S37505 and also bounty land warrant 2140-100 for his services. His second marriage was to Mary JUDD (born 1780) in Adair County, Kentucky on May 14, 1829. He died in 1847 (Ref: MS:2, RSK:29, KPR:1835).

WARREN. Charles WARREN and James WARREN, of Maryland ancestry, were in Nelson County, Kentucky by 1800. Charles WARREN settled on Cox's Creek and James WARREN settled in Bardstown. (Ref: KC:63, 114)

John WARREN, a possible relative of Charles and James, was born in 1759 and served in the Revolutionary War in Maryland (Ref: MRR:53).

WASHBURN. Anna WASHBURN, of Maryland, married Allen SHUTTLEWORTH, of Virginia, and their son, Dr. James A. SHUTTLEWORTH, was born in Marion County, Kentucky on May 19, 1812. By 1867 he was in Missouri (Ref: KM:115).

WATERS. Josephus WATERS was born in Maryland circa 1742, a son of John WATERS and Mary PLUMBER. He married Margaret Lancaster LANSDALE in 1788, had 14 children (unnamed) and died in Mason County, Kentucky in 1839. Also, the will of John WATERS in Mason County in 1800 was witnessed by James LANSDALE (Ref: KA 10:1, July, 1974, p. 48).

WATHEN. Jeremiah WATHEN was among the early Catholics who migrated from St. Mary's County, Maryland to Nelson County, Kentucky in 1785. He was a descendant of John WATHEN who was in Maryland in 1671. (Ref: KC:28; KPG 1:3, July, 1979, p. 48)

John WATHEN, Henry H. WATHEN, and Edward WATHEN were on Rolling Fork in Nelson County, Kentucky prior to 1800. and Charles WATHEN and Wilfred WATHEN were on Cox's Creek prior to 1800. (Ref: KC:111, KC:114)

Benedict WATHEN, M.D., was born in Baltimore, Maryland on August 15, 1801 and moved to Breckinridge County, Kentucky with his parents (unnamed), and his brother, Richard WATHEN, M.D., also moved with them. Benedict WATHEN married first Elizabeth CHAPEZE and then Eulalie CHAPEZE. Richard WATHEN married first Susan CHAPEZE and then Mary CHAPEZE. They were all daughters of Benjamin CHAPEZE of New Jersey, and granddaughters of Henry CHAPEZE, M.D., of France. Thus, two WATHEN brothers had married four CHAPEZE sisters (Ref: BCK:30-31).

WATSON. The will of Jonathan West WATSON was written on November 8, 1800 and probated on July 2, 1805 in Worcester County, Maryland. He mentioned his son Zadok WATSON and his daughter Mary WATERFIELD "that went to Kentucca." (Ref: Worcester County, Maryland Will Book JBR, pp. 241-244, and KA 5:1, July, 1969, p. 30)

The Frederick Independent American Volunteer newspaper on August 26, 1807 contained this obituary: "Died Tuesday, 21st ult., Miss Mary WATSON, of Fayette County, Kentucky, in the 65th year of her age, having lived in a state of celibacy." (Ref: WMNA 3:122).

WEBB. John WEBB was born in Maryland in 1764 and enlisted in the 7th Maryland Regiment under Capt. HARDMAN in 1778. He later moved to Garrard County, Kentucky where he applied for and received pension S37514 in 1828 (Ref: MS:40; MRR:53; KPR:1825. Source RSK:78 erroneously states he served in the Virginia Line).

WEDDING. Thomas WEDDING, a native of Maryland, was born of English parentage. He served in the Revolutionary War and migrated to Kentucky in 1811 where he died in 1838 around age 70. His son, George WEDDING, was born in Charles County, Maryland in 1786 and removed to Nelson County, Kentucky and then Ohio County in 1815. He was a Magistrate and Sheriff for many years, and died in 1845. His wife was Elizabeth RUNNER, who died in 1828 (Ref: KB 3:202--203).

WEINNAND. Philip WEINNAND was born in Reading, Pennsylvania on March 10, 1754 and enlisted in the Revolutionary War in Hagerstown, Maryland in 1776. After the war he lived in Little York, Pennsylvania and moved to Kentucky in 1797. He applied for and received pension S1267 in 1833 in Jefferson County, Kentucky (Ref: MS:52; RSK:101; MRR:53; KPR:1835).

WEIR. James WEIR was born in 1758 and living in Bucks County, Pennsylvania whn he enlisted in the Revolutionary War in 1778. He was married to Lydia RICHARDS in Frederick County, Maryland on March 10, 1793 by a clergyman of the Dutch Church. Lydia was born June 27, 1770. Their children were: John WEIR, born December 29, 1793; Polly WALKER, born 1799; Chloe WEIR, born 1803; Susanna STONE, born 1806; Nancy WEIR, born 1808; James WEIR, born 1811; and, Brice WEIR, born 1815. James WEIR applied for and received a pension in Adair County, Kentucky on November 7, 1820. In September, 1834, he requested a transfer to Sangamon County, Illinois, where all of his children had gone. He died there on February 12, 1837. In 1840 his widow applied and received pension W22569 or W22669 (Ref: MS:2, RSK:29).

WELLS. Richard WELLS was born in Maryland in 1775 and first married Nancy ----- in 1798 and second to Mary ----- (no date given) and his children were Isaac, John, Sarah, Margaret, Frank, William, Wilson, Samuel, Imuel, David, Richard, James, and Elijah. They lived in Henry County, Kentucky. (Ref: KPG 1:2, April, 1979, p. 60)

Thomas WELLS was born in Maryland on January 10, 1758 and died in

Kentucky on May 6, 1839. He is buried on the Wells farm on Strodes Run Pike in Mason County, Kentucky. (Ref: KCR:305. Source DAR:728 states he served as a Private in the Revolutionary War from Pennsylvania)

The Wells and Gaither families of Maryland intermarried and moved to Kentucky prior to 1800 (Ref: KA 2:2, October, 1966, p. 79).

WEST. Hezekiah WEST was born in 1763 in Frederick County, Maryland and moved with his parents to South Carolina in 1771 and settled on the Sandy River in the Camden District, now Chester County. His father, John WEST, served in the Revolutionary War in 1777 under Capt. Richard WINN and was killed at St. Tilles. Hezekiah WEST enlisted in 1779 after the death of his father and served under Capt. Robert FROST and Capt. John McCOOL. He moved to Jackson County, Tennessee in 1804, then lived in Kentucky from 1809 to 1811, and then moved to Johnson County, Illinois. He applied and received pension S34519 in 1832. He died July 29, 1845 in Illinois. (Ref: MS:31-32, and Roster of South Carolina Patriots in the American Revolution, by Bobby G. Moss, Baltimore: Genealogical Publishing Company, 1985, pp. 979-980).

WHEATLEY. Bennet WHEATLEY was among the early Catholics who migrated from St. Mary's County, Maryland to Nelson County, Kentucky circa 1786 and settled Hardin's Creek (Ref: KC:56).

WHERRITT. Thomas WHERRITT was born circa 1754 in St. Mary's County, Maryland and was a Private in the Maryland Line in the Revolutionary War. He married Margaret KING in 1792 (his second wife) and moved to Kentucky. A daughter from his first marriage, Nancy Ann WHERRITT, was born March 8, 1778 in St. Mary's County and married John FOUTCH in Kentucky in 1796 (Ref: MGS 15:1, February, 1976, p. 18).

WHITAKER. John WHITAKER was born on May 21, 1753 in (now) Harford County, Maryland, a son of Peter WHITAKER and Emele HITCHCOCK. He served in the Revolutionary War in 1775 under Capt. Aquila HALL and in 1776 under Capt. Francis HOLLAND. His wife, Ann DUNN, was born June 18, 1760. They were married on December 28, 1776 in Harford County and had two sons, John WHITAKER and Josiah WHITAKER. John and Ann lived in Harford County until 1784, in York County, Pennsylvania until 1789, in Washington County, Maryland until 1793, in Bourbon County, Kentucky until 1812, and then in Harrison County, Kentucky, where he died in 1833. Ann WHITAKER filed and received pension W9001 or W9101 in Harrison County where she was still living in 1840. (Ref: MS:48; RSK:91; HCP:237)

Thomas WHITAKER, a Scotchman, came to America in the 1790's and settled in Maryland. He became one of the earliest settlers in Butler County, Kentucky, and lived to be 104 years old. His son, Johnston WHITAKER, had a son Presley WHITAKER, who was born in Kentucky in 1825. (Ref: KB 3:53)

Another WHITAKER family migrated to Ohio County, Kentucky from Maryland after 1800 and were said to be of Welsh descent. Dorsey

WHITAKER married in Kentucky into the Benton family from Maryland, who were of English origins (Ref: KB 3:81).

WHITE. William WHITE was among the early Catholics who went to Nelson County, Kentucky from St. Mary's County, Maryland and settled on Cartwright's Creek (now Washington County) in 1785. (Ref: KC:80)

Aquilla WHITE was born on December 8, 1745 in Baltimore County, Maryland and enlisted in 1775 in Bradford County, Pennsylvania. After the Revolutionary War he moved to Montgomery County, Kentucky and received pension S37533 in 1819. (Ref: MS:58; RSK:127. Not listed in MRR:54)

Thomas WHITE was born in 1758 and enlisted in Frederick County, Maryland where he served in the militia. He later lived in Sullivan County, Tennessee and Monroe County, Kentucky, where he applied for and received pension S31474 in 1832 (Ref: MS:62; RSK:126; MRR:54; KPR:1835).

WHITTINGTON. William WHITTINGTON, of Maryland, had married by 1814 and was in Kentucky. His son, H. WHITTINGTON, was born April 13, 1814 in Woodford County, Kentucky. They were in Clay County, Missouri by 1835 (Ref: KM:167).

WHITTON. Elizabeth WHITTON, of Maryland, married Robert BESHEARS, of Virginia, and their son, William B. BESHEARS, was born August 24, 1814 in Montgomery County, Kentucky. They were in Pike County, Missouri by 1833 (Ref: KM:126).

WIGHT, WHITE. John WIGHT (WHITE) died in Prince George's County, Maryland in 1729. His wife was Ann GREENFIELD. They were the parents of Isle of WIGHT whose sons settled in the Blue Grass region of Kentucky. Isle of WIGHT, Jr. settled north of Bardstown in Nelson County and died in 1816. His brother William WIGHT (WHITE) married Rebecca BLANFORD in Prince George's County, Maryland in 1783 and settled in Washington County, Kentucky and died there in 1823. Their father was the Isle of WIGHT named as a son of John WIGHT who died in Prince George's County in 1829. William White's sons were: John B. WIGHT, who married Christiana ELDER, a daughter of Thomas ELDER and Elizabeth SPALDING of the Fairfield, Kentucky area; Thomas Noble WIGHT, who married Harriet LILY and settled in Breckinridge County, Kentucky; and, Richard Snowden WIGHT (WHITE), who married Mary WORLAND and lived in Springfield, Kentucky (Ref: Wight-White Family information compiled Mrs. J. W. Pikell of Lenexa, Kansas and published in Source KA 12:4, April, 1977, pp. 193-194).

WILLETT. John WILLETT was among the early Catholics who migrated from St. Mary's County, Maryland to Nelson County, Kentucky and settled on Cartwright's Creek circa 1785, now in Washington County. (Ref: KC:80)

Griffin (or Griffith) WILLETT also went from Maryland to Kentucky and settled on Pottinger's Creek, where his daughter Rebecca

WILLETT married Lewis STILES, and daughter, Mary WILLETT, married Jesse CRUME in Spencer County. (Ref: KB 5:267, KB 7:195)

Jettison (or Jefferson) WILLETT was born in Maryland circa 1807 and married Sophia -----, of Kentucky. They lived in Henry County (Ref: MGS 25:2, Spring, 1984, p. 202).

WILLIAMS. Abraham WILLIAMS was born in 1747 in Baltimore (now Harford) County, Maryland and first served under Capt. Abram JARRETT in 1775 and then as a Lieutenant in 1776 under Capt. Benjamin AMOS. He moved to Mason County, Kentucky in 1797 where he applied for and received a pension in 1832. Affidavits regarding his service were submitted by George BRIARLY, Walker REID, and Conquest Wyatt OWENS in September, 1832, in Mason County Court (Ref: MS:65; KP:181; MRR:54; KPR:1835; Mason County Court Order Book M, p. 4)

Amos WILLIAMS, of Maryland, married Rebecca COUCH, of Clark County, Kentucky, and their son, William WILLIAMS, was born October 25, 1822 in Montgomery County, Kentucky. They were in Jackson County, Missouri by 1857. (Ref: KM:129)

Benjamin WILLIAMS was born in Maryland in 1761 or 1762 and enlisted in Hagerstown, Maryland in 1780 under Capt. John SMITH in the 6th Maryland Line. He was in the Battles of Camden, Guilford Court-house, Eutaw Springs, and Cowpens. He applied for and received pension S40693 in Bourbon County, Kentucky in 1818. He requested that his pension be transferred to Highland County, Ohio in 1835 so he could "better his condition in life and to procure land for my children at a smaller price than I could get it in Kentucky." (Ref: MS:13; MRP:41; RSK:42; MRR:54; KPR:1835)

Gerard or Jarret WILLIAMS was born in Maryland on July 31, 1764 and volunteered in February, 1777 in Hagerstown, Maryland for three months under Capt. Basil WILLIAMS, his father. Gerard married Ruth CLEMMONS in Pittsburgh, Pennsylvania on February 2, 1792. She was born on March 26, 1774. Their children were: Phebe, born December 30, 1792; Levin, born April 12, 1794; Grissy, born October 23, 1796; Joshua, born September 24, 1800; Hannah, born August 10, 1802; James, born July 28, 1804; Jarret, Jr., born May 15, 1806; Robert Stockton, born July 1, 1811; Desey, born August 1, 1813; Charles Monroe, born December 1, 1815; and, Hester, born June 2, 1818. Gerard or Jarret WILLIAMS applied and received a pension in Fleming County, Kentucky in 1832. He died June 21, 1833. His widow applied in 1836 and received pension W2981. (Ref: MS:35; RSK:71; and, MRR:55 states he was born in 1759)

Lawrence WILLIAMS, son of Basil and brother of Gerard, or Jarret, was born in Maryland on February 28, 1758 and enlisted in June, 1776 for six months under Capt. John REYNOLDS in Washington County, Maryland. He reenlisted for one year as a Sergeant in February, 1777 under his brother, Capt. Nathan WILLIAMS, who was killed at Battle of Camden. Lawrence moved to Washington County, Pennsylvania and in 1779 he enlisted and served as a Spy and Ranger under Capt. David HOSIAS. In 1787 he moved to Stockton's Station in Kentucky.

He married Polly -----, in 1787 or 1788 in Mason County, Kentucky. Their children were: Eli, born June 20, 1791; Betty, born August 2, 1794; Hannah, born March 10, 1797; Nancy, born March 22, 1799; Benjamin, born February 22, 1803; Leaven, born March 22, 1805; Reason, born February 18, 1807; Samuel, born September 5, 1811; Sally, born January 11, 1819; Mariah, born August 18, 1823; Lawrence, born February 18, 1825; and, Harrison, born November 11, 1826. Lawrence WILLIAMS applied for and received a pension in Fleming County, Kentucky in 1832. He died September 14, 1834 and his widow applied and received pension W9018. (Ref: MS:36; RSK:71; MRR:55; KBG 7:1, Spring, 1980, p. 11)

John WILLIAMS was born circa 1755 (possibly in Maryland) and enlisted in New Jersey in January, 1779, but served during the war in the 1st Maryland Line under Gen. William SMALLWOOD. He married Molly ----- on February 8, 1784 in Prince William County, Virginia and their children were: Elizabeth, born November 7, 1785; Jason, born October 18, 1787; John, born January 19, 1789; Ann, born October 15, 1790; Jane, born May 18, 1798; Page, born August 24, 1798; George, born August 2, 1801; and, Polly, born March 5, 1803. He applied for and received a pension in 1825 and transferred such pension from New York in 1826, according to Source RSK:93. John WILLIAMS died June 7, 1831 and his widow died February 18, 1839 in Henry County, Kentucky, having received pension W9016, in which it was noted that her children were: Jane WILLIAMS; Ann CORN, wife of John CORN of Trimble County, Kentucky; Jesse WILLIAMS of Montgomery County, Iowa; and Page WILLIAMS of Bartholomew County, Iowa. (Ref: MS:50; MRP:41; RSK:93; MRR:55; KPR:1835)

Samuel WILLIAMS was born in Maryland and was an early settler in Washington County, Kentucky. His son, Thomas H. WILLIAMS, was born in 1812 or 1813 in Kentucky and married Sarah T. RODMAN, a daughter of David RODMAN of Maryland who also migrated to Washington County, Kentucky. Samuel WILLIAMS moved late in life to Marion County, Kentucky, where he died (no date given) at age 86. (Ref: BCK:442--443)

Kenrick WILLIAMS was among the early Catholics who migrated from St. Mary's County, Maryland to Nelson County, Kentucky circa 1785 and settled on Cartwright's Creek (now) in Washington County. (Ref: KC:80)

Jeremiah WILLIAMS was born in 1810 in Ohio County, Kentucky and died December 26, 1879. His parents (names not given) migrated to Kentucky from Maryland prior to 1800. (Ref: KB 3:205)

Another John WILLIAMS was born in Maryland and served in the Revolutionary War, after which he moved to Kentucky. His son, Alexander WILLIAMS, was in the War of 1812 and died in Owen County, Kentucky in 1865. He married Tamor JONES, daughter of Robert JONES and Martha BURNS, and their son, Robert WILLIAMS, was born September 13, 1824 in Owen County. (Ref: KB 8:177; MRR:55)

William Bayley WILLIAMS died in Henry County, Kentucky in 1817. He was probably related to William WILLIAMS who married Lucy Ann

BAYLEY in 1735 in Baltimore County, Maryland (Ref: MGS 23:4, Fall, 1982, p. 355; MM-1:197).

WILLMOTT, WILMOT. Robert WILLMOTT was a Lieutenant in Maryland in the Revolutionary War. His ancestors had settled in the Baltimore County and Anne Arundel County area in the late 1600's. Robert WILLMOTT, son of Robert, married Priscilla RIDGELY in 1781. In 1787 John WILLMOTT and Robert WILLMOTT moved to Kentucky. In 1790 Robert WILMOT appears on the Tax List of Bourbon County, Kentucky. He later received a pension under the Act of 1828 for his services during the war in Harrison's Artillery (Ref: RSK:43, MGS 7:21, and a chronology prepared by Margaret Wilmot Martin in 1962, is on file at the Maryland Historical Society in Baltimore).

WILSON. James WILSON was born March 12, 1763 and enlisted in Fredericktown, Maryland under Capt. Edward RILEY on March 2, 1781. He moved to Kentucky in 1804 and applied for and received pension S35727 in 1824. His wife (unnamed) was living, as were these children: Rachel, age 23; Thomas, age 16; Elizabeth, age 13; Moses, age 10; and, Susan, age 5. (Ref: MS:29; RSK:57; MRP:41; MRR:55; KPR:1835)

Robert WILSON was born in Maryland or Pennsylvania in 1752 and enlisted in the 6th Pennsylvania Regiment in 1775. He married Jane -----, on November 4, 1777 in Washington County, Maryland and later moved to Kentucky. He received a pension in Jefferson County, Kentucky in 1818 and died on September 10, 1835. His widow applied in 1835 and received pension W9010, naming these children: Emzer WILSON, now in Arkansas; Elliott WILSON, of Louisiana, now deceased, who left four daughters, including Jane WILSON and India WILSON; Patience BLUNK, wife of Joseph BLUNK, of Jefferson County, Kentucky; David WILSON, of Jefferson County; Daniel WILSON, of Jefferson County. (Ref: MS:52, RSK:100)

John WILSON of Montgomery County, Maryland, married Elizabeth -----, and died in Woodford County, Kentucky in 1831. Their children were: Samuel, William, Joshua, Lawrence (born 1779 in Maryland), Mary, Sally, Margaret, Nancy, and Ruth. (Ref: MGS 20:2, Spring, 1979, p. 175)

Micajah WILSON was born in Maryland in 1796, a son of Thomas WILSON and Nancy DUNN, and went to Kentucky with his parents in 1800, settling in Garrard County. Micajah WILSON married Elizabeth SCANLAND and died in 1875 (Ref: KB 4:252).

WIMSETT, WINSETT. Joseph WIMSETT, Raphael WIMSETT, and Stephen WIMSETT were Catholic settlers from St. Mary's County, Maryland who settled on Rolling Fork in Nelson County, Kentucky prior to 1800. (Ref: KC:111)

Raphael WINSETT was born in St. Mary's County, Maryland in 1754 and enlisted in the 1st Maryland Line in 1776. Raphael married Susannah CISSELL in 1783 and the following year they moved to Nelson County, Kentucky, accompanied by Frances PAIN, a neighbor who testified in behalf of Susannah when she filed for a pension in 1840. Raphael WINSETT applied and received a pension in 1818. He died May 25, 1828 and his widow later filed and received pension W621. Susannah WINSETT was 81 in 1840 when Sylvester WINSETT was appointed to take charge of her affairs (Ref: MS:59; RSK:132; MRR:55; KPR:1835).

WINGFIELD. Enoch WINGFIELD was born in Frederick County, Maryland on March 15, 1759 and enlisted in the Revolutionary War in Berkeley County, Virginia. After the war he moved to Staunton, Virginia and then to Kentucky where he resided in Woodford County. He applied for and received pension S16581 in 1833. Affidavit of service submitted by fellow soldier, Benjamin WHALEY, of Bourbon County, Kentucky (Ref: MS:54).

WINTER. Jane M. WINTER was born in Maryland in 1792 and married John GOODMAN (1779-1849) of Hersfeldt, Germany, who came to America in 1795 and settled in Savannah, Georgia. They met and married in Kentucky, and son John GOODMAN was born July 22, 1837, and became a physician. Jane GOODMAN died in 1844 in Frankfort, Kentucky (Ref: BCK:16-17).

WISE. Adam WISE was born in 1718 in Germany and came to America prior to the Revolutionary War, which he served in from Washington County, Pennsylvania. Some of his children were born in Pennsylvania and some in Maryland: Daniel, Abraham, Tobias (born 1779), and Catherine (born 1800 at Pipe Creek, Maryland) moved to Kentucky; and Jacob, Ulian (Julian?) and Judith may also have moved there. Tobias WISE married Mary GRIGSBY (born 1778 in Virginia) and she died in Ohio County, Kentucky on October 1, 1854 (Ref: Information from Jack Thornton of Dallas, Texas, and published in KPG 1:3, July, 1979, p. 45).

WOOD. Jonathan WOOD was born in Maryland in 1747 or 17488 and enlisted in 1775 in Fredericktown, Maryland for one year. He later moved to Nelson County, Kentucky where he applied for and received pension S11899 in 1832. (Ref: MS:59; RSK:133; MRR:56; KPR:1835)

Samuel WOOD was born in Maryland in 1744 and was a Private in the Maryland Line. He pensioned in Clay County, Kentucky in 1819 and died there on December 13, 1825. (Ref: RSK:59; KPR:1835. Not listed in MRR:56)

Thomas C. WOOD was born in Nicholas County, Kentucky on April 12, 1821, a son of Nimrod WOOD and Dryden MARSH. His paternal grandfather was John WOOD and his maternal grandfather was Beal MARSH of Baltimore County, Maryland. (Ref: KB 7:127)

Eli WOOD of Maryland migrated to Kentucky prior to 1800 and settled in Washington County, and later in Boone County. His son, Horatio R. WOOD, was born in Maryland and married Martha DOUDEN, daughter of Capt. John DOUDEN of the War of 1812 and Mason County, Kentucky. One of their eleven children, John A. WOOD, was born on March 6, 1833 in Boone County and became a physician (Ref: KB 8:179).

WOODALL. Jesse WOODALL was born in Maryland in 1760 and was a

Private and then a Sergeant in the Maryland Line during the Revolutionary War. He migrated to Rockcastle County, Kentucky where he received a pension in 1831 (Ref: RSK:146, KPR:1835).

WORLAND. Barney WORLAND, Sr. was born in Maryland circa 1780 and was one of the early pioneers in Scott County, Kentucky. His son, George L. WORLAND, was born about 1803 in Kentucky and was Sheriff of Scott County for a few years. His grandson, Barney T. WORLAND, was born on January 8, 1829 in Brandenburgh, Kentucky. George L. WORLAND moved to Lexington in 1836, and in 1841, he moved to Arkansas, but Barney T. WORLAND stayed with his aunt Catherine Hunter GREENWOOD in Meade County. Barney served in the Confederate Army under Gen. John Hunt MORGAN in Company D, 1st Kentucky Confederate Cavalry during the Civil War (Ref: KB 1:213).

WORTHINGTON. Thomas T. WORTHINGTON, son of Samuel, a native of England, was born in Baltimore County, Maryland and moved to Kentucky in 1796, settling in Mason County. Thomas married A. WHIPPS, daughter of John WHIPPS of England, and they had fourteen children. One son, Madison WORTHINGTON, was born in Kentucky and married Elizabeth BLEDSOE, daughter of Benjamin BLEDSOE. Another son, Henry WORTHINGTON, who was the youngest, was born on September 1, 1826. (Ref: KB 8:13, KB 8:180) The Samuel WORTHINGTON Bible record has been published in Source KPG:216-218 and spans the years 1734 to 1863. Part of that record follows: Samuel WORTHINGTON, born November 17, 1734; Mary TOLLEY, born March 12, 1740; Samuel WORTHINGTON married MARY TOLLEY January 29, 1758. Their children: John Tolley WORTHINGTON, born September 29, 1760, married Mary WORTHINGON, daughter of Brice WORTHINGTON, and died September 3, 1834; Comfort WORTHINGTON, born January 6, 1762, married John W. DORSEY, and died July 23, 1837; Ann WORTHINGTON, born November 29, 1763, married William RIDGLEY and Truman HAWLEY, and died June 29, 1827; Walter WORTHINGTON, born February, 1765, married Sarah HOOD; Vachel WORTHINGTON, born February 8, 1767, and died October 22, 1832; Elizabeth WORTHINGTON, born July 14, 1768, and died August 15, 1768; Charles WORTHINGTON, born September 22, 1770, married Sarah JOHNS, and died in 1847; Thomas Tolley WORTHINGTON and James Tolley WORTHINGTON, twins, born December 17, 1771 (Thomas married Misses WHIPPS; James married Miss S. JAMES and died in October, 1830); Edward WORTHINGTON, born June 18, 1773, married Elizabeth MADISON, and died in 1846; Martha WORTHINGTON, born April 9, 1775, married (1) Edward RIDGELY and (2) Dr. Thomas WORTHINGTON, and died January 23, 1846; and, Samuel WORTHINGTON, born September 23, 1776. Samuel WORTHINGTON, Sr. married secondly to his wife's cousin, Martha GARRISON, and died April 8, 1815. She died December 31, 1831. And, Abraham WORTHINGON of Missouri, late of Fleming County, Kentucky, died in Missouri in December, 1820 (Ref: KPG:216-218).

WRIGHT. Elijah WRIGHT was born on February 7, 1756 in Warrington Township, York County, Pennsylvania, where he enlisted in July, 1776 for 5 months under Capt. Jared GRAIFFE. He was released on January 26, 1777 and reenlisted in Cumberland County, Pennsylvania, serving a 3 year term. He then moved to Washington County, Maryland where he joined the Maryland Militia in August, 1781, for 4 months. After the war he moved to Bullitt County, Kentucky. He applied for and received pension S1273 in 1833. Affidavit (no date) by Edward HESSEY in Bullitt County stated that James WRIGHT was the only surviving heir of Elijah WRIGHT. (Ref: MS:17; MRP:42; RSK:48; MRR:56)

Henry WRIGHT, of Maryland, migrated to Kentucky at an early date. His daughter, A. C. WRIGHT, was born on January 23, 1820 in Simpson County. They moved to Hickman County in 1839 and to Texas in 1853. Henry soon after died in Texas of yellow fever, at age 62. A. C. WRIGHT married Richard LESTER in 1839 (Ref: KB 6:153).

YATES. Enoch YATES and Zachariah YATES were among the early Catholics who migrated from St. Mary's County, Maryland and settled in Nelson County, Kentucky. They resided on Rolling Fork prior to 1800. (Ref: KC:111)

Robert YATES was born in Maryland in 1738 and served as a Sergeant in the Maryland Line. He applied for and received a pension in 1818 while in Washington County, Kentucky (Ref: RSK:164; KPR:1835; MRR:56 states he was born in 1760).

YEISER. Phillip E. YEISER, a native of Wittenburg, Germany, came to American and settled in Baltimore, Maryland. A son, Daniel YEISER, was born in Baltimore in March, 1789, and in his childhood the family moved to Danville, Kentucky. Daniel became a physician at the Philadelphia Medical College and settled in Louisiana in 1809. He married Catherine SAMUELS of Orange County, Virginia and returned to Kentucky late in life and died in Boyle County in 1878. Phillip YEISER died in Danville, Kentucky of cholera in 1833 (Ref: KB 5:309).

YELLOTT. George YELLOTT, of Baltimore, Maryland, married Bethia BURRELL, of New York, at the Bourbon Furnace, near Lexington, Kentucky, on May 18, 1805 (Ref: KYM:7).

YOST. Sophia YOST was born in Maryland on July 19, 1799 and married Andrew SMITH (August 15, 1797 - December 20, 1877) in Kentucky. Their son, Willis B. SMITH, was born near Nicholasville, Kentucky on September 4, 1823. Sophia SMITH died on October 9, 1871 (Ref: KB 7:106).

YOUNG. Joseph YOUNG and William BRUCE, both natives of Maryland, migrated to Kentucky circa 1800 and settled in Henry County. Robert YOUNG, son of Joseph, and Elizabeth BRUCE, daughter of William, married in Kentucky and their son, Rev. John F. YOUNG, was born in Henry County, Kentucky on September 2, 1818. Another son of Robert YOUNG was James H. YOUNG, who was born April 11, 1813. Robert YOUNG served in the War of 1812 and died in 1842 (Ref: KB 7:268-269).

YOUNGER. Kanard YOUNGER was born in 1760 in Frederick County, Maryland and was drafted into the Revolutionary War in 1778. Soon after the war he moved to Louisville, Kentucky and then to Bullitt County. He applied for and received pension S32620 while living in Henry County, Kentucky. In 1850 he transferred to Ripley County, Indiana as he "wished to live with his step son-in-law." (Ref:

MS:50; MS:55; MRP:42. Source RSK:96 states he served in Virginia and MRR:56 states he served in Virginia and Pennsylvania).

ABELL Abner 1
  Absalom 1
  Alethia 136
  Barton 1
  Benjamin 1
  Ellen 1
  Ignatius 1
  James 1
  Janet 1
  Jesse 1
  John 1
  Margaret 1
  Mary 1
  Robert 1, 136
  Robert A. 1
  Samuel 1
  Susan 136
ACTON Nancy 1
  Smallwood 1
ADAMS --- 5
  Alexius 1
  Amelia 1
  Ann 2
  Bill 2
  Capt. 87
  David 131
  Eli 1, 2
  Elinor 2
  Evelyn 33
  Evelyn C. 33,
   88, 95
  Heland 2
  James Bowles 1
  James 1, 2
  James B. 2
  John 2
  John Quincy 5
  Joseph 1
  Josephus 2
  Malinda 2
  Martha 2
  Martin 2
  Nancy 1, 39, 131
  Nathan 60
  Otho 2
  Peter 2
  Richard 1
  Sallie 1
  Susan 2
AKER --- 109
  Elizabeth 2
ALDRIDGE Elizabeth
  2, 78
  Ellen 44
  William 2, 78

ALEXANDER Abigail
  B. 2
  Amanda 2
  Ann C. 14
  Charles Grandison
  2
  Dorcas 2
  Dorcas Reese 2
  Hannah 2
  Harriett 63
  James R. 2
  James Rankin 2
  John G. 2
  Joseph 14
  Mark 2
  Mary Sample 2
  Sarah 14
  Silas 2
  Walter 2
ALLEGRE Drucilla 78
ALLEN B. A. 8
  Ebenezer 35
  Levi 3
  Martha 104
  Rhodom 3
  Sarah A. 8
  Theophilus 3
  William 3, 35,
  113
  William Porter 2
ALLIN Nancy A. 136
ALLNUTT Sarah 73
ALLOWAY Elizabeth 3
  Joel 3
  William 3
ALVEY Anne 104
  Clement 3
  John 3
  Josias 3
  Mary 34
  Mary Ann 3
  Thomas Green 3
  Thomas S. 3
AMBROSE Ann 3
  Charlotte 3
  Isabel 3
  James 3
  Rachel 3
  William 3
AMOS --- 89, 123
  Abraham 3
  Ann 3
  Benjamin 3, 17,
  155
  Caroline A. 3

  Cassana 3
  Cassander 3
  Catherine 3
  Christiana 3, 95
  Ditto 3, 4, 109
  Elijah 3, 109
  Elizabeth 3
  Harrison 3
  Hester J. 3
  Margaret 4
  Martha 3, 4, 109
  Mary 3
  Mary A. 4
  Mordecai 3
  Nancy 3
  Nicholas Day 3, 4,
  39
  Rebecca 3, 109
  Sarah 4
  Thomas 3
  William 3, 4
AMOSS --- 3
  Isaac 146
  James 146
ANDERSON Archibald
  76
  Ruth 60
ANSON Elizabeth 79
ARMSTRONG Catherine
  22
  Mary 11
ARNOLD Joanna 87
ARTHUR Addie 4
  Eliza 4
  Etha 4
  William 4
  William E. 4
ASBURY Hannah 4, 37
ASH --- 33
  Polly 33
ASHCRAFT Henry 109
  Sally 109
ASHFORD Ally 137
  Michael 137
ASHLEY Amy 105
ASHURST Frances 85
  Jacob 85
ASSCHERICK Agnes 99
ATCHINSON Melinda 69
ATCHISON Hamilton 69
ATHERTON Letticia 33
ATKINSON Mary 129
ATWOOD Ann 100
AUD Ambrose 4
  Athanasius A. 4

Clotilda 4
James 4
Margaret 4
Nancy 4
Philip 61
Susan 61
Thomas 4
Zachariah 4
AUSTIN Catharine
125
Samuel 4
AYDELOTT
Christiana B. 4
George Howard 4
John 4
Sarah 4
AYRES Daniel 5
Dorcas 16
Matilda 5
Rebecca Dorcas 5

BACH William E.
111
BACON Elizabeth 53
Lucy 143
BADIN Father 122
BAGBY Nancy
Elizabeth 147
BAILEY Amelia
Elizabeth 14
Mary A. 5, 38
Robert 5
Ruth 142
Samuel 14
Stephen 5
Thomas 5, 38
BAILY Montjoy 148
BAIN Patterson 93
Rebecca 93
BAINBRIDGE Erastus
B. 52
Eusebius C. 52
Sarah M. 52
BAIRD Benjamin 5
Eliza A. 5
Margaret 5
Mary 5
Miles 5
Sarah Jane 85
Terrell 5
BAKER --- 33
Elizabeth 17
Henry 17
Mary 17, 56
BALD William 5

BALES W. E. 21
BANKS Cuthbert 13
Elizabeth 103
Gerard 103
BARCLAY John R. 5
Joshua G. 5
Sarah 5
BARKER Mary 136
Nancy 137
William 5
BARKLEY Elizabeth
Ann 28
BARKLOW Harriet 5
Leroy 5
BARNARD Ignatius P.
6
Joshua 6
William L. 5, 142
BARNES Alfred 6
Helen 6
James N. 92, 119
Jane 6
Nella 92, 119
Nellie 119
Nicodemus 6
Richard 60
Robert 6, 146
Robert W. 56, 139
S. T. 119
Stephen T. 92
BARNETT Daniel 6
James 68, 109
Lucretia 11
Margaret 4
Rosemary 109
Sarah 33
BARNEY Absalom 19
Frances 6
Harriet 6
Joshua 6
Thomas 19
William 6
BARR --- 6
Ann 6
Barbara 58
John Watson 6
Patsy 101
William 6
BARRETT Susan M. 6,
74
BARRICKMAN Ann 6
Eliza May 7
Jacob 6, 7
James Taylor 7
Jane 6, 7

Jennett Hannah 7
John 7
Keturah 7
Louisa 7
Martha 7
Mary 7
Nancy 7
Peter 6
Sarah 7
William 7
BARRON Matilda 15
Walter 15
BARTLETT Ebenezer
138
Eliza 138
Elizabeth 138
Franklin J. 138
Henry J. 138
Lucinda 138
Malinda 138
Mary Jane 138
Rebecca 138
Sally Ann 138
Sarah 138
Silas 138
William 138
BARTLEY Abijah 7
Benjamin 7
Elizabeth 7
George 7
Isaiah 7
Margaret 7
Martha 7
Sally 7
Thomas 7
William 7
BARTON Joshua 3
Mary 3
BATEMAN Hannah 7
John 8
Nancy 8
Polly 7
Rachel 8
Sally 7
Thomas 7, 8
BATESEL --- 8
Joseph 8
Malinda 8
Mary 8
BAXTER Nancy 67
Priscilla 31, 120
BAYLEY Lucy Ann 157
BEALE Nancy 34
BEALL David 11
George W. 8

James 8
James M. 8
Lucy 8
Margaret 46
Mary 8
Nathan 8
Sarah 8
Sarah A. 8
Sarah Ann 8
Sarah N. 8
Thomas 146
Walter 8, 11
Washington 8
BEAMS Jacob 8
BEAN Benjamin 97
  Bennett 9
  Charlotte 8
  Conrad 8
  Eda 8, 84
  Fanny 8
  Harrison 8
  Jacob 8
  Jane 8
  Jenny 8
  John A. 30
  John Albert 8
  Leonard 8, 84
  Letitia 8
  Matilda 8, 98
  William
    Gallenous 8
BEAR Elizabeth 19
  John 19
BEARD Charles 9
  John 9
  Mary 9
  Rachel 9
  Rebecca 24
  Sarah 9
  Thomas 9
BEASMAN Mary 62
BEATTY Adam 9, 59
  James 9
  Mary Dorothea 9,
    61
  Sally 9, 59
  William 9, 61,
    144
BEATY Alexander
  147
  Catherine 147
  William T. 147
BEAUCHAMP Annice 9
  Coston 9
  Elizabeth 9

Ellen 9
Jesse 9
Nancy 39
Newell 9
Robinson P. 9
BEAVEN Benjamin 10
  Charles 9, 10, 59
  Edward 9, 59
  Ellen 9, 59
  Richard 9
  Samuel 10
  Thompson 10
BEAVER Charles 10,
  134
BECK Adam 10
  Alexander 10
  Ann 10
  Beulah H. 10
  Elenor 10
  George H. 10
  James 10
  John 10
  Lewis G. 10
  Margaret E. 10
  Maria 10
  Nancy 10
  Thomas 10
  Thomas J. 10
  William G. 10
BECKETT Mary 28
BECKITT Thomas 11
BEIGER Jacob 54
BELL Capt. 128
  Clarissa 37
  D. D. 37
  David 11
  David 79
  Grace 93
  Henry 37
  John D. 11
  John D. 79
  John 93
  Mary 11
  Mary 79
  Rebecca 53
  Sydney S. 37
  Thomas 40
  Walter 11
  William 82
BELLAMY Matilda 18
BELMIRE Harriet 5
BELT George W. 11
  Joseph 11
  Joseph C. 11
  Joseph I. 11

Mary 11
Rachel 11
BENNETT Charles N.
  11
  Elijah 11
  Elizabeth 11, 56
  Emily 11
  Jesse 11
  John 11
  Joel 11
  Joseph 11
  Lucretia 11
  Margaret 11
  Mary 11
  Milton 11
  Moses 11
  Nancy 11
  Peggy 11
  Rebecca 11
  Samuel 11
  Saundra L. 7
  Serelda 11
  William 56
BENTLEY Hannah Ann
  32
  Isiah 32
BENTON --- 154
  Ann 150
  Joseph 150
  Nancy 150
BERGMANN Peter 6
BERRY Amelia 1
  Edward 11
  Eleanor 108
  Judson H. 11
  Thomas 133
BESHEARS Elizabeth
  154
  Robert 154
  William B. 154
BEVANS Juliann 109
BEVER Charles 10
BIBB Elijah 136
  Elizabeth 136
BICKETT Edmund G. 11
  Elizabeth 11
  Henry 11
BIDDLE Nancy 12
  Richard 12
BIGBY Mary A. E. 43
BIGGS Sarah 77
BIRKHEAD Ellen
  Amanda 14
  James R. 14

BROWNE Caroline E.
  48
  G. R. A. 48
  Stanley 48
BROWNING Malinda 8
BRUCE Elizabeth
  160
  Sarah 46
  William 160
BRUINGTON
  Elizabeth 19
  George 19
  James 19
  Mary Ann 19
BRUMBAUGH Gaius M.
  51
BRUNER Christian
  19
  David 20
  Jacob 19, 20
  Lydia 20
  Margaret 20
  Moses 20
  Peter 47
  Samuel 20
  Simon 20
  Solomon 20
BRUNT Chloe 20
  Peter 20
BRYAN Francis 20
  Nancy Ann 45
  William 20
BRYANT Allie 20
  Amanda V. 63
  Ben S. 20
  Rachel 148
  William 20
BRYARLY Elizabeth
  20
  Henry 20
  Isabella Jane 20
  John 20
  Margaret 20
  Margaret Ann 20
  Martha Mary 20
  Samuel W. 20
BUCKLEY Permelia
  20
  William 20
BUCKMAN --- 29
  Charles 44
  Clement 20
  Elizabeth 20
  Harry 20
  Ignatius 20

John Sims 20
  Joseph 20
  Joseph R. 20
  Martha S. 20
  William 20
BUCKNER George 82
BULL Margaret 102
BULLITT Benjamin 21
  William 21
BULLOCK --- 88
  Caroline 133
  Sarah 110
BURCH Anne 21
  Benjamin 21
  Chloe 21
  Eleanor 107
  Elizabeth 21
  Fanny P. 21
  John 21
  Joseph 21
  Landon J. 21
  Margaret F. 21
  Mildred 21
  Robert D. 21
  Romanus W. 21
  Walter 21
  William D. 21
  Zachariah 21
BURCHAM David 21
  Eleanor 21
  Rebecca 21
BURCHUM Bennaize 7
  Elizabeth 7
  Margaret 7
  Peggy 7
BURGESS Catherine
  22
  Cavon D. 22
  H. G. 22
  Henry D. 22
  J. Kate 22
  James B. 22
  John D. 22
  Joseph 115
  Joshua 22
  Lydia M. 22
  O. B. 22
  P. D. 22
  Thomas J. 22
BURK Sarah 62
BURNAM Curtis F. 22
  Edmond H. 22
  Eugenia 22
  John 22
  John Field 22

Lucinda 22
  Mary 22
  Thomas 22
  Thompson 22
BURNHAM John 22
  Margaret 7
  Mary Ann 22
BURNS Annie W. 48,
  116, 147
  Martha 156
BURRELL Bethia 160
BURRIS Sarah 22
BURT Franklin 59
  Sallie 59
  William 59
BURTON Allie May
  Moxley 106
  Robert J. 118
BUSKIRK Mary 27
BUSSEY Bennett 74
BUTLER Champness 23
  Elizabeth 23, 55
  John 23
  Sally 23
  Sarah 23
  Tobias H. 23
BUTTERFIELD Isabella
  Jane 20
  Nathaniel 20
BYRNE Ignatius 23

CAIN Enoch 53
  Mary 53
  Nathan 53
CALDWELL Elizabeth
  60
  John 60
  Sarah 150
CALENDAR Jane 69
CALHOUN Eliza 64
  Parker 64
CALMES Marquis 12,
  23, 82
  Nancy 23
CAMBRON --- 72
  Baptist 23
  Charles 23
  Charles C. 23
  Christopher C. 23
  Harry 23
  Henry 23
  James R. 23
  Margaret 23
  Margaret I. 23
  Martha A. 23

172

INDEX

DEAVER Aaron 33
  Deborah 38
  Delila 38
  Elizabeth 38
  George 38
  Mary Ann 38
  Micajah 38
  Rebecca 38
  Sarah 33
  William 38
DEBO Elizabeth 118
  Horatio 118
DEBRULAR John 38
  Mary 38
DECKER Abraham 81
DELASHMUTT Sarah
  T. 18
DENHAM Isaac 27
  Malvina 27
DENNIS Sarah 71
DENT Col. 63
DEVINE Mary 38
  Thomas 38
  William 38
DEVORE Catherine 3
DEWITT Nancy 33
DICKERSON Solomon
  38
DIMMIT Rebecca 39
DIMMITT Richard 39
DINWIDDIE Jane 56
DISNEY Solomon 121
DITTO Abraham 3,
  39
  Christiana 3
  Joseph 39
  Martha 39
  Nancy 1, 3, 39
  W. N. 1
  William 1, 39
DOLAN James 39
DONOVAN Alexander
  39
  Hannah 39
  Mary Mitchell 32
  Peter 39
DORA Benjamin 39
  Elizabeth 39
  Ferdinand 39
  Jesse 39
  John 39
  Nancy 39
  William 39
DORAN Edward 39
  Francis 39

  Margaret 39
  Nicholas 39
  Patrick 39
  Philip 39
  Thomas 39
DORCH William 40
DORRIS Katie 53
  William 53
DORSEY --- 139
  Archibald 93
  Comfort 159
  Edward 40
  Edward 87
  Elias 87
  John W. 159
  Leaven 40
  Lucy 139
  Mary 87
  Polly 93
  Rachel 89
  Susanna 40
DOUDEN John 158
  Martha 158
DOUGLASS Joseph B.
  40
  William 40
DOWDEN Clementius
  40
  James 40
DOWLING James 40
DOWNEY Andrew 41
  Calley 41
  Francis 40
  James 41
  John 40
  Mary 41
  Thomas 41
  William 41
DOWNHAM Annice 9
DOWNING Benjamin 41
  Elizabeth 41
  Francis 41
  Henrietta 41
  Isabella 41
  James 41
  John 41
  Nancy 41
  Rachel 41
  Samuel 41
  Sarah 41
  Sophia 41
DOWNS Benjamin 41
  James 41
  John 41
  Margaret 41

  Michael 41
DOYLE H. George 42
  John 32, 42
  Mary Ann Elizabeth
  42
  Patsey 32
DRAKE Agnes 27
  Charles 141
  George W. 141
  Mary 141
DRANE Anthony 42
  Catharine 42
  Frances 42
  Francis 42
  Frederick 42
  James L. 42
  John R. 42
  Judson Scott 42
  Lou 42
  Louisiana 42
  Margaret S. S. 42
  Martha 42
  Mary 42
  Mollie F. 42
  Priscilla Sprague
  42
  Richard K. S. 42
  Richard S. 42
  Sabrina S. 42
  Sallie 42
  Sarah 42
  Stephen 42
  Stephen T. 42
  Thomas 42
  Thomas J. 42
  Z. Taylor
DRURY Cecelia 15
  Charles 42
  Elizabeth 42
  Hilary 42
  Ignatius 42
  James W. 15
  Leonard 42
  Mary E. 74
DUCKER John 43
  Mary 43
  Nancy 43
DUCKETT Charity 43
  Jacob 43
  John 43
  Mary 43
  Sarah 43
  Thomas 43
DUDDERAR Catherine
  43

186   INDEX

Elizabeth 120
James 120
Nancy 88, 120
Nicholas A. 120
William 120
RAWLINGS Moses 36, 38
RAY Anna Isabel 22
John 120
Joseph F. 121
Lucinda 121
Margaret 120
Mary 120
Mary Ann 120
Nicholas 120
Nicholas S. 120
Polly 43
Polly A. 121
Presly S. 120
Samuel T. 120
Susan S. 120
READ Margaret 35
Walter 47
REARDON George 92
Sarah 92
RECORD Mary 78
REDDEN Esther 121
James 121
John 121
Leah 121
Mary 121
Nehemiah 121
Purnel Burch 121
Shadrach 121
Stephen 121
REDDING Amanda 150
REDMAN Nancy 123
REECE John 121
REED America 122
Andrew J. 121
Cynthiana 76
Emeline 121
George 121
Henry W. 121
Isaac 121
John P. 121
Mary J. 121
Rebecca 121
Sally 23
William 23
William Logan 121
REEDING Solomon 121
REES Lucy B. 33

REESE Daniel 121
Elizabeth 121, 122
Mary 147
Samuel 91
REID Walker 155
REMINGTON James 41
REBEAU Martha P. 27
RENICK Betsey 122
Rachel 12
Strother 122
William 122
RENICRID Elizabeth 133
REVEL America 122
William 122
REYNOLDS Ann 42
Barnaby 42
John 42, 155
Margaret 147
Mary 147
Monica 42
William 147
William M. 122
RHINEHART Sallie 122
Sarah 122
Thomas C. 122
William 122
RHODES Abram 122
Agnes 122
Bennet 122
Elias 122
Elizabeth 51
Ellen 122
Ely 122
Eve 51
Francis 122
John 122
Margaret 122
Mary 122
Nancy 122
Nelly 122
Richard 122
Thomas 51, 122
Winifred 122
RHORER Frederick 79
Henry 75
Jacob 122
Mary 75, 122
Thomas J. 75
RICE David 85
Katherine 85
RICH Nancy 43
Stephen 43

RICHARDS Ann 47
Chloe 29
Lydia 152
RICHARDSON Benjamin 35
Daniel 122
David 123
Edward 40
George 123
John 123
John T. 123
Jonathan 123
Joseph Crowley 123
Malinda 123
Margaret 123
Marion 142
Mary H. 123
Moses 123
Nancy 123
Noble 123
Rebecca 123
Robert S. 123
Samuel Q. 123
William 123
RICHEY John 123
RICKETTS --- 124
John 123
Margaret 123
Nathan 123
Phoebe 123
Robert 123
Susannah 123
Thomas 124
RIDGE Benjamin 124
Charles 124
Cornelius 124
Eden 124
Elizabeth 124
Ephraim 124
Katherine 124
Levi 124
Rebecca 124
Susan 124
William 124
RIDGELY Edward 159
Frederick 13
Martha 159
N. H. 48
Priscilla 157
RIDGLEY Ann 159
William 159
RIEVES Olivia A. 63
RIFFE Christopher 124
Elizabeth 124